Technology, Economic Growth and Crises in East Asia

*Dedicated with love to Milan Lin*

# Technology, Economic Growth and Crises in East Asia

G. Chris Rodrigo
*Associate Professor, School of Public Policy*
*George Mason University, Arlington, VA, USA*

Edward Elgar
*Cheltenham, UK • Northampton, MA, USA*

Published by
Edward Elgar Publishing Limited
Glensanda House
Montpellier Parade
Cheltenham
Glos GL50 1UA
UK

Edward Elgar Publishing, Inc.
136 West Street
Suite 202
Northampton
Massachusetts 01060
USA


A catalogue record for this book
is available from the British Library


**Library of Congress Cataloguing in Publication Data**

Rodrigo, G. Chris, 1942-
    Technology, economic growth and crises in East Asia / G. Chris Rodrigo.
        p. cm.
    Includes bibliographical references and index.
    1. Technological innovations–Economic aspects East Asia. 2. East
Asia–Economic policy. 1 Title.

    HC460.5.Z9T47 2001
    338'.064'095–dc21                                      2001031532


ISBN 1-85898-477-7


Printed and bound in Great Britain by Biddles Ltd
*www.biddles.co.uk.*

# Contents

# Figures

# Tables

# Acknowledgements

I wish to express sincere thanks to everyone who helped me with this project, first to acquire the experience, knowledge and insights necessary and then to bring it to a successful conclusion. First among these are the members of my doctoral committee at Cornell, Erik Thorbecke, Henry Wan Jr. and Robert Massson. Erik Thorbecke inducted me into the complexities of developing economies through three years of apprenticeship. Henry Wan helped me work out the subtler connections between theory and empirical reality in the first draft of the study. They all helped in many ways to develop my understanding of economics. Thanks must also go to Karl Shell who stimulated an enduring interest in growth theory.

The book itself evolved out of my first dissertation essay begun at Cornell University around 1992 and completed in 1994. But the abiding curiosity that generated and sustained this effort and indeed my turn to a professional career in economics began earlier. It originated in a quest to understand how four countries in East Asia worked out strategies for catching-up with industrially advanced countries, a task that then seemed beyond the grasp of most other developing nations without a major restructuring of the international political order. The fact that something quite extraordinary was taking place in East Asia was first thrust into my consciousness by William Nordhaus in a macro-economics course he conducted at the Yale School of Organization and Management in 1979. My own subsequent direct experience of East Asia more than justified his early insight.

I first encountered Singapore and Hong Kong in 1983–4 , while working for IBM in Asia. In late 1992 and early 1993, I visited Seoul, Taipei, Hong Kong, Singapore and Jakarta to gather information and perspectives from East Asian economists and business executives about their perceptions of the sources of growth in East Asia. Financial support for this study tour from the Cornell Graduate School, the Mellon Foundation and the Mario Einaudi Center for International Studies, is gratefully acknowledged. Since then many visits have been made to the region including China. From 1994–5 I taught economics at the National University of Singapore, thereby gaining valuable first-hand experience of this city-state. Throughout the period 1983–2000, my apprehension of East Asian growth has benefited from numerous exchanges with academics, business executives, consultants and technologists located in or having experience of this region. This real-world nous, the experience and insights gathered and developed, were highly valuable in sifting through and integrating the stories told in the purely academic literature, especially those reliant on economic models.

Such contributions cannot be individually acknowledged or cited, because they are too numerous and details of origin are anyway lost in the evolving synthesis of ideas. Instead, I list the institutions to which the individuals who helped me most were affiliated to. In Taipei, I benefited from exchanges with a number of scholars at the Chung-Hua Institution for Economic Research, the Institute of Economics of Academia Sinica, the National Science Council, and the Departments of Economics at both the National Taiwan University and the National Central University. In Seoul, I received similar assistance from individuals at the Korea Development Institute, the Department of Economics of Yonsei University, the Korea Institute for Industrial Economics and Trade, the Ministry of Finance, the Korea Labor Institute, the Bank of Korea, the Korea Research Institute for Human Settlements and IBM Korea.

Information and useful insights were provided by scholars and business executive in Hong Kong affiliated to the School of Business of Hong Kong Baptist College, the Department of Economics at the Chinese University of Hong Kong, the Centre of Asian Studies at the University of Hong Kong, the Hong Kong Polytechnic University, the US Commercial Service, the Hong Kong and Shanghai Banking Corporation and JP Morgan Securities Asia. My understanding of Singapore's economy and development strategies were significantly enhanced by discussions with former colleagues and associates in the Departments of Economics, Business Policy and Engineering at the National University of Singapore, in the School of Business at Nanyang Technological University and at IBM Singapore.

The reworking of the initial draft into the final product was carried out at George Mason University from 1997 to 2000. I am grateful to the University and the School of Public Policy in particular, for providing an environment supportive of research. During this period, I have benefited from interactions with colleagues at George Mason University and economists at the World Bank, the IMF and the Brookings Institution. The Washington-area has been a very good location from which to study developments in East Asia and, in fact, any topic that falls within the broad sweep of political economy.

Many arguments in this book have been drawn from or based on the work of a number of scholars spanning different schools of thought – though mostly within the economics profession. The list is long because a primary objective has been to work at integrating ostensibly conflicting perspectives. Richard R. Nelson of Columbia University and Sanjaya Lall of Oxford University, deserve special mention on account of the extent to which my own thinking has been formed by their writings. I offer them my heartfelt gratitude for having laid out analytical pathways that made my own progress easier and for generous encouragement with regard to this book and other research efforts. The third person from whose writings I have drawn heavily in this book is Joseph Stiglitz, of Stanford University and until recently the chief economist at the World Bank. Though I have had no personal contact with him, I take this opportunity to acknowledge a large intellectual debt.

My debt to some others who provided special encouragement needs to be acknowledged individually as well. Though my assessment of East Asian growth differs radically from his own, I have been greatly stimulated by the scrupulous work of Alwyn Young, of the University of Chicago, beginning with a stirring presentation of his famous 'Tale of Two Cities' at a 1992 Cornell graduate seminar. I am deeply grateful for his generous words of encouragement on the initial draft of the manuscript which may well have persuaded the publisher to consider it seriously. Thanks must also go to Will Martin of the World Bank and Philippe Scholtes of UNIDO for involving me in projects that helped develop my competence as a real-world economist. Philippe's kind words of encouragement with regard to this book itself and early optimistic assessment of the author's potential, are much appreciated.

I am very grateful to my colleagues at George Mason University's School of Public Policy, Ken Reinert, Frank Fukuyama and Connie McNeely for help with this book. Ken and Frank, along with Ron Herring of Cornell University and Jesus Felipe of the Georgia Institute of Technology, provided valuable comments on some chapters of the book. Connie McNeely's pithy advice and encouragement were critically important in taking this book across the final psychological barrier and her support is gratefully acknowledged. My warm thanks also go out to the staff at Edward Elgar, to Dymphna Evans, Julie Leppard, Matthew Pitman and Edward Elgar for unfailing good humour, sympathy and inexhaustible patience in dealing with my shortcomings. It has really been a delight to work with you.

Needless to say the usual disclaimer applies: none of the individuals or institutions acknowledged are responsible for my views or shortcomings.

My final words of warmest gratitude are offered to my wife Milan to whom this book is dedicated. She has endured much on account of the work that I put into this book and my study of economics in general, extending over a ten-year period. Despite her own heroic struggles, she has continued to provide an environment of affection and support beyond the call of duty, even at times when my academic efforts did not seem to be yielding much success. I owe her more than I can put down here or anywhere else.

# Acronyms

| | |
|---|---|
| AMF | Asian Monetary Fund |
| APF | aggregate production function |
| BMP | black market premium |
| CES | constant-elasticity-of-substitution |
| CRS | constant returns to scale |
| DBPF | domestic best practice frontier |
| DEA | data envelopment analysis |
| EA | East Asia(n) |
| EA-NIE | East Asian newly industrializing economies |
| EAM | *East Asian Miracle* (book) |
| ERP | effective rate of protection |
| FDI | foreign direct investment |
| FEM | Far Eastern Method |
| FTC | firm-level technological capability |
| GDP | gross domestic product |
| GM | General Motors |
| GNP | gross national product |
| HD1 | homogeneity of degree one |
| HPAE | high performing Asian economies |
| I/GDP | investment/gross domestic product ratio |
| IBPF | international best practice frontier |
| IC | integrated circuits |
| ICP | international comparison program |
| IEEE | Institution of Electrical and Electronic Engineers (USA) |
| IMF | International Monetary Fund |
| IRS | increasing returns to scale |
| ISI | import substitution industrialization |
| ISTP | investment-specific technological progress |
| LP | labour productivity |
| LPG | labour productivity growth |
| LTCM | Long-Term Capital Management (US hedge fund) |
| MNC | multi-national company |
| MRW | Mankiw-Romer-Weil (growth model) |

| NTC | national technological capability |
| OBM | own-brand manufacture |
| ODM | own-design manufacture |
| OECD | Organization for Economic Cooperation and Development |
| OEM | original equipment manufacturer |
| PPP | purchasing power parity |
| PWT | Penn World Table (data set) |
| R&D | research and development |
| SEA | South-East Asia(n) |
| SEA-NIE | South-East Asian newly industrializing economies |
| SFPF | stochastic frontier production function |
| SME | small and medium enterprises |
| SMME | state monopoly of major exports |
| SSA | stabilization and structural adjustment |
| SWW | Second World War |
| TC | technological capability |
| TFP | total factor productivity |
| TFPG | total factor productivity growth |
| WDR | *World Development Report* (various issues) |
| WM | Western Method |

# 1. Aspects of the East Asian puzzle: miracle growth and crises

## 1.1 INTRODUCTION

This book is partly an attempt to apprehend the economic actions, linkages and strategies that have driven extraordinary economic growth in East Asia. It draws from numerous existing analyses of the economic performance of the original newly industrializing economies (NIEs) of South Korea, Taiwan, Hong Kong and Singapore. But the main objective here is to draw general lessons about processes of technological change and economic growth, rather than to further analyse the growth record of these economies. Despite current and past problems, these four economies have exhibited the most successful strategies of industrial catch-up in recent history.[1] Their exceptional success has given rise to similar strategies in many other countries, but the East Asian achievement still remains largely unmatched in its depth and scope.

In business journals and the popular press, euphoric assessments of miraculous growth have, in the 1997–8 period of crises, been replaced by analyses that are excessively pessimistic. The financial crises in East Asia led many to conclude that either the era of rapid growth had ended, or even further, that there was something hollow, fragile or ersatz about the entire strategy of East Asian growth, despite manifest achievements.

The post-1997 wave of reassessment is understandable; we tend to project current perceptions backwards into history as much as we compulsively extrapolate patterns of the moment into the future. The bearish backlash was in proportion to the excessive bullishness of the past. That seems to be the way expectations are driven in intellectual discourse as well as in financial markets. If the crises have toned down the rhetoric and cleared the ground for a sober reassessment of long-term gains, then that is all for the better.

---

[1] By virtue of its super-growth in the 1945–73 period, Japan could also be grouped with the 'miracle' EA-NIEs (Hayami 1998, Pilat 1994). Japan is seen not only as the precursor of the East Asian mode of growth but also as a key facilitator of economic success in Taiwan and Korea along the lines of the 'flying geese' model (Hobday 1995, Chakravarty 1987). But Japan was a major industrial country before 1945 and its inclusion raises awkward issues.

1

Contributing to the harsh verdict of financial markets were the rebukes that Asian hubris elicited from prominent Western intellectuals. Some East Asian leaders had begun making excessive claims about their superior model of development based on some 'Asian values,' which stressed authoritarian political structures over the principle of democracy. The theory itself had some strictly utilitarian plausibility when expounded by Singapore's leaders desirous of finding a political bridge to Beijing. It lacked credibility when echoed in Kuala Lumpur or Jakarta, where achievements were decidedly on a more modest scale. Cut from a different cloth altogether, leaders in Malaysia and Indonesia were seen as squandering public resources to build pyramids or enrich family and friends. The patent absurdity of these claims have goaded Western thinkers across the political spectrum to pour scorn on the idea of a superior Asian path.[2]

Perhaps the most influential refutation of the 'miraculous' nature of East Asian growth has been Paul Krugman's 1994 article in *Foreign Affairs*. Drawing on empirical assessments made by Alwyn Young (1992) and Kim and Lau (1994), Krugman argued that the impressive growth record could be explained quite adequately by measurable factor inputs of capital and labour, education, and structural change. Hence there was no significant residual of efficiency advance and therefore no need to invoke any special mechanisms to explain the high rates of growth.

Though in a later article Krugman (1997) clearly stated that he was not questioning the 'awesome reality' of East Asia's impressive growth sustained over several decades, the impression created was that Asian super-growers would collapse much like the former Soviet Union. In fact, the association with the Soviet Union was explicitly drawn in the 1994 article, much to the surprise of other well-known economists.[3] But few could match Krugman's extensive reach through articles in academic and business journals and the popular press and his interpretation has come to be seen as timely and prescient in the aftermath of the financial crises of 1997–8.

Krugman's critique has been reviewed in many academic fora and journals and in leading newspapers from North America to Singapore and Hong Kong. For aficionados of economic growth, it is gratifying that an argument about how to apportion observed growth over its various sources should elicit such wide public interest. Perhaps this is a general trend arising

---

[2]See Fukuyama (1998) for a short, sharp analysis of the issues. More detailed criticisms are to be found in Sen (1999). It is possible that ultra-Westernized Singapore is driven by a need to reclaim a lost Asian identity.

[3]Sachs (1995) states that unlike Russia, Singapore produces goods sold in world markets. He identifies the real miracle as Singapore's ability to invest near 40% of GDP for decades and still maintain high returns to investment. Pack (1992) makes the same point for Taiwan.

out of expanded investment opportunities for investors, deriving from the spectacular rise of East Asia? If that is the case, then the economic profession has anticipated this need by a decade or so, to judge by the rapid growth of 'new growth theories' from around 1986.

For growth economists the aftermath of financial crisis is a particularly good time to discuss the sources of growth. Previously, extra-high growth in East Asia was seen as an unstoppable phenomenon spreading contagion-like from Japan and the original four NIEs to Malaysia, Indonesia, Thailand and beyond. This was succeeded by the new contagion of rampant financial crisis, which in turn has given way to a new period of consolidation and reform. Now, it is easier to hold attention with a more balanced assessment of real achievements and manifest shortcomings, which were revealed by the crises.

Even a well-informed layperson experiences some conceptual dissonance when trying to relate the revealed institutional weaknesses in East Asian societies to the extraordinary record of sustained growth. It seems that similar incongruous associations of rapid growth episodes punctuated by crises in the history of industrial nations do not spring to mind in the first instance. By the turn of the 19th century, the USA was already the productivity leader in the industrial world. Yet five decades of extraordinary growth by the standards of that time ended in the Wall Street crash of 1929 and the financial crisis of 1931 which ushered in the great depression.[4]

The recent crises in East Asia show very clearly that economic growth is most usefully comprehended as an evolutionary process with punctuated equilibria (Hodgson 1993), in which episodic crises or disruptions bring to the fore the structural and institutional flaws that need to be corrected to restore the momentum of growth. This is indeed a characteristic of capitalist, market-driven, growth everywhere especially in the major industrial nations. However, recovery and regeneration are not at all 'determined' or inevitable, since its realization depends crucially on the mobilization of the necessary political will and consensus, which sometimes does not happen.

It is in the aftermath of crises that political consensus is organized to set in place laws and institutions needed to dampen the inherent instability of financial markets or push through other needed reforms. Japan, Korea and other countries, having long resisted the lessons drawn from the experience of older industrial nations, are now forced to repeat that learning experience in more painful ways. The evolutionary perspective does not imply that there is anything automatic about the mobilization of political will to overcome the obstacles. Quite often political stalemate prolongs gridlock and sets the stage

---

[4]Krugman (1998a) writes of this period, 'the United States was not only subject to panics, but unusually crisis-prone compared with other advanced countries, during the very years that it was establishing its economic and technological dominance.'

for a truly catastrophic turn of events.

An important lesson that derives from the above argument is that East Asian events cannot be adequately apprehended except by locating them in the general context of growth since the industrial revolution, i.e. economic growth has always been punctuated by episodic crises. But the emphasis here is on sources of long-term growth rather than short-term instabilities, even though they may be connected at a rather more fundamental level, as discussed later in Chapter 8.

## 1.2    THE REGIONAL CONTEXT

This introductory chapter attempts to place East Asian growth in the general context of long-term growth since the industrial revolution, its magnitudes, tempo and character in relation to the broad historical experience. The analysis of observed growth in terms of its constituent sources, factor accumulation, technology, human capital, social and institutional reform and other determinants is taken up in subsequent chapters. The role of opening out to export markets in promoting sustained high growth is examined in some detail as are various channels of technological capability acquisition.

Growth is still an important component of economic development, despite more recent and eminently justifiable concerns about equity, limits to growth, environmental degradation and the broader issue of global ecological sustainability (Wade 2001, Van den Berg 2001). Since the focus of this book is long-term growth, issues of distribution and macroeconomic stability are of interest mainly as enabling conditions that promote or hinder the growth process.[5] The discipline of economics itself originates with this problem, which is to explain rationally the economic power or 'wealth' of nations. Beginning with Adam Smith's *Inquiry into the Nature and Causes of the Wealth of Nations*, economists have sought to identify the driving forces of economic advance and the conditions for sustained long-term growth.

Maddison (1995) estimates that in the years 1950–73, the 'golden age of unparalleled prosperity,' world GDP grew by 4.9% per year. When corrected for a population growth rate of 2%, the per capita GDP growth rate works out

---

[5] In extending the list of development objectives, it becomes clear that some 'outcomes' such as a stable macroeconomy, health and human capital, are also very important conditions for rapid economic growth. The existence of such two-way causality in economics, indeed in all social science, is now well established (Sah and Stiglitz 1989, Stiglitz 1992, 1995, 1996, Arthur 1994). In the terminology of control theory, these are 'positive feedback loops' the existence of which are pervasive in economic and social processes. It is these that generate 'virtuous circles' and 'vicious circles,' terms commonly used in early economic literature.

to 2.9% per year. Thereafter, growth slowed down everywhere except in Asia. Maddison's estimates of per capita growth for Asia as a whole, excluding Japan, are 2.6% during 1950–73 and 3.6% in 1973–92. In India and Sri Lanka which are among the worst performers in Asia, per capita growth averaged approximately 2% for the entire period 1950–92.

The striking exceptions to the above general pattern are the first-tier East Asian (EA) economies of Taiwan, South Korea, Hong Kong and Singapore, which establishes their importance for a study of the sources of growth. Table 1.1 shows that the East Asian economies sustained per capita growth rates averaging between 6 to 7% per annum from 1960 to 1997, far above the norm for the rest of the world. When added to population growth rates of 2–3%, absolute GDP growth is raised to 9–10% in the 1960–73 period for the EA four. Thereafter population growth falls significantly for all except Singapore, but absolute GDP growth drops only slightly to around 7–9%. The second-tier South East Asian (SEA) set of Indonesia, Malaysia and Thailand exhibit a growth pattern intermediate between the EA economies and India.

*Table 1.1 Average GDP/capita/year growth for selected economies*

| Period | 1960–73 | 1973–85 | 1985–97 | 1960–97 |
|---|---|---|---|---|
| Japan | 8.5 | 2.7 | 2.6 | 4.7 |
| Singapore | 8.4 | 5.1 | 6.2 | 6.6 |
| Hong Kong | 7.5 | 5.2 | 5.3 | 6.0 |
| Taiwan | 6.7 | 5.4 | 6.6 | 6.2 |
| South Korea | 6.6 | 6.1 | 7.7 | 6.8 |
| Indonesia | 2.1 | 5.9 | 4.3 | 4.0 |
| Malaysia | 4.6 | 4.1 | 5.3 | 4.7 |
| Thailand | 4.4 | 3.4 | 6.1 | 4.6 |
| China | 2.1 | 4.5 | 5.5 | 4.0 |
| India | 0.2 | 2.4 | 3.6 | 2.0 |
| Sri Lanka | 0.0 | 4.2 | 2.2 | 2.0 |

*Source:* PWT 5.6 series data for 1960–92, supplemented by IMF World Economic and Financial Surveys data for 1993–7.

This relatively isolated achievement, geographically confined to East Asia, sprang into view around 1980 because of the manifest failure of most other developing countries. The Third World of former colonial regions had been expected to develop rapidly once the colonial yoke was lifted; but this did not happen for the great majority. Instead, the period of globalized crisis that began with the oil price hike of 1973 and culminated in the debt crisis of the eighties revealed the general failure of inward-oriented development strategies from Africa and Latin America to India and China (Gore 2000).

The significance of the EA economies lies in their outstanding record of rapid economic growth sustained over many decades. Despite continuing problems in South Korea and Taiwan, these countries are now generally considered to have integrated with the advanced industrial world or at least to be on the threshold of integration. This claim is supported by Figures 1.1 and 1.2 which show the evolution of GDP/capita[6] for these four countries. The patterns for the USA and India are included to frame the East Asian pattern of 'catch-up' within the broader context; India is replaced by China in Figure 1.2. The EA countries appear to emulate Japan's own explosive growth episode of 1945–73 with a lag, but in fact the sources of growth are not the same.[7] Interestingly, the lag is about two decades for South Korea, 15 years for Taiwan, 10 years for Singapore and only five years for Hong Kong.

While the four EA countries appear to converge to US-Japan levels of per capita real income, the performance of the SEA countries, shown in Figure 1.3, is not so impressive. China, however, exhibits an EA-type pattern beginning around 1990, nearly a decade after its 1979 market-friendly reforms. Pack and Page (1994) and World Bank (1993) lump the EA and SEA economies along with Japan as the 'high performing Asian economies' or HPAEs. They point out that all are significant exporters of manufactures and have experienced common patterns of internal structural transformation, which indicate that they have experienced a historically unique and coherent pattern of growth. However, it is questionable whether the SEA countries have experienced anything close to the thoroughgoing reforms of Taiwan and South Korea (Campos and Root 1996). The SEA economies exhibit weaker growth trajectories which do not appear to cohere well with the EA patterns for the period under review.

In terms of PPP (purchasing power parity) adjusted income per capita, South Korea is as rich as Portugal, Hong Kong is on par with Norway and Singapore is very close to the USA (World Bank 1998). Taiwan and Korea

---

[6]GDP/capita is plotted on a log scale so that the growth rate is proportional to the slope of the graph. In such a representation, a constant growth rate appears as a straight line.

[7]Japan's growth specifics are very different since it was already an industrial country before the Second World War. An examination of its growth trajectory since 1880 shows that the super-growth of the 1945–73 period was in part a catch-up bonus deriving from the sharp drop in output resulting from the War. Hence the slower rate of growth since 1973 is a reversion to the more normal pattern seen in the 1880–1940 period (Ito 1996, Hayami 1998).

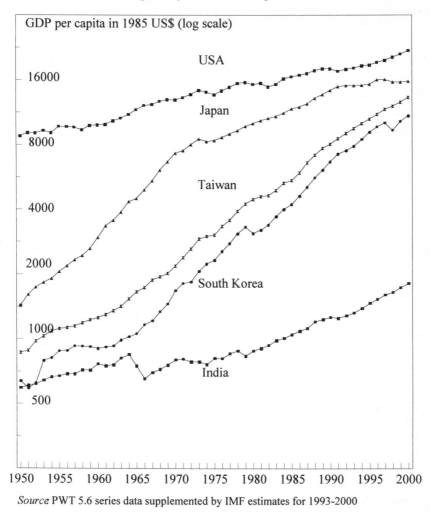

GDP per capita in 1985 US$ (log scale)

USA

16000

Japan

8000

Taiwan

4000

2000

South Korea

1000

India

500

1950   1955   1960   1965   1970   1975   1980   1985   1990   1995   2000

*Source* PWT 5.6 series data supplemented by IMF estimates for 1993-2000

*Figure 1.1 Growth patterns of Japan, Taiwan ROC and South Korea framed within the growth trajectories of the USA and India*

are somewhat behind the city states of Hong Kong and Singapore.[8] The extent of their achievement is highlighted sharply when EA economies are compared to rich nations such as Saudi Arabia and Kuwait which derive their

---

[8] A wealth of specific detail about the extraordinary achievements of these four economies can be found in special survey supplements of the *Economist* (May 21, 1988; November 16, 1991; October 10, 1992; November 12, 1994; March 7, 1998; October 21, 2000).

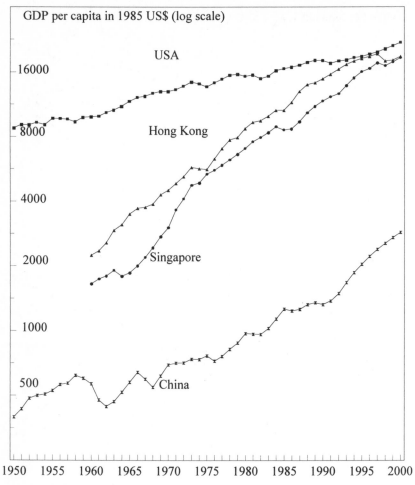

Source: PWT 5.6 series data supplemented by IMF estimates for 1993-2000

*Figure 1.2  Growth patterns of Hong Kong and Singapore framed within the growth trajectories of the USA and China*

wealth almost entirely from petroleum resources. The strength of the EA nations, based on the productive capacities of their workers and the élan of its entrepreneurs, is clearly more durable than prosperity based on natural resources which are exhaustible or may be devalued by technological change.

Impressive as they are, these statistics do inadequate justice to the real magnitude of the achievement. South Korea, a nation of 48 million people, has spawned a clutch of multi-national companies that exercise a near global

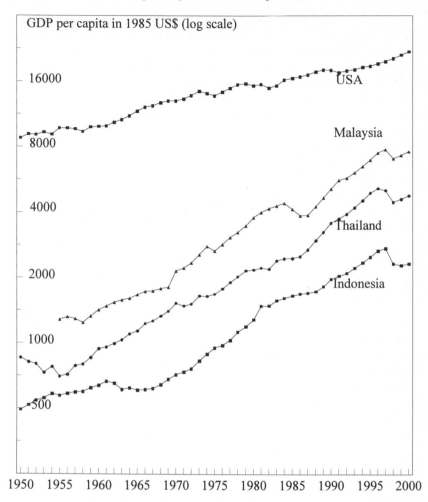

GDP per capita in 1985 US$ (log scale)

*Source* PWT 5.6 series data supplemented by IMF estimates for 1993-2000

*Figure 1.3  Growth patterns of Malaysia, Thailand and Indonesia compared to the growth trajectory of the USA*

presence. They, and firms from Taiwan, have mastered some of the most complex technologies being currently deployed (Chapter 7). The success of East Asia has thrown the failure of the planned economy model into sharper relief. The long-term viability of a social system depends crucially on the productivity of labour deriving from its economic base relative to that of competing systems. Productivity in turn depends on technical skills accumulated in the workforce, the creative energy of its innovators and the technologies embodied in machines and other physical capital which produce the goods and services demanded by society.

Productivity also depends, in complementary fashion, on the nature and quality of the socio-economic institutions which promote or hinder economic activity. Institutions are built up over time and therefore successful societies acquire the ability to reform institutions adaptively. Most planned economies, including the Soviet Union and pre-1978 China, were unable to build viable, productive economies with continuously evolving institutions, despite impressive achievements in basic science and military-space technology. China alone after 1978 has developed the ability to adapt and evolve along East Asian lines. An insight, usually ascribed to Darwin, is that the species – and by extension the societies – that succeed are not the biggest or even the strongest, but those most capable of adapting to change.

## 1.3    GROWTH IN THE FIRST INDUSTRIAL NATIONS

An overview of the growth record of the leading industrial nations over the last few centuries is provided by Maddison (1991, 1995). He shows that from around 1820, the striking characteristic of industrial capitalism in the First World was a sustained expansion of labour productivity and real income per capita, achieved by a combination of innovation and accumulation. From 1820 to 1950 per capita GDP grew around 0.8–1.2% per year for Britain, 0.8–1.3% for France, 0.7–1.6% for Germany and 1.5–1.8% for the USA.[9]

By comparison with the near stagnation that prevailed in preceding millennia in Europe and elsewhere, these figures represent extraordinary growth, a decisive break with the social stasis of pre-industrial society.[10] The above growth rates are, of course, quite modest by post-war standards for Japan and East Asia. As is to be expected, the average rates of growth rise along with the progress of industry during the 19th and 20th centuries.

---

[9]These estimates, and much of the data on long-term growth used in this study, are taken from the pathbreaking work of Angus Maddison (1995). Estimates for periods prior to 1950 are broad averages. Maddison (1982, 1987, 1991) has compiled economic statistics that enable relatively reliable comparisons of the long-term growth experience of 16 major industrial nations stretching back to 1820, i.e. to the beginning of the era of industrial capitalism. In his 1995 book, he has refined previous estimates and extended his coverage to other nations in Europe, Asia and Africa. A supplementary perspective is provided by Hayami (1998).
[10]For example, Maddison (1991, Table 3.1) estimates that before the Meiji reforms, GDP/capita in Japan grew at the insignificantly low rate of 0.1% per year from 1820–70. After the reforms, the rate jumped to 1.4% for 1870–1913 and then rose to a dizzying 8% per year during the 1950–73 period. See also Hayami (1998).

It is clear from Maddison's exposition and Easterly and Levine (2000) that economic growth is uneven across geographical space and unsteady in time, on whatever scale we choose to examine it. Changes in the tempo of long-term economic growth between countries often persist and build up into glaring disparities. Uneven development in turn invariably leads to political responses. In the past this response often took the form of territorial annexation, such as the acquisition of colonies by leading industrial powers.

But there is another common and longer-lived political reaction: when recognized in time, economic disparity spurs laggard nations to exert extraordinary efforts to catch up with the leaders. This often involves the forced modernization of social institutions to whip them into forms more conducive to contemporary economic processes.[11] Such was the logic of reform in Bismarckian Germany and Meiji Japan. Episodes of forced 'catching up' through state-directed reform are an integral part of the rise of Germany and Japan as major economic powers. This is a pattern of behaviour that many less developed nations have attempted since 1945, with widely varying degrees of success.

Following the Second World War, the rates of growth of real GDP/capita in the First World, consisting of Japan, Western Europe, Australia, Canada and the USA, accelerated to an average of around 4% per year during the golden years of the 1950–73 upswing and then fell quite abruptly to around 2% per year for the 1973–89 period. The growth figures quoted here and in the previous paragraph are only marginally different if expressed in terms of labour productivity or GDP/work-hour, as in Baumol et al. (1989) and Maddison (1995).

Numerous studies have established the relative coherence of this First World group. These countries enjoy high levels of real income and productivity that are closely clustered, deriving from over 150 years of significant productivity growth. Nevertheless, their progress is by no means characterized by a simple, secular rise of productivity; there are clearly periods of fast growth (1870–1913 and 1950–73) and slower growth (1913–50 and 1973–to the present).[12]

---

[11]See Vernon (1989) and North (1990) for details. Economic history has been studied from the standpoints of the rise and fall of nations or that of institutions; the former perspective is adopted by Thorstein Veblen and Mancur Olson and the latter by Marx and North. An approach that integrates both perspectives is proposed by Elster (1986).

[12]Within this group there has been convergence of real incomes, productivity and even patterns of growth, from 1950 (Maddison 1991, Baumol et al. 1989). Using data from Maddison, Fagerberg (1994; pp.1156–7) has shown that GDP per man hour for an aggregate of 15 industrialized countries, relative to the USA, has fallen steadily from around 65% in 1870 to 45% in 1950. From 1950, however, relative productivity has risen sharply to around 80% of US levels in 1987. Detailed statistics of post-war catch up in particular industries, are

Indeed these patterns have given rise to various 'long wave' theories of growth. Despite the intrusion of major political and economic crises, such as the World Wars and the great depression of 1929–33, the existence of an underlying pattern of distinct secular phases or stages of growth is established by Maddison (1987, 1991). However, he rejects the theory of long waves, or Kondratieff cycles with a periodicity of 50–60 years, which posit a purely deterministic explanation for fluctuations in the growth momentum.

Maddison shows that at every stage there is a distinct leader country, which maintains technological leadership. The Netherlands was the lead country from around 1600 to the Napoleonic wars. Then with the defeat of Napoleon, leadership passed to Britain around 1820 at the height of the first the industrial revolution which began in Britain. From 1890, technological leadership shifted over to the USA which has maintained it since. Typically productivity levels are higher in the leading country than in the 'followers' since it operates nearest to the 'international technical frontier.'

The genesis and progress of the first industrial revolution in Britain is naturally different and more protracted than the progress of industrialization in follower countries, though some features are shared in common. The story of the British industrial revolution is related in detail in Mokyr (1999) where it is shown that the process was both more complex and further extended in time than is commonly believed.

Productivity growth is often higher in the follower countries which are 'catching up' with the frontier technologies in the lead country. Maddison (1991, p. 30) argues that 'The forces animating a lead country are more mysterious and autonomous than in the followers, whose growth path can be more easily influenced by policies to mimic the achievements of the leader and exploit the opportunities of relative backwardness.'

Some qualifications and questions need to be added to the basic Maddison scenario. Once leadership is achieved, it tends to persist in the lead country. This appears, partially at least, to be the result of 'natural' economic forces, that is to say an economic tendency that does not require exogenous intervention or conscious political action. It results from the self-organizing tendency of economics systems which derive from agglomeration effects.

Agglomeration economies derive from increasing returns to spatial association and contiguity. Such effects are generated by various positive feedback economic mechanisms involving the propagation of industrial skills and information. They underlie the formation of cities within nations and the geographical clustering of industries: hence they tend to amplify and extend

---

to be found in the McKinsey Global Institute (1993) survey of manufacturing productivity. Nelson and Wright (1992) supply the detailed story behind these episodes of technological 'falling behind' followed by 'catching up.'

the unevenness of development. These effects were understood by classical economists but ignored by mainstream theory, until recently, when spatial analysis and clustering have been brought again to the forefront of attention and their importance reasserted with contemporary analytical rigour.[13]

## 1.4    ASSIMILATING THE EAST ASIAN EXPERIENCE

The East Asian phenomenon impinges on problems or issues at the forefront of economic analysis and theory development, as explained below. These issues are expanded on in later chapters and very briefly summarized here in the same sequence as in the book. Each chapter is devoted to a salient area affected or a well-defined problem, as far as possible. The *raison d'être* of this book is, in fact, the clarification of the conceptual and theoretical challenges posed in assimilating the East Asian experience. This is a task that has been taken up by increasing numbers of economists over the last two decades or so. In the aftermath of the East Asian crises the theoretical alternatives have begun to be stated with much greater power and cogency.[14]

This book attempts to develop a synthesis of the best insights that can be pulled together to understand industrialization and growth in developing economies by drawing heavily from the East Asian experience.[15] There is now an extensive literature on which to draw, one that has grown by leaps and bounds since this work was begun around 1992. It is impossible to cover all of the literature and, very likely, some important works have been left out. This shortcoming is arguably mitigated by the emerging consensus on the way technology, institutions and productivity growth interact and co-evolve, at least among the most active researchers in this area. One could even hazard that the emerging challenge to mainstream thinking has developed to the point where we may be on the threshold of a paradigm shift; but that is a transition which is still very much in the making.

The area of economics that bears most directly on the subject under study here is growth theory, from the old neoclassical theory of Solow and Swan to the new models of endogenous growth. Closely related to growth theoretic papers are the data-oriented exercises in growth accounting and the various econometric panel studies of groups of countries. The basic theory relating

---

[13]David (1988), Glaeser et al. (1992), Arthur (1994), Henderson et al. (1995), Stiglitz (1995, 1996), Fujita and Thisse (1996) and Easterly and Levine (2000).

[14]See in particular Stiglitz (1998a). The challenges posed to orthodox development thinking are discussed in detail in Chapters 7, 8 and 9.

[15]A broader-based account of economic growth and development integrated with the progress of technology and institutions is to be found in Van den Berg (2001).

to economic growth and growth accounting is summarized in Chapter 2. This is followed in Chapter 3 with a review of the best-known growth accounting exercises and related analyses of the East Asian experience. The main theme linking together the discussion in these and all chapters is the nature and extent of technological change in East Asia.

A comment needs to be made here about new developments in growth theory. Many experienced analysts of technology and growth hold that new growth theory has provided few totally new insights into growth processes (Stern 1991, Pack 1994, Nelson 1997). But most agree that crucial questions about the sources of growth have been posed more sharply as a result of the new developments. If such is the case, then the failure of new growth theories to measure up to the challenges is an issue that itself needs to be taken up, as in Nelson (1998).

In the above-cited papers, Nelson has argued that because economic processes are complex, theorizing proceeds at two levels of abstraction at least, above the ground level of empirical data collection. The first level of abstraction is 'appreciative theorizing,' which closely tracks empirical work and is expressed mostly in words. But here, causal relationships are established between the key variables selected, while other variables are dropped because they are considered less important. Thus appreciative theorizing develops or imposes a certain logical structure which is articulated verbally and stays closely linked to empirical observations.

The second level of abstraction is formal theorizing, where logical relationships based on a set of 'stylized facts' are expressed in mathematical terms. The role of formal theorizing is to explore logical connections to the utmost. Formal theorizing proceeds at a level of abstraction much higher than that of appreciative theorizing in relation to the base empirical material. When well formulated, formal theory should express the causal or deterministic essence of economic processes. It is this capability that gives economic science its power to analyse, predict and derive policy prescriptions that go beyond the mere extrapolation of experience.

Nelson (1997, pp. 34–5) argues that empirical findings seldom influence formal theory directly but most frequently through the intermediate level of appreciative theorizing. Empirical work and appreciative theorizing would work well together and formal theorizing should take up the challenges posed by appreciative theorizing. This means that the formal models 'identify gaps or inconsistencies in the verbal stories and suggest new mechanisms and connections to explore.' In the best of all possible worlds, these cross-level interactions should sustain each other in symbiotic harmony

The reality today is that mainstream formal theorizing has worked itself into a cul-de-sac, largely resisting influences from appreciative models. For example, Nelson (1997, p. 35) states that 'new growth theory, while advertising its break from traditions, in fact, has stayed very close to the status quo ante.' The key concepts and growth mechanisms popularized by new growth theory are outlined in Chapter 2 in relation to growth in East Asia. The formal growth models themselves are not discussed, since they are not seen to add insights that are useful for the analyses developed here. In any case, the discussion in this book is pitched mostly at the level of Nelson's appreciative theorizing.

The decomposition of the sources of growth in terms of the contributions of physical capital, labour, human capital and technical advance is a standard technique of economic analysis, as indicated in the introduction above. This analytical technique derives from the underlying theory of economic growth and is also taken up in Chapter 2. Maddison, a master of the art, describes it as the identification of the 'proximate sources of growth.' It is, in fact, the starting point for much of the discussion presented in this book. Chapters 2 and 3 also take up the important question of the significance of measures of total factor productivity growth which is still commonly taken as the measure of technological change; that view is comprehensively challenged there.

Going beyond the proximate sources of growth, there is the fundamental question of development economics: what set of economic policies lead to the fastest possible growth? This is an old debate going back to the early 1950s; it was revived with particular intensity in the late 1980s by influential economists associated with the World Bank. They argued for the superiority of the outward-oriented model of development purportedly exemplified by East Asia, based on liberal trade policies and market-oriented development.

Opponents of the neo-liberal view emphasized the role of the powerful development-oriented state, with industrial policies and the 'governing of markets,' as the crucial determinant of East Asian success. Now, at the start of the new millennium, the debate about development policy appears to have reached closer accord in some areas, incorporating important elements from both sides. In particular, the growth-promoting value of a relatively open relationship with the world market, stable macroeconomic conditions and the active promotion of domestic market forces, is now accepted by all except small minorities on the extreme right and the left (Stiglitz 1998a). These debates, the extent of the consensus and outstanding differences are summarized in Chapters 4 and 5.

The role of technological change is discussed in some detail in this book, since it is crucial to the process of growth. It is clear that technical advance in East Asia has occurred largely in catch-up mode. Yet the conclusion of mainstream analysis that technical advance has not been a significant source of growth in East Asia flies in the face of all other assessments of technological change. As an alternative to the old and new theories of growth, Chapter 6 pulls together insights drawn from the best-known appreciative studies of East Asian growth. These studies establish that technology assimilation and productivity growth take place as a series of multi-level learning processes, in work teams, firms, organizations and even nations. The story developed here is richer and more complex than the simple neoclassical model of consumption-foregone savings invested in physical and human capital and new designs through R&D activity.

Chapter 7 develops an integrated view of various aspects of technological capability acquisition based on the East Asian experience. The learning processes involved are conceptualized as the acquisition of 'social capability' by various productive units and nations. The accumulated aggregate of these non-physical capabilities, along with physical capital invested in equipment, machines and infrastructure, are then seen as determining the productivity of the national economy or its 'national technological capability.'

The accumulated non-physical capabilities, which are equivalent to the 'social capability' of Abramovitz (1995), are explicitly conceptualized as forms of non-tangible capital, much as the human capital that is seen to reside in individual agents. It is in a  sense the social equivalent of human capital which working in tandem with the technology hard-coded in physical investment, i.e. machines, equipment and physical infrastructure determine the productive potential of the economy. National differences in economic performance are then seen to depend on both forms of accumulation. The accumulation of social capability is governed by the nature of competition, success in world market penetration and the building of domestic institutions, which are in the nature of public goods. Social capability and its economic consequence are then no longer the automatic outcome of tangible, physical investments alone, but depend on the intangible investments made in human capabilities and supporting institutions.

The generalized financial crisis that engulfed the East Asian region from the middle of 1997 to 1998 has raised many important questions about the viability of outward-oriented models of development and the desirability of trade and financial liberalization. Some of these are old questions, such as the capacity of world markets to absorb expanding volumes of manufactures exports from NIEs. It is likely that China's emergence as a major exporter has generated competitive pressures for Thailand, Indonesia and Korea which contributed to the crises. Newer questions have arisen about the destabilizing effect of global financial markets, especially short-term capital flows. The extent of corruption and cronyism, along with the weakness of  financial institutions in East Asian countries, are crucial deficiencies in the institutional structure which inhibit  growth beyond a certain threshold of maturity.

The nature, origin and possible modes of resolution of financial crises in East Asia are discussed in Chapter 8 and compared with the experience of financial crises in Latin America and in the early USA. While there are new features associated with the current crises in Asia, there are also other features that are common to financial crises in capitalist economies everywhere. Crises sometimes constitute the mechanisms of renewal and reform in capitalism, but on occasion could lead to deep and prolonged social and political crises. The possibilities latent in the present situation in Asia, are discussed along with the longer-term significance of episodes of crisis.

The economic success of the first-tier East Asian economies has induced many developing countries to reorient their policies in line with the perceived elements of East Asian development strategies. Yet few countries seem to be progressing along on similar growth paths to date. The performance record of the second-tier SEA economies of Malaysia, Indonesia and Thailand fall well short of the first-tier East Asian standard, as discussed in section 1.2 above. The general question raised is whether the more modest achievements of the emulators derive from internal causes, such as failure to push through needed reforms, build essential elements of capability, or from external constraints.

It could also be argued that the first-tier East Asian nations exploited a historically specific window of opportunity in the world economy that has now passed. But even if that is true, the fact remains that they built up the capabilities to benefit from the opportunity, whereas other developing nations did not. So the substantive question remains of how such capabilities are built up. In any case, the possibilities of producing for a liberalized global market appear to be growing with time, though undoubtedly competition is getting more intense as well.

Chapter 9 concludes with a discussion of the broad theoretical and public policy issues arising out of the analysis of technological change and economic growth developed here on the basis of the East Asian experience. An important question in this respect is the use of industrial policy to promote or direct technological change, in crucial phases of the transition. This question is still an unresolved and sensitive issue in the mainstream of the economic profession. It is well known that South Korea, Taiwan and Singapore actively promoted technical advance through state-directed industrial policies. However, industrial policy has not worked well in many other countries; hence most economists do not support anything more than broad functional interventions to build educational levels, infrastructure and other public goods and services.

The conclusion reached in this study is that there is no alternative to intervention if the development needs of the great majority of presently poor countries are to be addressed expeditiously. Such intervention needs to be much more carefully crafted than the development policies practised in the past. While 'government failure' is still a very real possibility, it is argued that there is no alternative to governmental action. International agencies and transnational corporations can, however, play a key supplementary role in strengthening the capabilities of public and private agencies involved in building up the technological capabilities of developing nations.

# 2. Sources and measures of growth

This chapter provides a brief introduction to prevailing economic growth theory and measures used in the literature to compare long-term economic growth and technological change across industries and countries. The chapter begins by defining the different concepts of productivity and linking them to the theoretical model. Growth accounting methodology is then briefly taken up, followed by a review of the relationship between capital accumulation and technical change. Some empirical test of the theory are considered next, followed by a discussion of the key insights brought in by the endogenous theories of growth. The chapter concludes with some important criticisms of mainstream theory raised in the recent literature. Additional criticisms are also taken up in section 3.5. Broader surveys of the growth literature are to be found in Temple (1999) and Van den Berg (2001).

## 2.1 ECONOMIC GROWTH AND PRODUCTIVITY

Statistics measuring long-term economic progress are commonly presented in the form of output per capita, or as labour productivity (LP), which is output per unit of labour input. When tracking the growth record of an economy, or when comparing growth across nations, the common practice now is to use international comparison program (ICP) data for measures of GDP, which are corrected for purchasing power parity (PPP).[1] The growth rates of labour productivity and output per capita differ somewhat because the ratio of working to total population varies with time and across nations, especially for rapidly industrializing countries. While labour productivity tracks the productive capacity of the domestic economy, GNP/capita is the better measure of potential welfare for its citizens.

Economic growth, of course, is only a necessary condition for economic development. It is widely accepted that declining inequality in distribution, poverty alleviation and environmental sustainability are crucial indicators of

---

[1]Details of measurement issues are to be found in Maddison (1995, 1991), Baumol et al. (1989) and Summers and Heston (1991).

the broader objective. One could add to this list other desirable outcomes: human capital accumulation, health care and PQLI (physical quality of life index) levels close to those of the advanced nations, civil liberties, security and democratic freedoms (Sen 1999). These measures are crucial 'ultimate' goals of development, whereas sheer output growth is merely an intermediate or 'proximate' target; this distinction is explained below. Furthermore, progression from proximate to ultimate is not at all automatic. Wade (2001) argues that uneven growth has widened global inequality to the point where it threatens the political sustainability of the system. While acknowledging their importance, such considerations are beyond the scope of the present analysis, which focuses mostly on economic growth and technological change, rather than the much more complex issue of development.

To facilitate comparisons of relative economic performance, raw growth data have to be corrected for varying levels of factor inputs. This is usually accomplished by computing labour productivity, as described above and total factor productivity (TFP) which is described below. Occasionally capital productivity is also used. Most of the time it is the annual growth rates of these measures that are useful rather than their absolute 'level' values. The corresponding rates are referred to here as TFPG and LPG, where the 'G' stands for the annual rate of growth. Furthermore, given the nature of the inquiry here, the emphasis is mostly on medium to long-term growth rates. Thus short-term cyclical effects such as labour hoarding and capacity utilization, which are important in a different context, are not considered.

Maddison (1991, pp. 10–11) explains that in analysing growth, causal analysis can be pitched at two levels, the 'proximate' and the 'ultimate': 'The investigation of ultimate causality involves consideration of institutions, ideologies, pressures of socio-economic interest groups, historical accidents, and economic policy at the national level.' He argues that it also involves 'consideration of the international economic order, exogenous ideologies, and pressures or shocks from friendly or unfriendly neighbours.' Analysis of proximate causes would take off along the lines presented in Chapter 5.[2]

Proximate analysis attempts to explain growth in terms of the measures, models and concepts developed in contemporary economic theory. This is the approach adopted in the literature on cross-country analyses of medium-term economic growth. The explanatory variables driving growth are then labour, physical and human capital, natural resources, benefits from transactions with foreign countries, such as trade and technology transfer, scale effects and structural change. Detailed discussion of the various proximate determinants are provided by Maddison (1987, 1991) and Temple (1999).

---

[2]Examples of analyses that focus more on ultimate determinants are Braudel (1984), Kennedy (1987), Vernon (1989), Tunzelmann (1995), Landes (1998) and Mokyr (1999).

This study also begins with issues of proximate analysis, especially in this chapter. However, to explain growth completely it is found necessary to consider issues of 'social capability,' i.e. the human and social factors which determine the efficiency with which tangible inputs are used in production. The discussion then necessarily moves on to broader analyses of the social and political institutions that promote faster accumulation of critical inputs, and how these are changed by deliberate human activity. In other words, to explain economic change completely, we have to move beyond the purely formal models of economic theory. Such issues are taken up in later chapters.

As explained above, aggregate labour productivity (LP) is the commonly used measure of the economic progress of a nation. But this index does not say anything very specific about the way it is realized. Thus the extent of capital accumulation, both physical and non-physical, in relation to active labour, which is the driving force behind labour productivity, remains hidden from view. It seems intuitive that if two nations achieve the same LP growth with different levels of physical investment per capita, then the one that uses less tangible capital is more efficient. For a measure of economic efficiency, it is necessary to go beyond LP and correct for capital used in production.

The measure of economic efficiency[3] used most often in standard theory is total factor productivity (TFP) or multi-factor productivity. In general terms, TFP is the ratio of aggregate output to a composite measure of the inputs used in production. However, TFP needs to be distinguished from 'efficiency' per se, which is a technical concept used in production, where inputs and outputs are defined in purely physical terms. TFP, by contrast, is an economic concept with inputs and outputs aggregated into common units using value or cost weights. The two measures would be identical in the case of a single output, single input system (Norsworthy and Jang 1992, ch. 1).

But TFP has a significance transcending its use as a measure of economic efficiency. Since technological change cannot be measured directly, TFP is often taken as a surrogate index for technology. More explicitly, TFPG, or the rate of TFP growth, is used as a measure of the rate of 'technical progress,' or efficiency gain that cannot be explained by factor accumulation alone. The justification for this association is that for it to be effective, technological change must generally be productivity enhancing, which implies a one-to-one monotonic functional relationship between TFPG and technological change. These concepts are examined further in Chapter 3.

---

[3] The use and limitations of alternative productivity yardsticks is discussed by Baumol et al. (1989, ch. 11). They argue that TFP must not be construed as a better alternative to labour productivity; they are complementary measures of different aspects of economic growth: 'while TFP is undoubtedly the better index of efficiency of input use ... labor productivity is the more illuminating measure of the result of the process for its human participants.'

Absolute TFP, as distinct from its growth rate, can be defined by equation 2.1 below for the case of a production unit with outputs characterized by physical quantities $y_j$ and inputs by physical quantities $x_i$ which include labour. TFP is the ratio of aggregate gross output to aggregate purchased inputs expressed in real terms, so that quantity and price of all inputs and outputs are adjusted for quality change. The logic is that the measure must capture only the total factor productivity of the technology associated with the production process, excluding any quality change in the inputs that takes place outside the 'black box' of the production process.[4]

$$TFP = \Sigma_j v_j y_j / \Sigma_i w_i x_i \qquad (2.1)$$

Competitive market conditions are assumed initially. In the above equation, $v_j$ is the share of output $j$ in total revenue and $w_i$ is the share of input $i$ in total cost. If $q_j$ is the price of output $j$ and $p_i$ is the price of input $i$, $v_j = q_j y_j / \Sigma_j q_j y_j$ and $w_i = p_i x_i / \Sigma_i p_i x_i$. The assumption of profit maximization in competitive markets, subject to the production function, can be relaxed to variable cost minimization, with outputs and fixed inputs determined exogenously, subject to a cost function. When the rate of change of TFP is calculated, the factor shares and output shares are assumed to change with time in the most general case, along with input and output quantities. The arithmetic aggregation of inputs and outputs, however, is a matter of convention; geometric, or log-linear, aggregation could be used as in the Cobb-Douglas form.

## 2.2   THE SOLOW-SWAN GROWTH MODEL

Total factor productivity (TFP) has a very simple interpretation in the conventional, Solow-Swan growth model. This model, which is widely used in TFP estimation, is based on an aggregate production function for the nation, which is often assumed to have the Cobb-Douglas form. Following Harberger (1998), a similar form can be derived as a value relation, without assuming an aggregate production function. Harberger starts from the simple intuition that output growth is the sum of economic rewards to capital and labour input changes plus an unexplained residual, as expressed in the first order, value accounting equation 2.2.

$$p\Delta Y = w\Delta L + (\rho + \delta)\Delta K + R \qquad (2.2)$$

---

[4]See Norsworthy and Jang (1992, ch. 1) and Baumol et al. (1989, ch. 11) for details. The more comprehensive Divisia index of TFP growth, $TFPG = \Sigma_i v_i\, d\ln y_j / dt - \Sigma_i w_i\, d\ln x_j / dt$, is applicable here, albeit under more restrictive conditions, as discussed in Baumol et al.

Here, $\Delta Y$ is the change in output (GDP) during the appropriate time period, which is usually one year. $\Delta L$ is the change in labour input and $\Delta K$ is the gross increase in the capital stock $K$. Also, $p$ is the initial general price level, $w$ the initial real wage, $\rho$ the initial real rate of return to capital, $\delta$ the rate of real depreciation of capital and $R$ is the residual of output growth presently unexplained by increase in the standard factor inputs alone. All variables except $\delta$ are assumed to be functions of time. Labour and capital are paid their marginal products which reflect their contribution to net output.

$$\Delta Y/Y \;=\; \Delta A/A \;+\; \alpha \Delta K/K \;+\; \beta \Delta L/L \tag{2.3}$$

When equation 2.2 is divided throughout by $pY$, it yields the familiar growth accounting formula of equation 2.3, where $\alpha = (\rho + \delta)K/pY$ and $\beta = wL/pY$ are the income shares of capital and labour in gross national income which is assumed to be the same as the value of output $pY$. The share of the residual $R$ in gross output, $R/pY$ is redefined as $\Delta A/A$, the fractional increase in a productivity index $A$. This term can then be identified as the change in total factor productivity TFPG, since it represents output growth not explained by the input growth of capital and labour in the above accounting identity. It is conventionally attributed to Hicks-neutral, ' disembodied technical progress.'

By deriving the concept of TFPG from the strongly intuitive value accounting equation 2.2 above, Harberger links the 'growth residual' to 'real cost reduction' in producing output out of capital and labour. Harberger's value-based approach appears to sidestep conceptual difficulties associated with the existence of an aggregate production function.[5] It is also particularly helpful in understanding the logic behind growth accounting which allocates the residual $R$ to its various cost reducing causes. The implicit assumption that these causes can be combined additively is taken up later in this chapter. If the factor shares $\alpha$, $\beta$ are now assumed to be independent of time, then equation 2.3 can be integrated with respect to time to yield the familiar Cobb-Douglas production function of equation 2.4, which is the log-linear form of the more common $Y = AK^\alpha L^\beta$.

$$\ln Y \;=\; \ln A \;+\; \alpha \ln K \;+\; \beta \ln L \tag{2.4}$$

The usual procedure is to start from equation 2.4, and then derive growth

---

[5] If factor shares are assumed to be determined by marginal productivity, then this approach is not that different from the aggregate production function (APF) approach. See Fisher (1993) for a discussion of the aggregation problem and the comments of Felipe (1999) on the APF and the aggregation problem. The question of allocating the residual between capital and labour is not resolved if competitive market conditions are assumed.

accounting implications, along the following lines. When productivity $A$ is static, it is generally assumed that balanced increments of $x\%$ in $K$ and $L$ would result in $Y$ increasing by $x\%$ as well. This is the constant returns to scale (CRS), or homogeneity of degree one (HD1), assumption which implies $\alpha + \beta = 1$. Usually, these coefficients are assumed to be independent of $t$. By differentiating $Y$ partially with respect to $K$ and $L$ in equation 2.4, it is easily shown that $\alpha$ and $\beta$ represent the elasticities of output with respect to capital and labour respectively. Competitive factor market conditions imply that factors are paid their value marginal products, thus ensuring that $\alpha$ and $\beta$ are income shares of capital and labour in accordance with standard neoclassical production theory.

$$\ln Y/L \;=\; \ln A + \alpha \ln K/L \;=\; \ln A + \alpha \ln k \qquad (2.5)$$

When equation 2.5, obtained by subtracting $\ln L$ from both sides of equation 2.4, is differentiated with respect to time $t$, equation 2.6 is obtained in terms of the intensive variables $y$ ($Y/L$) and $k$ ($K/L$). Here the fractional growth rate of any variable $x$ is written $\hat{x}$ which is shorthand for $x^{-1}dx/dt$, which is also $d(\ln x)/dt$. Equation 2.6 is an expression for labour productivity growth LPG, in terms of $\hat{A}$ and $\hat{k}$. Here $\hat{A} = A^{-1}dA/dt$ and $\hat{k} = k^{-1}dk/dt$, are the growth rates of TFP $A$ and the capital/labour ratio $k$, respectively.

$$\text{LPG} \;=\; d(\ln Y/L)/dt \;=\; \hat{y} \;=\; \hat{A} + \alpha\hat{k} \qquad (2.6)$$

Equation 2.6 confirms the simple economic intuition that welfare growth as measured by LPG can be realized by pure technical progress or by raising the capital/labour ratio, or by a combination of both. The above derivation of total factor productivity can be made consistent with the more basic form given in equation 2.1. Starting from equation 2.1 for a single output system, TFPG is defined as the fractional rate of growth of $Y/X$, where $Y$ is output and $X$ is a scalar index of the factor inputs $K$ and $L$, defined as $X = aK + bL$, where $a$ and $b$ are cost shares. With the usual neoclassical assumptions of constant returns to scale, the expression for TFPG reduces to the rate of technical advance $\hat{A}$, where $\alpha = aK/X$. A similar expression could be derived with geometric (log-linear) aggregation of inputs, which is more in line with the basic Cobb-Douglas form of the production function.

$$\text{TFPG} \;=\; d[\ln(Y/X)]/dt \;=\; \hat{y} - \alpha\hat{k} \;=\; \hat{A} \qquad (2.7)$$

The Cobb-Douglas form carries the assumptions that capital and labour are indefinitely substitutable, with a substitution elasticity equal to one, and that their contribution to output is additively separable, as in equation 2.2. In fact, a specific objective of Solow's work was to overcome the rigidities of the Harrod-Domar model which derived from the absence of substitutability between capital and labour in that model. The production function can also be generalized to the CES form or, as is more common, to the translog form, to bring in variable elasticity of substitution between factors and introduce interaction terms. In fact the entire theory of TFP can be easily generalized for more flexible functional forms (Felipe 1999, Hulten 2000).

The dynamics of the Solow model can be derived from equation 2.8 which is obtained by equating the growth rate of the capital stock $dk/dt$ to the fraction of income saved less the investment required to sustain a population growth rate $n$ and a depreciation rate $\delta$. In this equation $s$ is the savings rate and $y = A.f(k)$ is the production function of equation 2.4 expressed in terms of the commonly employed intensive variables $y$ and $k$.

$$dk/dt \ = \ s\,Af(k) - (\delta + n)k \tag{2.8}$$

Human capital is often factored into the original model by considering $K$ to be an aggregate of physical and human capital. Labour productivity growth then derives from investments in capital, both physical and human, and from technological change. But the transient growth component deriving from rising $K/L$ tapers off to zero on account of diminishing returns implicit in the form of $f(k)$. It is assumed that returns to human capital exhibit diminishing returns and follow depreciation patterns just as physical capital.

Capital accumulation per unit labour input is assumed to cease when $k$ reaches a steady state value $k^*$. The steady relationship of equation 2.9 is derived by putting $dk/dt = 0$ in equation 2.8, assuming that the technology-productivity factor $A$ is fixed. Beyond that, $y = Y/L$ ceases to grow, but $Y$ grows at the same rate as the population, $n$. Hence the only long-term source of per capita growth is technological change, which is generated exogenously.

$$sAf(k^*) \ = \ (\delta + n)k^* \tag{2.9}$$

Empirical estimations of long-term economic growth indicate that both $k$ and $y$ do indeed continue to grow, albeit unevenly, in almost all countries. Hence growth in $A$ is absolutely vital to any explanation of long-term growth in this 'exogenous growth' model. The fact that the key variable governing long-term growth is exogenous to the model is a serious shortcoming, one that the endogenous models of growth have sought to remedy by relating technical progress to real investment in R&D. Solow (1994, p. 48) points out that the crucial question is whether formal models of economic growth can shed any light on this uncertainty-ridden process.

## 2.3    GROWTH ACCOUNTING

The objective of growth accounting is to apportion observed labour productivity growth in an economy to its main proximate sources. Maddison (1995) lists the main sources as technological progress, physical capital, improvements in skill and education or human capital, and productivity gains deriving from organizational change and closer integration with the world economy through trade, investment and other business-related interaction. There is generally little disagreement about the various sources of growth.

Later in this book, an argument is made that the evolution of business-friendly institutions and advances in organizational and business efficiency also contributes to productivity gains. These overlap somewhat with sources of technological advance identified by Maddison. He adds three other effects commonly invoked in the literature as promoting productivity growth: scale effects at industry or national level, structural change from less productive to more productive economic activities and availability of natural resources. Other effects such as energy availability, labour hoarding or dishoarding and capacity utilization, have also been employed by various analysts.

The first step in growth accounting is to obtain TFPG as a residual by subtracting the contributions of physical capital and labour from LPG, as explained in section 2.2 above. Then the residual is allocated to its various sources according to its estimated contribution to 'real cost reduction.' In practice, with annual or quarterly data for output and inputs, the Törnqvist discrete approximation to the continuous Divisia measure of TFP is used. In this index, varying factor shares are approximated by the average of starting and ending values for each period. If the underlying production function is translog, this index turns out to be an exact measure of TFPG.[6]

Much of the discussion about the significance of residual TFPG[7] originated in the 1950s when a number of studies found that only about half of the observed growth of US productivity could be explained by factor growth. Many later studies for a number of European countries and Japan confirmed the finding that the major part of observed growth had to be attributed to an unexplained residual. Kendrick, Denison, Jorgenson, Griliches, and other researchers took up the challenge of 'squeezing down the

---

[6]TFPG estimation is described in Fuss and Waverman (1990, pp. 103-7) and Hulten (2000).
[7]Griliches (1996) states that the concept of an output/input index of TFP originated as far back as 1937, but the first actual measurement was carried out by Tinbergen in 1942. Accounts of the origins of growth accounting theory are given in Hulten (2000), Griliches (1999), Maddison (1987, 1995), Fagerberg (1994) and Nelson (1997). Nelson suggests that most of the concepts underlying growth accounting and even contemporary growth theory are already prefigured in a 1952 review article on economic growth by Abramovitz (1952).

residual,' and a rich growth accounting literature has developed out of these efforts. Griliches (1999) provides an excellent comprehensive survey.

Estimating even the contribution of labour input is not quite as easy as it seems in theory. In the advanced countries, estimates of hours put in are not very accurate before 1950 or so. For newly industrializing countries in their early stages, when a significant amount of economic activity is carried out in household units, labour input is necessarily an approximate measure.

Capital stock estimates are built up by the perpetual inventory method in which successive investments are aggregated over the years on the basis of some assumption about effective depreciation. Apart from the problems inherent in this procedure (Hulten 1996, Kendrick 1993), there is a serious conceptual issue which is rarely highlighted. Griliches (1988, p. 126) notes that while most of the available measures of capital are in the form of value data, what is most useful for productivity estimates are quantity estimates, since the production function should be seen as a relationship between quantities. Hence procedures have to be developed for aggregating capital services based on various adjustments, such as hedonic price indices (Jorgenson and Landau 1989, Hulten 1996).

As far back as 1961, Schultz suggested that 'human capital' be used as a factor of production. Abramovitz had argued in 1952 that education and research should be included in the growth accounts. In recent years this idea has gathered support and is now widely accepted. However, while human capital must include acquired skill and health care levels in addition to education, it is purely education that is most often used as an index because of the difficulty of measuring the other two attributes. Furthermore, increase in education is usually accounted for as an improvement in labour quality rather than as a factor in its own right (Maddison 1995, ch. 2).

Maddison illustrates these procedures by going through successive steps in the growth accounting methodology for the USA, France, Britain, Germany, the Netherlands and Japan, for five distinct periods ranging over 1820–1992. For the periods 1950–73 and 1973–92, TFPG clearly accounts for the lion's share of LPG. He then adjusts for the effects of foreign trade, structural change and labour hoarding or dishoarding and economies of scale to get at the unexplained residual of technical change.

Maddison's procedures seem closer to the eclectic methodologies of Denison and Kendrick than to the more rigorously neoclassical approach of Jorgenson and associates, who have attempted to narrow down the residual as much as possible by means of quality adjustments made to disaggregated factor inputs. This is achieved by augmenting factor inputs for effectiveness, labour for higher skill levels and capital for more productive, later vintages.

The estimates of TFPG and the technical change residual obtained by Maddison are substantial for the countries studied in the 1950–92 period, though the values for the USA are smaller because it is the technology leader. The other countries benefit from a catch-up bonus except for Britain in the period 1950–73. Britain does not appear to have the social capability to benefit from its position as a follower country until the 1970s.[8]

Maddison finds that accumulation of physical capital has been quite considerable as well. There are two components: one is capital 'widening' which is the provision of capital goods for the expanding population. There is also substantial 'deepening' of capital, reflected in rising capital/labour ratios, to accommodate many new technologies developed in these periods. In the USA, for example, the capital stock had risen faster than output growth in the period 1820–1913 but slower in 1913–73. Maddison states that without the advance of technology, accumulation of physical capital since 1820 would have been much more limited.

The results of various growth accounting exercises carried out for the East Asian economies are considered in Chapter 3. Problems arising from the fundamental assumptions underlying the methodology are discussed below and elsewhere in the book. A crucial issue is whether the various effects listed above are additively separable in the form assumed by growth accountants. To resolve this issue, it is necessary to look more closely at the underlying mechanisms of accumulation and technical change.

## 2.4   ACCUMULATION AND TECHNICAL CHANGE

A major shortcoming of the simple neoclassical model is its representation of technical change as independent of the accumulation of capital. This separation is necessary because diminishing returns to accumulable capital is expected to eventually choke off investment-driven growth. Yet it flies in the face of the simple intuition that most technological innovations need to be embodied in new equipment to take effect. Invoking a lesser-known model of Solow (1960), Greenwood and Jovanovic (1998) and Gort et al. (1999) find that 'investment-specific' technological change accounts for about half of labour productivity growth. This argument and other radical departures from the neoclassical growth model are taken up later in Chapters 3 and 7.

Hulten and Srinivasan (1999) show that subtracting the contribution of $K/L$ growth from LPG, as in equation 2.7 above, yields an underestimate of

---

[8]Britain's anomalous behaviour indicates that 'catch-up' is not automatically determined by the existence of a technology gap. The potential for catch-up needs to be actively sought by a readiness to reform existing institutions and practices, a task that was difficult for Britain while basking in the after-glow of empire and heroic victory in the SWW. This issue is taken up in Chapters 7 and 9 in the context of the forces driving growth in developing countries.

technological change $A$. While a rise in $A$ makes the entire production function shift upwards, $K/L$ growth involves movements along the function for a fixed $A$. Since the production function is but one equation in a system of equations determining the growth trajectory, they argue that $K/L$ is an endogenous variable and part of its rise is 'induced accumulation' caused by the rise in $A$. In other words, as $A$ rises, it will induce an increase in capital to support the higher level of $A$ in a steady-state equilibrium.

The above argument is easily established for the steady state represented by equation 2.9. Suppose that the technology parameter $A$ changes by an amount $dA$ when the economy is in its steady state. Since this change in $A$ would shift the production function upwards, the capital/labour ratio $k$ has to rise to a higher value $(k + dk)$ to reach a new steady state, for the same rate of depreciation. With a basic Cobb-Douglas production function $\ln y = \ln f(k) = \ln A + \alpha.\ln k$, equation 2.9 can be invoked to yield a simple relationship between the fractional growth of variables $y$, $k$ and $A$, if it is assumed that the new equilibrium is reached relatively quickly.

$$\frac{dy}{y} = \frac{dk}{k} = \frac{dA}{(1-\alpha)A} \qquad (2.10)$$

If $\alpha = 1/3$, then a 1% rise in $A$ would generate a 1.5% rise in $y$ and $k$. *Ex post* growth accounting would attribute $1.5\alpha$ or 0.5% of the growth in $y$ to capital accumulation as a separate source of growth, when the change in $k$ is entirely ancillary to the change in technology. Hulten and Srinivasan (1999) show that when induced accumulation is taken into account, calculated TFPG/LPG ratios of 54%, 62% and 59% for South Korea, Taiwan and Hong Kong, respectively, turn into 77%, 83% and 95%. This is the Harrodian concept of TFPG which measures the shift in the production function along a constant capital/output line rather than the conventional constant $K/L$ line; it accounts for the lion's share of the observed growth in labour productivity.

Criticisms of the basic assumptions of the Solow-Swan model and growth accounting methodology have been made very forcefully by Nelson in a series of articles from as far back as 1964.[9] Nelson points out that even in a neoclassical production model, growth is 'super-additive' in the sense that the growth of one input augments the marginal contribution of the others. Growth can be attributed separately to factors only for very small changes. Marginal analysis is misleading when large finite changes of inputs are involved. Nelson shows that growth accounting makes sense only if complementarity between physical capital, human capital and technical change is not very

---

[9]Nelson (1964, 1973, 1981, 1998). Strong complementarity between technical change and investment is supported in Solow (1960) and reiterated in Greenwood and Jovanovic (1998).

significant. The existence of strong complementarity invalidates any attempt to separate out the contributions of each factor.

The above problem is linked to the way human capital is seen to operate in promoting growth. Human capital, usually proxied by years of education, is seen as contributing to growth by simply augmenting the capital stock or the quality of labour input. Contemporary views see human capital as consisting of skill and knowledge acquired in the process of design and production, supported by adequate formal education (Chapter 7 and Lucas 1993). These basic criticisms are developed in greater detail in Chapters 3 and 7 in an alternative conception of productivity growth.

There are other problems with some of the standard procedures. Thus quality improvements in labour, capital and intermediate inputs represent embodied technological change. If technical change is computed as a residual with input contributions corrected for quality enhancement, then the residual is reduced and embodied technology is not accounted for. Further, structural change, such as the movement of labour from agriculture to more productive industrial activity, is an important source of growth in rapidly industrializing countries. This must involve a widening of the capital stock to accommodate the shift and so capital investment is linked to productivity growth.

Nelson observes that positive feedback links exist between investment and technical innovation, which link them together in boom periods as well as slumps. These positive feedback linkages manifest themselves in the form of increasing returns to scale in manufacturing industry, particularly in the production of durable goods. Nelson and Pack (1999) and Rodrik (1998) have also argued that if the elasticity of substitution between capital and labour is less than one, then estimates of TFPG will be biased downwards. These criticisms are taken up in section 3.5 in the next chapter, since they are made in the context of TFPG estimation in East Asia.[10]

## 2.5   SOME EMPIRICAL TESTS OF THE ASSUMPTIONS

Econometric analyses have shown that other basic assumptions of the neoclassical framework are questionable, such as the assumption of perfect competition and CRS (constant returns to scale). Hall (1990) found large markups and increasing returns to scale (IRS) in many US industries. The Solow residuals were also found to be procyclical, thereby negating the assumption of Hicks-neutral technical progress. Hall also establishes that the

---

[10]Felipe (1999) has pointed out that the existence of an aggregate production function itself is questionable as is the procedure for aggregating various kinds of physical capital. This important issue is not taken up directly in this book, but addressed obliquely in Chapter 7.

non-neutrality of the residual does not depend on the existence of market power. He concluded that either IRS exist or firms enjoy thick-market externalities when output is high.

Building on Hall's approach, Caballero and Lyons (1990) have estimated returns to scale separately for individual industries at the two-digit level and for aggregate manufacturing, for a number of European countries. They find strong evidence of IRS at the aggregate level for Germany, France, Britain and Belgium. But at the disaggregated level, with the external effects between industries extracted, there is very little evidence of IRS; if anything, the estimates suggest decreasing returns.

However, evidence of external economies is established for all four countries. There are specification problems with the Caballero and Lyons procedure. They assume that external effects are internal to each country. But a number of industries, in particular the auto industry, benefit from economies of scale for the entire European Common Market. The procedure also assumes that TFP growth or technical progress is disembodied. If TFPG is correlated with investment then the model is not properly specified.

Bartelsman et al. (1991) extend the above approach for US manufacturing industry. They attempt to separate external interactions into short-run cyclical (thick-market) effects and long-run growth-related effects.[11] In addition to the investigation of external interactions between the aggregate and two-digit levels they examine linkage between two-digit and four-digit levels, to find the extent to which external effects are localized to particular sectors.

In all of their estimations they find internal returns to scale to be very close to unity. But strong evidence of both short-run cyclical and long-run growth-oriented externalities is found.[12] For the former, the linkage is largely mediated through demand for industry output. Further, once the inter-industry linkage is specified, cyclical effects do not depend on sectoral proximity. For growth externalities, the dominant linkage is that between an industry and its suppliers, suggesting an important role for intermediate goods, either through specialization or knowledge embodiment.

More recent studies (Burnside et al. 1995, Basu and Fernald 1997) correct for Hall's use of value-added data and other problems. Use of gross output data reduces returns to scale and markups, but confirm significant increasing returns at higher levels of aggregation as do earlier studies. At the industry level, Basu and Fernald find evidence of significant increasing returns only

---

[11]The long-run effects are assumed to operate thorough knowledge spillovers, direct or mediated through intermediate goods linkages, hinging on specialization in intermediates or transmission of technological progress (see Rosenberg 1982 for details).

[12] Evidence of productivity correlation across industries within the same country is found by Costello (1993), which further supports the existence of growth externalities.

in durable goods manufacturing industries. The output of durable goods industries are also found to be more procyclical than the average.

Overall, the somewhat mixed results of econometric studies indicate that a resolution of the question of returns to scale at the industry level has still not been reached. Hall (1995) suggests that the weight of evidence indicates mild increasing returns, a view that is supported by the analysis of Basu and Fernald (1997). Increasing returns are clearly found at the aggregate level, indicating strong externalities. Of course, the absence of IRS within narrowly defined industries in the USA and Europe does not mean that this is also true for newly industrializing countries at a very different stage of development.

The residual is also not neutral or disembodied as assumed. De Long and Summers (1991, 1992) suggest it is correlated with investment in capital equipment. It very likely includes the effect of externalities not captured by a misspecified production function. Srinivasan (1995) says 'it is in general difficult to identify separately the effects of returns to scale and technical progress – either one can be used as a substitute explanation for the other.'

## 2.6    THEORIES OF ENDOGENOUS GROWTH

There has been a very rapid expansion of the literature on new models of economic growth since the first tentative steps taken by Romer (1986, 1990) and Lucas (1988). Attempts to endogenize growth began earlier with Arrow (1962), Shell (1966, 1967, 1973) and others.[13] The main thrust of these and subsequent efforts has been to rectify the arbitrary way in which long-term growth is made to depend on exogenous technical progress, as described above. In the new models, sustainable growth is endogenized by one or other of the basic processes described below. The essential elements in the models that enable sustained growth are examined at the end of this section.

Elements of the Romer constructs are present in earlier attempts to extend the Solow-Swan model by Arrow (1962) and Sheshinski (1967). Indeed, continuities are quite strong, as detailed in Stern (1991), Romer (1994) and Aghion and Howitt (1998). Arrow developed a 'learning-by-doing' model in which productivity-enhancing knowledge is accumulated as an unintended externality, arising out of successive investments in capital goods. The idea that investment and technological knowledge are quite intimately linked was raised in the earlier discussion of the dynamics of the Solow model as well. Clearly new designs need to be embodied in new vintages of capital goods.

---

[13]Surveys are given in Amable (1994), Barro and Sala-i-Martin (1995), Jones (1998) and Aghion and Howitt (1998). Shell (1973) flags even earlier attempts to endogenize growth.

Sheshinski's non-vintage version captures the essence of the Arrow model as well. The production function of each firm is $Y_i = F(K_i, AL_i)$. The level of technical knowledge is $A = (\Sigma K_i)^\gamma$, where $\gamma < 1$ is the elasticity with which new knowledge grows as a result of growth in the aggregate capital stock of the entire economy. Romer's equation (2.11 below) can be construed as a variant of this model in which $\gamma = 1$ and human capital in the research sector replaces the aggregate capital stock. Both models generate a steady-state growth rate of $n/(1 - \gamma)$ where $n$ is the growth rate of the workforce.

In Romer (1986), a fraction of productive resources in each firm is diverted to research or knowledge production by means of a research technology which exhibits diminishing returns. Knowledge is treated as a form of capital which combines with physical capital and labour to generate output. The production function for output is CRS (constant returns to scale) in physical capital, labour and produced knowledge. Hence, a competitive equilibrium can be sustained. But since knowledge is nonrival and not entirely excludable,[14] the production of knowledge by one firm has a positive external effect on the productivity of other firms. In other words, the spillover of knowledge generates a positive (Marshallian) externality which yields increasing returns to scale in all inputs at the aggregate level when all firms are generating knowledge. In this model, investment in knowledge capital need not have a diminishing marginal product.

The endogenization of technological knowledge $A$ is made more explicit in Romer (1990). Here the engine of growth is not inter-firm learning externalities, but continuous increase in the variety of producer durable goods incorporating new designs. This model has three sectors: an R&D sector for the production of new knowledge or designs, an intermediate capital goods sector and a final goods sector. In the intermediate goods sector, which is imperfectly competitive, each firm produces a single good out of existing designs. As a consequence, firms reap monopoly rents which are the reward for technological progress.

The essence of the model is described by Romer (1990) as follows. Overall production is represented by $F(A, X)$, where the vector $X$ represents the rival inputs, labour, capital and human capital $H$. $A$ represents the total stock of designs or knowledge which every producer is free to use. Therefore $A$ is nonrival. The production function for final consumption goods is assumed CRS in X by a simple replication argument, which means $F(A, \lambda X) = \lambda.F(A, X)$. But if $A$ is productive, it follows that $F(\lambda A, \lambda X) > \lambda F(A, X)$, which leads to increasing returns in all inputs.

Romer recognizes that human capital $H$ is a composite measure of

---

[14]A *rival* input cannot be used in more than one production site. If a nonrival input, such as technological knowledge, can be withheld from other potential users, it is *excludable*.

education and on-the-job training, which is therefore a rival component of knowledge, associated with individual workers. $H$ is distinct and quite separate from $A$, the nonrival, 'technological' component, which is not associated with individuals. For model simplicity, Romer keeps $L$ and $H$ constant. But new knowledge $\Delta A$ is produced from a portion $H_A$ of $H$ assigned to the research sector, on the basis of existing knowledge $A$, according to the following equation.

$$\dot{A} = \delta H_A A \qquad (2.11)$$

The evolving stock of nonrival knowledge is incorporated in capital goods produced as described above. The capital goods are assumed to be perfect substitutes in use. Final output is produced from these capital goods, labour and residual human capital $H - H_A$ by a Cobb-Douglas production function. Other details of the model are not given here, since they do not add much to the understanding of the engine of growth.

There are, of course, many strong simplifications made, such as the separation of human input into raw labour and disembodied human capital in the R&D sector, or the assumption that all capital goods are perfect substitutes. Romer keeps human capital fixed because investment in this resource would eventually run into diminishing returns, just as physical capital does, and therefore could not contribute a long-term component to growth. But this means that the human capital stock is unaffected by the continually growing stock of technological knowledge in society, which is unlikely. The decisive issue, however, is whether the model represents an advance on the neoclassical growth model.

The more detailed specification of the knowledge production system certainly indicates an advance on the Solow-Swan conceptions. The final result obtained by Romer for the long-run growth rate is $\delta H_A$ beyond a minimum threshold value below which there is stagnation. But this is the growth rate of $A$, already implicit in equation 2.11 above, which is still surely in the nature of an 'exogenous' assignment. Romer finds that the proportion of $H$ assigned to design development under optimal conditions depends on the interest rate and other parameters of the model. Nevertheless, one is left wondering whether the formal model as such has advanced insight much beyond the Solow-Swan baseline.

Lucas (1988) is technically similar to Romer (1986). In his first model, there is no change in technological knowledge $A$; instead, human capital, which is taken as the skill level, augments productivity in two ways. The human capital of each worker expands the effectiveness of raw labour directly. In addition to this 'internal' effect the average level of human capital augments the value of $A$ as a human capital externality in the production function which is CRS in direct inputs. The externality induces increasing returns to scale as in the other models. Human capital itself is built up deliberately by diverting a fraction of labour to its production in a separate education sector, and it grows in direct proportion to the raw labour diverted.

Lucas develops a second model in which human capital is built up involuntarily in a learning-by-doing process induced by the production of two consumer goods, one of which generates more human capital than the other, mimicking the dichotomy between a high-technology sector and a low-technology one. This model lends itself to the analysis of the effects of a subsidy to the high-tech industry. It can also be used to study the evolution of trade relations between two countries when one specializes in the high-tech good and the other in the low-tech one.

An influential approach that rejects both externalities and deliberate industrial innovation as the engine of growth, is that of Mankiw, Romer and Weil (1992), hereafter MRW. The MRW model extends the basic Solow framework by augmenting physical capital with human capital as another accumulable factor built up by the diversion of a part of savings. The model assumes a Cobb-Douglas production function in physical capital, human capital and effective labour. Technical change is entirely labour-augmenting and assumed the same for all countries. Savings rates and population growth rates are exogenous for each country. The savings rate for physical capital is proxied by investment/GDP, assuming that there are no inter-country capital flows. The 'savings rate' for human capital is proxied by the fraction of working-age people in secondary school. It is also assumed that depreciation rates are the same for both forms of capital, and for all countries.

MRW derive steady-state conditions for this model and then estimate the steady-state equation for output per unit labour from the Summers-Heston ICP data set. They find that the augmented model explains 78% of the cross-country variation, much better than the original Solow model. The estimation also yields coefficients for the terms involving the savings rates that imply elasticities for human capital and physical capital (roughly one-third each) that accord well with observed returns to these factors.[15] The coefficients are such that the observed variation in savings rates is enough to explain the range of variation of per capita output observed across a wide range of countries. Since this was not possible with the original Solow form, the MRW model overcomes one major problems associated with the former.

---

[15]These results indicate that the elasticity of output with respect to total capital is around two thirds, a value that is closer to econometrically estimated values which range between 0.4 and 0.6, rather than physical capital's share of income which is closer to one-third (Pack 1994). Though the measures of capital in these estimates cover only physical investment, the results are still valid if it is assumed that human capital is roughly proportional to physical capital.

De Long (1997) remarks that today the modal view held by most economists conforms to the MRW model. If so, the likely reason is that the MRW model is only a step removed from the very familiar Solow model. Yet there are serious problems with the MRW model. It does not really overcome the problem of diminishing returns to accumulation; it simply stretches out the time to adjustment to steady state from about 25 years to about 50 years (Mankiw et al. 1992, Mankiw 1995). It is, therefore, highly likely, that most countries in the data set are very far from steady state. Other assumptions of the model are also hard to accept, such as a common rate of technological progress for 98 countries over a 25-year period. When the regression set is confined to the 22 OECD countries for which the data are likely to be more reliable, the adjusted $R^2$ drops from 0.78 to 0.28 (Grossman and Helpman 1994).

Other serious objections to the MRW model have been voiced at a Brookings presentation by Mankiw (1995). Phelps (1995) remarks that the rather mechanical representation of human capital as analogous to a physical stock does not capture the dynamic processes of learning, which are contingent on market opportunities and entrepreneurship, and the role of property rights and institutions in general. This criticism is, of course, applicable to all deterministic models, including the endogenous growth models, and has even been raised elsewhere by Lucas (1993). A fuller discussion of this problem is deferred to Chapters 7 and 9.

Romer (1995) takes serious objection to Mankiw's representation of technology as a public good, which he sees as the principal determinant of variation for per capita national income worldwide. Romer probably means 'technological capability,' a broader concept discussed in more detail in Chapter 7, rather than technology in a narrow sense. This is indicated by his invocation of Fagerberg's (1994) comprehensive review of the literature on technology and international differences in growth rates. Romer (1995, pp. 313–20) categorically states that 'unnecessary reliance on this neoclassical model has hampered clear thinking about growth' and that what is needed is 'an extended theoretical framework that lets us take technology seriously.' He also finds quantitative inconsistencies in the MRW model, some of which Mankiw has recognized as well.[16]

Perhaps the really fundamental objection to the widely held MRW model of growth is the way in which human capital is conceived and proxied. Human capital should be replaced by a measure of overall national technological capability (discussed in Chapter 7) rather than just education. But technological capability includes productivity-enhancing gains in

---

[16]Romer (1995) argues that the model implies that skilled labour in poor countries should receive wages that are ten times larger than wages received by skilled labour in the USA.

organization and management, economic institutions facilitating business activity, the strength of the network of organizations supporting technical education, research and development, and so on (Lall 1990). It is then clear that the term 'human capital' must be replaced or at least supplemented by broader concepts such as 'social capability,' 'social infrastructure' or 'social capital.' The above caveats, indeed criticisms, of the neoclassical system of analysis go back over many decades (Fagerberg 1994, Nelson 1997).[17]

What has been discussed so far are the most widely quoted models of the new growth theory. Grossman and Helpman (1994) observe that the wide range of endogenous growth models can be categorized into three basic types. The first type continues to see 'capital accumulation' as the main engine of growth with the concept of capital broadened to include human capital, as exemplified by the MRW model. The second type sees external economies as the key factor supplying an external productivity boost which sustains long-term growth in the face of diminishing returns to physical or human capital investment. This mechanism is invoked in Arrow (1962), Romer (1986) and Lucas (1988). The third approach sees deliberate improvements in technology, i.e. industrial innovation *à la* Schumpeter, as the principal engine of growth behind 'perpetually rising standards of living.' This last approach is exemplified by Romer (1990), Grossman and Helpman (1991a) and Aghion and Howitt (1992).

The innovation models posit private, profit-seeking agents that invest in new technological knowledge with the object of capturing monopoly rents. As a result, these models incorporate increasing returns and monopolistic competition, which is typically modelled by an increasing variety or quality of intermediate capital goods embodying knowledge developed in an R&D sector, such as in the Romer (1990) paper. The outlays for R&D are recouped from monopoly profits. Details are given in Grossman and Helpman (1991b) and Aghion and Howitt (1998). The models that employ an increasing variety of intermediate inputs also explain the positive effects of international trade as deriving from access to a wider range of specialized capital goods from abroad.

Increasing returns, whether derived from external economies or from the replication of nonrival technological designs, provide the mechanism by which the tendency to diminishing returns in investment is overcome.[18] If it is strong enough to exactly offset the tendency to diminishing returns, the

---

[17]Now, however, they are being made much more insistently in reviews of and reactions to the explicit formulations of the new growth theory (Stern 1991, Pack 1994). The discussion following the above-quoted Mankiw (1995) presentation is a case in point.

[18]See Romer (1994) for a lucid account of the evolution of the concept and Amable (1994) for a more detailed summary of the mechanics underlying endogenous growth.

result is constant returns to accumulable factors, $K$, alone. This situation is captured by the formula $Y = AK$, which harks back to the fixed coefficient production function of the Harrod-Domar model. In any '$AK$' model, there are no transitional dynamics and the growth rate of output $\hat{Y}$ is given by equation 2.12 below, where $\delta$ is the depreciation rate, $s$ the savings rate and $A$ is an index of technology.

$$\hat{Y} = \hat{A} + sA - \delta \tag{2.12}$$

Though it is customary to see $AK$ growth as 'steady' and a razor's edge possibility, this is only true if it is assumed that $A$ is constant. From the above equation, it is clear that the growth rate can rise if $A$ is rising. If increasing returns are more than enough to offset the decreasing returns to capital, then the growth rate keeps increasing all the time even with a constant $A$. As a result, growth is explosive (see Amable 1994).

The conclusion of many reviews (Stern 1991, Fagerberg 1994, Pack 1994, Nelson 1997, Solow 2001) is that the new endogenous theories of growth have not advanced appreciative insights significantly beyond what was already understood before the new wave began. But it is fair to say that the right questions are being asked, and that the problem is being posed in a systematic, theoretically consistent way. In particular, it is worth noting that the investigation is leading researchers such as Romer and Lucas to question fundamental tenets of the neoclassical system in an attempt to explain the diversity of observed growth.[19]

The insights provided by the above developments in endogenous growth theories are the starting point for the examination of East Asian growth undertaken in this book. The East Asian super-performers figure prominently in the literature surveyed here for obvious reasons. But East Asian issues are not taken up here since these are discussed in Chapter 3 and later chapters. Some of the phenomena important for the understanding of East Asian growth, such as structural change, technical efficiency advance and the acquisition of technological capability (discussed in Chapter 6), are inadequately treated in the endogenous growth literature.

---

[19]Pack (1994), for example, remarks that the innovation models establish an internally consistent link between the empirical literature on R&D pioneered by Schmookler, Griliches and Mansfield in the 1950s and 1960s, and general equilibrium models of growth, which incorporate the operation of labour and capital markets, imperfect competition with rents from R&D and household inter-temporal optimization.

# 3.    The puzzle of TFP growth in East Asia

This chapter reviews the more widely discussed analyses of the proximate sources of growth in East Asia carried out through the methodologies of growth accounting or cross-country regression. There are now so many such published cross-country analyses that it is not possible to consider most of them in one chapter. Instead, the strategy adopted here is to cover those studies that have generated the most controversy or have been quoted most frequently in the literature. More detailed accounts of the various analyses of productivity growth in East Asia up to around 1998 are to be found in Chen (1997) and Felipe (1999).

Some of the sharpest debates about the sources of growth in East Asian NIEs have been generated in response to the *East Asian Miracle* study by the World Bank (1993). The 'miracle' economies are identified as eight high-performing Asian economies (HPAEs) which are the first eight economies listed in Table 1.1. These are Japan, the four EA-NIEs (Taiwan, South Korea, Hong Kong and Singapore) and the three SEA-NIEs (Indonesia, Malaysia and Thailand). The choice is determined by their extraordinary growth records, ability to maintain or extend equity in income distribution and other features described in section 1.1 and Chapter 4.

The Miracle study (as it is now commonly referred to in the literature) attempts to identify key elements of HPAE success as policy prescriptions for other less developed countries. These conclusions, and the criticisms elicited, are discussed in detail in Chapter 5. The objective here is to delineate the sources of growth analyses on which the broader arguments are based. The analyses and arguments of the Miracle study are developed more concisely by Pack and Page (1994a), who were key members of the study team. Hence it is appropriate to focus on this paper rather than the Miracle study itself, as the latter was reportedly modified to steer it through the political process of the World Bank.[1] The Miracle study, however, is much more detailed and descriptive; it contains a wealth of supporting data.

[1] A fascinating account of the origins and progress of the *East Asian Miracle* study is to be found in Wade (1996). John Page was the leader of the team and the Pack and Page (1994a) paper is the final version of a working paper that was circulated in 1993.

The Pack and Page results are followed by the analyses of Alwyn Young who categorically refutes the idea that there is anything miraculous about the growth record of the East Asian economies. Some other analyses of East Asian growth are then briefly discussed including the extensive study of Collins and Bosworth. The chapter concludes with a critical review of TFP analyses and the insights provided for understanding growth in East Asia.

## 3.1    PACK AND PAGE ON THE EAST ASIAN MIRACLE

Pack and Page (1994a) examine growth statistics for a group of 118 countries taken from the Heston-Summers 1988 ICP compilation, World Bank data and other data on human capital and trade openness. They find that the HPAEs stand out as extreme outliers in this set, as does the Miracle study.[2] Real income per capita over the period 1960–85 is found to be consistently high for the four EA-NIEs and Japan. In addition, the three SEA-NIEs also exhibit extra-ordinary growth for the 1970–85 period, but slower growth for the earlier 1960–70 period, suggesting that these countries experienced 'take-off' around a decade later. The growth paths of GDP/capita for all these countries, shown in Figures 1.1, 1.2 and 1.3, bear out these statements.

From the above data, Pack and Page derive cross-sectional measures of total factor productivity growth using a neoclassical production model with human capital (see Chapter 2 for details). They regress GDP/capita growth for the 1960–85 period against average investment/GDP, the primary enrolment rate in 1960, the rate of growth of the economically active population and per capita real income in 1960 relative to that of the USA. The last variable is expected to capture gains deriving from the migration of factors to higher productivity sectors. The residuals are interpreted as TFP change not explained by any of these determinants of growth. Since the TFP change consists of technological change plus the advance of technical efficiency (see section 6.2 and appendix 6.A), they make the strong assumption that the former is constant at around 1% per annum across all countries and therefore attribute the variability in the residuals entirely to technical efficiency change.

Just as the GDP/capita data, the residual plots are widely dispersed for the developing countries and there is no pattern of convergence as a whole. As

---

[2]In a plot of GDP growth through the 1960–85 period against 1960 per capita GDP/capita, the more developed countries cluster around a relatively narrow 2–4 % per year band, while the less developed countries are widely spread from – 2% to 7%, with no discernible pattern. The HPAEs are clustered at the upper end in a 4–8 % band. The levels of investment and educational attainment in the HPAEs are also substantially higher than in other countries at similar levels of development (World Bank 1993).

expected the HPAEs fall on the high side of all scatter plots. More interestingly, the HPAEs separate into two distinct groups. The 'investment- driven' economies of Thailand, Malaysia and Indonesia have normal TFPG rates indicating that their high growth derives mostly from factor accumulation. The 'productivity-driven' economies of Singapore, Hong Kong, Taiwan, South Korea and Japan have unusually high rates of TFPG for low and middle-income countries, in addition to high rates of investment. They find these results are closely correlated with other independent studies of TFPG.

Pack and Page find the overall fit of the regression to be good and the coefficients significant at the 5% level. Their results also indicate that when controlling for investment in human and physical capital, poor countries grew faster than rich ones, indicating conditional convergence. They suggest that the results indicate that TFPG could partially derive from structural change, i.e. the shift of factors to higher productivity sectors, such as from agriculture to industry, in the earlier period. When equipment investment is substituted for total investment, the regression fit is found to improve somewhat, in line with the findings of De Long and Summers (1991, 1992).

When the explanatory variable set is expanded to include the share of manufactured exports in total exports and the share of manufactured exports in GDP, the corresponding coefficients are found to be positive and highly significant. They find that these measures and other measures of trade openness are strongly correlated with productivity, indicating a link between high productivity and the export of manufactured goods.

The final conclusion of the study is that superior HPAE growth can be explained on the basis of high, sustained levels of investment in human and physical capital, with an extra productivity premium being captured by the EA-NIEs through the strong promotion of manufactured exports. They also go on to discuss the various channels through which a strong export orientation contributes to the faster growth of productivity. These channels are discussed further in Chapter 4. In the more ideologically slanted Miracle study, the above combination of policies is identified as reliance on economic fundamentals with market friendly trade and macroeconomic policies.[3]

## 3.2   ALWYN YOUNG'S CONTRARIAN VIEW

The Pack and Page analysis described above and the World Bank perspective of productivity growth in East Asia are vigorously contested by Alwyn

---

[3]The validity of this interpretation has been sharply criticized by many analysts, who argue that the Bank study understates the importance of state-directed industrial policies. These issues are taken up in later chapters, since this chapter focuses more on technical issues.

Young (1994a). Young shows that once factor accumulation is properly accounted for, residual TFP growth in the East Asian NIEs is unremarkable, except for the case of Hong Kong. He argues that the high TFPG values obtained by Pack and Page for the HPAEs derives from methodological errors, which are described below. Since the case made explicitly against the Pack and Page paper is similar to analyses developed in more detail in other papers (Young 1992, 1994b, 1995), they are all considered together.

In his most detailed analysis, Young (1995) measures technical change in the EA-NIEs as total factor productivity growth (TFPG), computed from a two-level, value-added translog production function, using the discrete time extension of the Divisia index described in section 2.3. Inputs of capital and labour are, in turn, aggregated from finer sub-categories using a translog index of sub-inputs. Constant returns to scale are assumed at both levels of aggregation. Capital inputs are subdivided into five categories: residential and non-residential buildings, other durable structures, transport equipment and machinery. Labour inputs are adjusted for seven attributes: income, education, age, sex, hours of work, industry and class of employment.

TFPG is computed as the residual of output growth that cannot be explained by the value share weighted contributions of capital and labour inputs. This procedure is exactly equivalent to separating output growth into movements along the production function predicted by factor growth inclusive of various adjustments, and shifts of the production function which are usually identified as 'disembodied technical change.'

Young (1994a, 1994b) begins with a comparison of output/capita growth for 118 nations in the Summers and Heston Mark V data set for the period 1960–85. As expected the EA-NIE 4 appear right at the top of the table with approximately 6% annual growth each, beaten only by diamond-endowed Botswana. When adjusted to yield output/worker growth (which Pack and Page fail to do), the figures appear less spectacular, ranging from 4.3% for Singapore to 5.5% for Taiwan. The roughly 1% fall in the growth rates derives from rising labour participation rates which are extraordinarily high in the 1960–85 period for the four East Asian economies.

The proximate cause of rapid growth is also made patently clear: the EA-NIEs, with the exception of Hong Kong, sustained an extraordinary acceleration of investment to GDP (I/GDP) from around 10% in 1960 to 25–40% in 1970 and beyond. In Hong Kong alone I/GDP stayed around 20% for the 1960–90 period. These investment patterns are depicted in Figure 3.1.

When TFP growth is computed for the 1970–85 period, the ranking of the EA-NIEs and SEA-NIEs drop further, blending indistinguishably into the broad spectrum of nations. Taiwan and Thailand drop to 1.5%, South Korea and Indonesia to 1.2%, Malaysia to 1.1% and Japan to 0.9%. Singapore at 0.1% gets bracketed outrageously between the sluggish South Asian nations of India and Sri Lanka, right at the bottom of the table. Hong Kong alone at 2.4% retains its stellar ranking in relation to other developing countries in the sample. On the basis of Young's calculation of TFPG, the HPAEs cannot be identified as a coherent group of outliers by any stretch of the imagination.

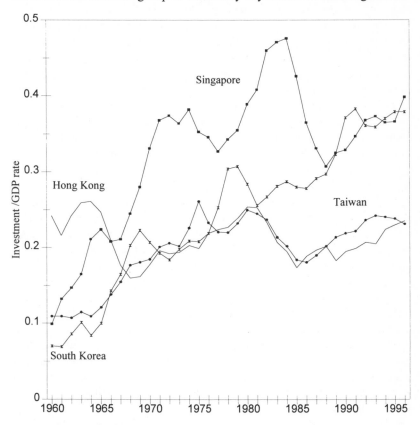

Source: PWT 5.6 series data supplemented by IMF estimates for 1993–6.

*Figure 3.1 Savings/GDP rates for the East Asian economies (1960–96)*

In the later paper, Young (1995) refines the analysis of the EA-NIEs and obtains somewhat higher TFPG values of 2.3% for Hong Kong, 1.7% for South Korea, 2.6% for Taiwan and 0.2% for Singapore, for the 1966–90 period. These values are essentially the same as those obtained by the simpler procedures. With the exception of Singapore, the TFPG values are similar to contemporary values for the advanced industrial countries (Maddison 1995). They are low only in relation to high rates of per capita output growth.

He also computes manufacturing output per worker and shows that the performance advantage of the EA-NIEs over the rest is smaller than that for aggregate output. South Korea, however, is the exception since its manufacturing output/worker exhibits 7.3% growth over the 1979–90 period, well ahead of the rest of the pack. With the exception of Hong Kong, they also maintain very large 5.5–5.7% growth in manufacturing employment over the 1970–90 period, which is well ahead of most developing countries. Young concludes that rapid, sustained factor accumulation explains the 'lion's share' of East Asian growth, but concedes that 'outward orientation' could well have contributed to promoting the demand and supply conditions necessary to sustain heavy factor accumulation for such long periods of time.

Young (1994a) also upbraids Pack and Page for using the Mankiw, Romer, Weil (MRW) model for data that is not consistent with the MRW assumptions. The MRW model is premised upon a constant savings rate, whereas the rates of investment in the HPAEs have changed substantially over the period under review as is clear from Figure 3.1 above.

MRW assume uniform technological change for all countries, whereas Pack and Page work with varying rates of TFPG. Young does not comment on the Pack and Page assumption of a uniform rate of technological change related to progress of the best practice frontier, attributing TFPG variation entirely to changes in technical efficiency. There is no provision for the latter in the MRW model. Finally, Young argues that the significance of exports of manufactures in the regression does not imply a causal connection, since any variable common to most members of a selected subset of rapidly growing economies will show up as significant in a cross-sectional regression.

Pack and Page (1994b) respond to Young's criticisms as follows. First, they point to the manifest technological achievements of South Korea and Taiwan, corroborated by detailed studies of labour productivity and TFP convergence with US industries, such as Pilat (1994). Next they argue, on the basis of neoclassical production theory, that the high rate of investment should necessarily have attenuated the marginal product of capital by 8% per year amounting to a total fall of 81% over a 20-year period. This catastrophic decline in the return to capital is inconsistent with continuing heavy investment, unless rising TFP offsets diminishing returns to physical investment.

Pack and Page also point out that some differences derive from Young's use of the 1970–85 period rather than the 1960–85 span used by them and by his use of accumulated capital stock rather than the investment/GDP measure they use. They point out that on the basis of Young's calculations, Burma, Bangladesh and Uganda show a record of technological advance, proxied by TFPG, comparable to that of the East Asian NIEs, a conclusion that strains credulity to say the least. They do not, however, suggest the more obvious conclusion  that TFPG must be seen as a grossly inadequate measure of technological change. As regards the role of manufactured exports, they point to the results of Levine and Renelt (1992), discussed in section 4.3.

## 3.3    YOUNG'S TALE OF TWO CITIES

Young's TFP analyses of East Asia were developed in the earlier, highly stimulating 'Tale of Two Cities' (Young 1992). This detailed comparison of the post-War growth experience of Singapore and Hong Kong finds significant TFP growth for the former and none for the latter.[4] Operating under a *laissez-faire* economic regime, Hong Kong moved leisurely through a succession of dominant industries with the movement to higher value-adding industries impelled by pristine market forces. Each industry begins with fast growth followed by slowdown and eventual decline when it is overtaken by the next leader industry, though not completely displaced. The economic impetus was provided by refugee textile entrepreneurs, technical workers and factory foremen from the mainland, mainly from Shanghai.[5]

In the initial post-Revolution decade the dominant industry was textiles. This was overtaken by clothing and plastics (toys) in the next decade and by electronic products in the succeeding cycle. Finally in the 1980s, entrepôt trade and banking moved into first place as Hong Kong became the principal conduit for trade and investment flows into post-reform (i.e. post-1978) China. This tale of success is related with some zest by Young who describes the quite extraordinary ingenuity of Hong Kong's entrepreneurial class in responding to changing opportunities in the world market.

---

[4]Young chose these two city states purposively. Their backgrounds are very similar as is the composition of their populations. Both have developed large export dependent manufacturing sectors and passed through similar industries. GDP per capita were very close in 1960 and since then has grown at roughly 6% per annum for both counties.

[5]Hong Kong has benefited from sources other than the invisible hand. First, a large part of Shanghai's textile entrepreneurs, bringing with them foremen and skilled workers, descended on this small island after the 1949 Revolution, thereby significantly raising its entrepreneurial temperature. The industrial skills of *émigré* Shanghainese were crucially complemented by the trading skills of British, Chinese and Indian merchant and financial companies already ensconced in Hong Kong. These companies had spread their trading tentacles throughout the international networks of the British Empire and possessed well over a century of commercial experience. Amsden (1999) points out that Hong Kong benefited from Commonwealth trade preferences against Japan. When the 1950 UN economic blockade closed China's markets to its products, Hong Kong's business barons launched an intensified export drive which eventually led to an export-oriented, transnational production network straddling South-East Asia. More recently Hong Kong has benefited enormously from being the major conduit for China's exports and imports and the principal entrepôt for the rising flood of investment finance into China (Lall 1991, Enright et al. 1997, Yu 1998).

Singapore embarks on its growth trajectory almost 15 years later, but with a significantly lower endowment, especially of human resources: its initial educational levels are much lower and it has practically no domestic capitalist class. Yet under the powerful impetus of a comprehensive state investment programme the economy takes off decisively around 1968. Young remarks that in contrast to Hong Kong's *laissez-faire* policies, Singapore has 'pursued the accumulation of physical capital via forced national saving and the solicitation of a veritable deluge of foreign investment.'

The initiative of the Singaporean state is highly successful in drawing foreign direct investment at accelerating tempos into partnership with state-owned corporations. Singapore then cycles through the same sequence of key industries as Hong Kong, but at roughly double the speed. The stimulus here is not the market but the government's industrial targeting system which provides tax benefits and other subsidies to the target industries. Nowhere else in the annals of economic history has an emergent state cooperated with foreign capital so easily, so efficiently and to such spectacular effect.

On the basis of TFP analysis Young concludes that Hong Kong guided by market forces has been using capital efficiently whereas Singapore, by forcing the pace of technological change, has been wasting capital. Young's analysis is supported by an earlier study by Tsao (1982); she found negative TFPG for the Singapore economy as a whole during 1972–80 and for 28 manufacturing industries on average, for the period 1970–79.[6] The argument is that technologies and associated physical capital are displaced well before the learning potential associated with each new technology is exhausted. This argument is based on Young's (1991) model of bounded learning-by-doing which is discussed in section 6.4.

Nevertheless, there is now a common perception in Hong Kong and Singapore that starting from a lower level of human capital endowment, Singapore has matched or even surpassed Hong Kong by means of its unique industrial policy.[7] Here it seems that physical capital investment along a rising technological trajectory has served as a powerfully effective vehicle for crucial human capital accumulation, or more precisely for the accelerated building-up of social capability (as defined in Chapter 7). The argument that

---

[6]Stiglitz has pointed out that calculation of TFP in Singapore is problematic: 'not only are factor prices noncompetitive because of government control, but state-owned firms, which are major investors, do not necessarily optimize in the neoclassical sense. As a result the production function coefficients assumed for such countries may be meaningless' (Discussion comment in De Long and Summers 1992, p. 209).

[7]In 1993 the author found economists and senior business executives in Hong Kong who were critical of the Colony's administration for failing to pursue a more aggressive policy of industrial development. Their impression was that Singapore was now ahead of Hong Kong in technological capability, a point made also in Lall (1992) and IEEE Spectrum (1991).

the latter is a much more important developmental goal than immediate high growth and income targets is developed later on in this book. It follows that TFP growth is not by any means the ultimate measure of success. This argument raises fundamental questions about the nature and meaning of economic growth and the neoclassical measures of efficiency that continue to be employed by most analysts, which are taken up in later chapters.

But other aspects of Singapore are not that positive; for example, the low level of domestic entrepreneurship seems related to heavy reliance on MNCs and the heavy hand of the state. This may prove a serious constraint now that Singapore is expanding rapidly into its regional hinterland through 'growth triangles' and suchlike (Krause et al. 1987, Lee 1991). Hong Kong businesses are also expanding rapidly, not only into China, but into many parts of the world. Unlike Singapore, however, Hong Kong clearly enjoys a surfeit of entrepreneurial talent (Lall 1991, Yu 1998).

## 3.4   OTHER ANALYSES OF TFP GROWTH

The results of the growth regressions of Kim and Lau (1994) are frequently quoted in the literature, partly because they support Young's findings. This analysis is an extension of an earlier Boskin and Lau study (1991, 1992) to take the EA-NIEs into the sample set. Like Young, Kim and Lau use a very general value-added, aggregate meta-production function in their cross-country estimation. No assumptions are made about constant returns to scale, neutrality of technical progress or the maximization of profit. The production function is assumed to be universally applicable provided output Y, capital K and labour L are measured in efficiency units. The efficiency unit measure corrects for different productivity levels in different countries and for specific efficiency levels of capital and labour.

A reduced form obtained by reformulating the original production function is regressed against data for a sample of nine countries, France, Germany, Britain, the USA, Japan and the four EA-NIEs. The period covered is 1949–90. The results confirm the basic Boskin and Lau findings. These are, first, that the hypothesis of a single meta-production function applicable to the entire sample cannot be rejected, though it is clear that the two groups operate on very different parts of the function. The hypothesis of a Cobb-Douglas production function is rejected. Additionally, constant returns to scale, neutrality of technical progress and profit maximization with competitive output and input markets are separately rejected subject to the assumption of a single meta-production function. The homogeneity of the production function also does not hold up in the regressions.

The most striking result obtained by the Kim and Lau analysis is that technical progress is zero for the EA-NIE group. In a later account of the 1994 study, Lau (1996) reports that 63% of growth is explained by capital accumulation, 17% by human capital and the remaining 20% by labour. For the developed country group, TFP accounts for 58% of growth if the embodied portion of technical progress is not attributed to capital, otherwise it accounts for only 6%. Without embodiment, capital accumulation accounts for 34% of growth and human capital for 8%. If embodied technical progress is assigned to capital, its share goes up to 86%, but the share of human capital remains unchanged.

Finally, for all countries in the sample Kim and Lau find that returns to scale decrease steadily from the beginning of the period to the end. For Taiwan and South Korea the fall is from about 1.0 in the mid-1950s to about 0.85 in 1990. The developed countries seem to have dropped down to returns to scale of around 0.75 by 1990. This indicates that the production function is such that returns to scale are initially close to 1.0 and then diminish with increasing capital intensity.[8] Labour elasticity is at around 0.5 in the developed countries and capital elasticity is low at 0.2–0.3, in 1970. In the EA-NIEs labour elasticity is around 0.42 and capital elasticity around 0.5, also in 1970.

Kim and Lau are puzzled by their finding of zero TFP growth for the EA-NIEs, which contradicts most other estimates. They offer some possible reasons. They explain that until recently, industries in the EA-NIEs were not knowledge or technology intensive and little R&D was done locally. Most of the technology was imported fully priced so that the acquisition and royalty costs offset the realized productivity gains.

Further, the capital goods installed are of older vintages and the potential for indigenous improvement was limited. They also suggest that the 'software' component deriving from better managerial methods, institutional developments and supporting infrastructure, induced by capital investment, lags behind the 'hardware,' and so the full benefits of the investments have not been realized. The authors conclude that further research is needed to resolve the puzzle, especially as human capital levels are very high in the EA-NIEs.

Collins and Bosworth (1996) employ a simpler procedure based on the Cobb-Douglas production function with labour-augmenting human capital, but extend the analysis to cover 88 countries in six groupings. They are thus able to compare EA-NIE performance with that of other developing countries

---

[8]The observed decline in the returns to scale could be the result of the missing factor, land. Land prices typically rise with economic growth and absorb an increasing share of the total returns, an outcome consistent with decreasing returns to the remaining factors.

and industrial countries, especially those among the latter that were catching up fastest with US technological levels after the Second World War. In their main growth accounting exercise, they use a fixed weight of 0.35 for the capital share of the entire set of countries. They supplement the accounting exercises with regression analysis to better examine the relationship between growth rates and its determinants.

Like Young, they use a measure of capital stock aggregated out of a perpetual inventory estimation with a geometric depreciation rate of 0.4. They find the mean investment rate a poor proxy for the rate of capital accumulation with no significant correlation between the two measures over the 34-year period (1960–94) covered. Human capital is factored into the analysis by means of a labour quality index which augments pure labour. The index is constructed by aggregating the average levels of schooling for each country weighted by relative earnings for each educational group, based on constant returns to schooling levels across all countries. The indices are worked out for 7% and 12% rates of return for each extra year of schooling.

The results of the growth accounting exercises are reported for various sub-periods of 1960–94, for individual countries in East Asia and for the main regional groupings. The summary results for the entire 1960–94 period are shown in Table 3.1. Collins and Bosworth too find that TFP growth is a relatively small component of overall LPG for East Asia. They state that their results are very similar to those of Young allowing for their inclusion of agriculture.

But as Rodrik (1998) has remarked, East Asia's TFP is still 'quite respectable,' being higher than that of the USA, South Asia, the Middle East and Latin America and Africa. It equals the TFP performance of 'other industrial countries.' China's high rate is believed to be the result of overestimated official data on output growth (Collins and Bosworth 1996). In short, the results reported do not indicate that East Asia's TFP growth is significantly inferior to that of other regions or countries in this study. The East Asian TFP figures are small only *relative* to the very high overall growth rates for these countries.

TFP growth close to the highest international rates is exactly what one would expect if it reflects universally accessible, productivity-enhancing disembodied 'knowledge' in the sense of Mankiw, Romer and Weil (see section 2.6). If TFP growth is expected to be proportional to the rate of accumulation, which seems to be the implicit assumption, then it must be induced by physical and human capital growth. This particular inconsistency in the interpretation of the estimates of TFPG appears not to be noticed in the original studies discussed above.

*Table 3.1    Collins and Bosworth decomposition of the sources of growth (percentage growth rates per year for the period 1960–94)*

| Country or region | Output per worker | Contribution of each component | | |
|---|---|---|---|---|
| | | Physical capital per worker | Education per worker | TFP |
| Taiwan | 5.8 | 3.1 | 0.6 | 2.0 |
| South Korea | 5.7 | 3.3 | 0.8 | 1.5 |
| Singapore | 5.4 | 3.4 | 0.4 | 1.5 |
| Indonesia | 3.4 | 2.1 | 0.5 | 0.8 |
| Thailand | 5.0 | 2.7 | 0.4 | 1.8 |
| Malaysia | 3.8 | 2.3 | 0.5 | 0.9 |
| Philippines | 1.2 | 1.2 | 0.5 | −0.4 |
| East Asia (all of above) | 4.2 | 2.5 | 0.6 | 1.1 |
| China | 4.5 | 1.5 | 0.4 | 2.6 |
| South Asia | 2.3 | 1.1 | 0.3 | 0.8 |
| Africa | 0.3 | 0.8 | 0.2 | −0.6 |
| Middle East | 1.6 | 1.5 | 0.5 | −0.3 |
| Latin America | 1.5 | 0.9 | 0.4 | 0.2 |
| USA | 1.1 | 0.4 | 0.4 | 0.3 |
| Other industrial | 2.9 | 1.5 | 0.4 | 1.1 |

*Source:* Collins and Bosworth (1996).

Further, Collins and Bosworth include Malaysia, Thailand, Indonesia and the Philippines in their 'East Asia' category, which depress the aggregate TFP measure below the rates for the top three EA-NIEs. The TFP growth obtained for Taiwan, South Korea and Singapore are 2%, 1.5% and 1.5%, respectively. Young's accounting yields 2.6%, 1.7% and 0.2% for these countries in the same order. The results for Singapore are significantly different, especially when compared along the same sub-period. Since this city-state has no agricultural sector to speak of, that could not be the source of the difference between the results of Collins and Bosworth and Young.[9]

---

[9]Young (1992) uses a capital share of around 0.55 for Singapore in the 1966–80 period and 0.5 in the 1980–85 period. Since Collins and Bosworth use 0.35, this is the likely source of the higher TFPG values obtained.

The persistently negative TFP growth figures obtained for Africa, the Middle East, Latin America and the Philippines, are unfortunately quite typical for developing countries in which heavy investments are sustained. Pack (1992) points out that a remarkable feature of the EA-NIEs is their ability to maintain positive TFPG performance in spite of heavy investment in physical capital over many decades. He attributes the negative TFPG of many developing countries to excessively capital-intensive technologies adopted in line with import-substitution policies. By contrast, the Collins and Bosworth results show a distinct tendency for TFPG in the East Asian economies to increase over the sequence of sub-periods from 1960–94.

Collins and Bosworth recompute their estimates for capital shares of 0.3 and 0.4 and for higher 12% returns to education. As expected, the higher share increases the contribution of capital and lowers the TFPG estimate, as does a higher imputed return to education. But the overall relative pattern of TFP growth among the different countries and regions is not affected. This sensitivity analysis highlights a weak point in the Collins and Bosworth approach in assuming constant factor shares of 0.35 for all countries. Since capital shares are somewhat larger in developing countries, this assumption would actually overstate the estimated TFPG values. Other sources of TFPG misestimation are discussed below in section 3.5.

Collins and Bosworth also use regression analysis to relate economic growth to basic initial conditions and external environment. They find higher educational levels and life expectancy account for some of East Asia's superior growth. Measures of trade openness and macroeconomic stability are found to be significant. Investment share as a proxy for accumulation is less significant than capital stock.

They find that in the 1960–73 period, TFPG in industrial economies is high and somewhat correlated with capital per worker growth, but this relationship vanishes in the 1973–94 period. In the 1960–73 period, most industrial economies were rapidly catching up with the USA; investment was a major source of technological learning. Catch-up growth seems to have been exhausted by 1973, when the entire industrial world entered a period of much slower growth with lower levels of TFPG as well.[10]

The pattern is reversed for the non-industrial countries. There, TFPG is lower on average and uncorrelated with capital per worker growth for the 1960–73 period. But after 1973–94, a 'modest correlation emerges,' though TFPG levels remain relatively low. Collins and Bosworth express surprise that for their sample as a whole, TFPG is largely orthogonal to the growth of capital per worker. This could indicate that the in-phase component of TFPG

---

[10]Greenwood (1999) attributes this productivity slowdown to the learning and adoption costs associated with a third industrial revolution based on information technology industries.

is factored out by the regression analysis as a part of capital's share.[11]

In addition to the studies discussed above, there are many analyses that are focused more narrowly, but at greater depth, on the sources of growth in particular countries. These include Dollar and Sokoloff (1990) on South Korea, Dollar and Wolff (1993), Pack (1992) and Thorbecke and Wan (1999) on Taiwan, Pilat (1994) on South Korea and Japan and others. Most of these are summarized in Chen (1997) and Felipe (1999). Rao and Lee (1996) argue that TFPG has been picking up in Singapore in later years and that initial low values were a necessary consequence of accelerated capital investment.

## 3.5   EXPLANATIONS OF THE TFP PARADOX

The idea of low technical progress in the EA-NIEs is so hard to reconcile with the manifest reality that other theorists with a stronger feel for practical relevance reject it out of hand. Stiglitz (1998b) posits errors of measurement and imperfect factor markets as the reason for low estimates, rather than the association of technological advance with TFPG.

> Any visitor to the cities and factories in East Asia comes away impressed by the enormous technological progress in the last decades. The Young, Kim, Lau, et al. results are simply not very robust. When a country is accumulating capital rapidly, small changes in the estimate of the capital share can result in a large shift in estimates of the contribution of total factor productivity. Estimating these shares is very problematic, especially in East Asia where the assumption of perfect competition in labor and product markets is inappropriate, at least in some economies. There are also problems in the measurement of human and physical capital. Moreover, we must remember that technology is both the cause and the consequence of investment. Without improving technology, diminishing returns would have set in, and it is hard to believe that investment could have been sustained (Stiglitz 1998b).

Comprehensive surveys of the problems associated with measuring TFP, going back to the earliest efforts, are provided by Chen (1997) and Felipe (1999). Chen identifies the measurement of capital input as the greatest problem of all. In the standard growth accounting framework the capital growth term subtracts the contribution to overall growth made by technology

---

[11] These results relate to the analyses of De Long and Summers (1991, 1992) who find equipment investment to be a better predictor of growth than total investment. TFPG is found to be strongly associated with equipment investment for a range of realistic capital share coefficients and net rates of return to investment. They also find no strong association between TFPG and schooling. They suggest that this reflects learning-by-doing triggered by equipment investment. However, these gains are not automatic, and seem to accrue to outward-oriented countries that export a significant proportion of output. The relationship between trade and growth is taken up in detail in later chapters.

embodied in capital. Since this embodied technology is pre-packaged and paid for, it is not taken as contributing to technological change in the entity (firm or country) that imports it. This point is discussed below in more detail.

Since physical capital cannot be measured directly it has to be measured in terms of value or more precisely resource cost. But capital equipment prices may not accurately track quality change generated by technological advance in the capital producing country. Much of the capital goods used in developing countries are imported. Hence the contribution of physical capital could be overstated or understated. The same argument can be made for the labour-enhancing effect of human capital which is computed in terms of wage compensation over and above the rate for unskilled labour. Chen shows that 'non-proportional' quality improvements, scale effects, the uncertainty of the relationship between compensation and real human capital, etc. would bias the estimation of TFP.

Chen (1997) and Felipe (1999) list other well-known sources of error in the measurement of physical capital. These are capital composition errors (i.e. deciding exactly what constitutes capital), capacity utilization errors, and errors arising from the assessment of effective depreciation. Chen quotes the results obtained by Jorgenson and Griliches (1967) who cut estimated TFP for the USA for the period 1945–65 from an initial tally of 1.6% in a total output growth of 3.5%, to a negligible 0.1% when correcting for these errors.

Chen concludes that disembodied, Hicks-neutral, technical change as measured by the TFP residual is an arbitrary concept, highly sensitive to the growth accounting procedure. In short, while the index of overall labour productivity growth (LPG) can be measured with reasonable accuracy and taken as an indicator of overall technological change, it is very difficult to separate out disembodied technical change from that embodied in the inputs. Chen suggests that the confusion arises from the fixation of analysts with TFP and their inability to see LPG as the major indicator of technological advance in East Asia.

Chen's conclusion is consistent with arguments advanced by Greenwood and associates.[12] They show that roughly half of per capita economic growth in post-war USA is fuelled by investment-specific technological progress (ISTP). ISTP is reflected in the fall in price of new producer durables relative to the price of new consumer nondurables. They quote price declines of 3.2% for equipment and 1% for structures per year in the USA and estimate that 37% of per capita economic growth derives from ISTP in equipment and 15% from ISTP in structures; disembodied TFPG accounts for the remaining 48%.

The conclusion is inescapable that ISTP must represent a much larger

[12]Greenwood et al. (1997), Greenwood and Jovanovic (1998), Gort et al. (1999) and Greenwood (1999).

share of technological progress in EA-NIEs and TFPG only a small part. The high variability displayed by the various cross-country patterns of TFPG obtained from different studies indicate that the estimation procedure is also not robust. In general, 'crude' TFP estimation procedures yield significant values for East Asia, but when thoroughly adjusted for differentiated inputs as in Young (1994a, 1995), the resulting values are relatively small.

Arguments that invoke a misspecified production function have been advanced by Rodrik (1998) and Nelson and Pack (1999) to explain the peculiar TFP results for East Asia. They point out that if the elasticity of factor substitution is less than one, then large cumulative investments on the scale of what took place in the EA-NIEs could significantly lower the marginal productivity of capital. Collins and Bosworth assume that the capital share remained constant at 0.35. But if the elasticity of substitution were less than one, then this figure would decline significantly. As a result TFP growth estimated by the standard accounting procedure would be much larger than when estimated under the assumption of invariant capital share.

The observed share of capital has remained remarkably steady and high in the East Asian NIEs. But this does not invalidate the argument. Consider a linearly homogeneous production function $F(BK, AL)$ with time-varying technical change that differentially augments labour and capital through time-varying coefficients $A$ and $B$, respectively. If the function has the usual properties assumed in microeconomic theory and competitive market conditions prevail, then it is easy to show that the capital share $s_k$ evolves as in equation 3.1. Here, as in Chapter 2, the $^\wedge$ symbol stands for the growth rate of the variable qualified and $\sigma$ is the elasticity of factor substitution.

$$\hat{s}_k \ = \ (1 - s_k)(\sigma^{-1} - 1)[\hat{A} - \hat{B} - (\hat{K} - \hat{L})] \qquad (3.1)$$

If $\sigma$ is constant, then the above expression can be integrated to yield the simpler expression of equation 3.2 in which $\mu$ is a constant and $\rho = (1-\sigma)/\sigma$. From this expression it is clear that if $A = B$ (Hick's neutral technical change, or $A > B$ (labour-saving technical change), then capital share $s_k$ would decline as the capital/labour ratio rises. Since $s_k$ does indeed decline as countries industrialize (Chenery et al. 1986, Hayami 1998), this result is consistent with what is known about the nature of technical change in developing countries.

$$s_k \ = \ (1 + \mu[BK/(AL)]^\rho)^{-1} \qquad (3.2)$$

Starting from equation 3.1, Rodrik argues that $\sigma = 1$ is only one explanation of a stable capital share $s_k$. But if $\sigma \neq 1$, then the effect of a rising $K/L$ ratio in reducing $s_k$ can be offset by technical change that is relatively labour-saving, i.e. if $A$ grows faster than $B$. In this case, if the ratio $BK/(AL)$ remains approximately constant, then the capital share $s_k$ will again be stable. Rodrik shows that even though Young's translog production function does not constrain the elasticity of substitution to unity, the use of the Törnqvist index introduces a bias into the estimation of TFPG. This downward bias is zero only when $\sigma = 1$ (i.e. the production function is Cobb-Douglas) or the ratio $A/B$ remains constant, which is equivalent to assuming that technical change is Hicks-neutral, not discriminating between capital and labour.

In East Asia where well-developed technologies were implemented, rising $K/L$ ratios are most likely to have been accompanied by labour-saving technical change.[13] It is also likely that $\sigma < 1$. If these conditions hold, then TFPG measures will be biased downwards with greater underestimation for the higher investment countries such as Singapore. Rodrik also shows that the bias is cumulative with greater bias for longer estimation spans. Rodrik (1998) and Nelson and Pack (1999) argue that it is not possible to separately identify the contributions of accumulation, deriving from rising $K/L$, and technical change through TFPG analysis.[14]

Felipe and McCombie (2001) estimate the extent of the likely bias for four EA-NIEs for elasticities of substitution varying from 0.2 to 1.2. In an estimation over a 30-year period, when $\sigma$ is reduced from 1.0 to 0.2, the proportion of output growth accounted for by TFPG rises from 34% to 52% for Hong Kong, from 27% to 45% for Taiwan, from 16% to 35% for South Korea and from 2% to 29% for Singapore. The order of magnitude change for Singapore is particularly striking, bearing out Rodrik's expectations quoted immediately above. Also, as is to be expected, the bias is larger for larger periods of estimation.

The Felipe and McCombie estimations depend on the capital share in 1966 being taken as the datum from which TFPG is calculated over various time spans. The initial year is important since the capital share would decline in the absence of technical change, or if technical change was Hicks-neutral, as a result of a rising $K/L$ ratio, as is clear from equation 3.2. Felipe and

---

[13]Hayami (1998) shows that high capital elasticities ranging from 0.4 to 0.5 in the EA-NIEs combined with very high rates of growth of $K/L$ ratios, indicate a capital-using, labour-saving bias relative to high-income economies where capital elasticities are 0.3 or lower and K/L growth rates are much lower. He argues that all NIEs go through this 'Marx pattern' of growth in which measured TFPG/LPG is low before graduating to a 'Kuznets pattern' of advanced country growth in which TFPG/LPG is relatively high. He shows that Japan moved from a Marx pattern into a Kuznets pattern in the 1920–37 period and then jumped back into a hybrid Marx-Kuznets super-growth pattern in the 1958–70 period as it rapidly assimilated technologies in the West. Japan's 1950–70 growth, shown in Figure 1.1, which is much like the catch-up patterns of the EA-NIEs, confirms Hayami's construction.

[14]See section 2.5 for Nelson's earlier comments on the problems associated with standard TFPG estimation procedures.

McCombie note that if the datum is extended back far enough into the past, then virtually all of the contribution of $K/L$ growth would have to be ascribed to TFPG. Again, the conclusion is that it is not possible to definitively separate out TFPG from per capita output growth, an idea that harks back to Hulten and Srinivasan's (1999) arguments about induced accumulation, discussed in section 2.4.

Rodrik (1998) concludes that the crucial point is the existence of a 'tight relationship' between capital accumulation and economic growth. Nelson and Pack (1999) emphasize the enormous deployment of human effort required to sustain the extraordinary rates of accumulation seen in East Asia. They argue that 'accumulationist' theories miss the difficult innovation and learning processes needed to 'assimilate' the modern technologies that are only potentially accessible through physical investment. The 'assimilationist' viewpoint raises fundamental issues about technology and economic growth, which are treated more comprehensively in Chapter 7.

The debate about the meaning and estimation of TFPG appear to have entered a rather sharper phase at the present time. Hsieh (1998, 1999) has computed TFPG for the EA-NIEs using a price-based formulation that is the dual of the usual quantity-based form. Since real wages have risen strongly and the return to capital, as measured, has remained steady, the dual estimates yield relatively high values of TFPG. The stability of returns to capital in Singapore, found by Hsieh, also speak against Young's argument about excessive investment there. Young (1998a) has responded vigorously to Hsieh, arguing that when computational and methodological errors are corrected for, dual estimates based on Hsieh's data are not that different from Young's own estimates. In a riposte to an earlier version of Nelson and Pack (1999) and Rodrik (1998), Young (1998b) argues that their procedures raise a Paasche-type index of TFP but lowers a Laspeyres-type index.

The problems listed here have yet to be resolved within the theoretical framework of neoclassical production theory. The important outcome is that TFPG, measured as a residual of what cannot be explained by the production function, is not an adequate measure of technological change. The conclusion deriving from the discussions in this chapter and Chapter 2 is that investment in physical capital is more an indicator of growth rather than an autonomous source, an idea supported in Easterly and Levine (2000). They state that available evidence suggests that human capital accumulation and high savings are also both driven by growth. The tentative conclusion here is that technological change is carried by investments in both physical and human capital. A fuller discussion of this issue is deferred to Chapters 7 and 9.

# 4.    Empirics of the trade-growth nexus

There are now many empirical studies that attempt to establish a link between the nature of the trade regime and the growth performance of countries through econometric analysis. A selected set of these, which are considered to have been the most influential, are summarized here. Reviews of previous studies are to be found in Edwards (1993, 1998a) and Rodriguez and Rodrik (1999). Earlier studies attempted to link output growth to exports, while more recent analyses regress growth against a set of variables that include various measures of openness to trade. This topic is included here because of its importance for the apprehension of East Asian growth. But the empirical studies covered are not confined to the countries of this region alone.

The issue is clearly important as evident from the debates summarized in Chapter 5. The role of trade in promoting economic growth poses some of the most contentious questions in economic analysis and public policy. Yet the idea that trade and integration with the global economy are potentially the source of immense real benefits is a cardinal principle on which there is widespread agreement across the spectrum of economic thought. The idea is intuitively obvious, confirmed by all theoretical analyses and well established by historical studies going back over millennia. It is therefore mildly irritating that empirical analyses are unable to definitively confirm the validity of this almost axiomatic proposition.

The issue has come up again in the Rodriguez and Rodrik (1999) critique of the Sachs and Warner (1995) study. This continuing problem indicates that there may be fundamental flaws in the way the empirical studies themselves are conceptualized. One obvious stumbling-block has already been flagged: the existence of two-way causality between growth and trade. While trade promotes growth by boosting productivity through greater specialization, growth also promotes trade through lower output prices which derive from productivity growth that accompanies rapid output growth. This two-way causality needs to be handled in dynamic conceptions which look more closely at specific country strategies. Cross-country econometric analyses, pitched at highly aggregate levels, seem not to have been successful in providing satisfactory answers.

## 4.1    EXPORTS AND OUTPUT GROWTH

The earliest of the frequently cited references on the trade-growth linkage is Michaely (1977). He used simple rank correlation to check whether the exports/GDP ratio was correlated with output growth for a sample of 41 countries; the idea was to avoid spurious results deriving from the fact that exports are a component of GDP. His results yielded significantly positive Spearman rank coefficients. This result was also obtained by Balassa (1978) using pooled data for 11 countries. Edwards (1993) notes that these studies have been criticized for leaving out the effect of other important factors, for not distinguishing sufficiently between endogenous and exogenous variables and for using inadequate theoretical frameworks.

Feder (1983) based his investigation on a two-sector disequilibrium model with neoclassical production functions and a positive export externality. He introduced a productivity differential across sectors such that the export sector is more productive than the domestic sector. He analysed a sample of 31 semi-industrialized countries and found that marginal factor productivities were higher in the export sector; but export externalities were relatively more important than productivity differentials. Feder made no attempt to test the robustness of his results or consider the econometric problems associated with the analysis.

A host of conceptual issues are raised by these empirical approaches, which are discussed by Edwards (1993). First there is the question whether a critical minimum threshold of per capita income has to be attained before the benefits of export growth take effect. Some studies find that middle-income countries benefit more, but other studies do not. There have also been attempts to relate threshold effects to the trade structure alone, rather than the economy as a whole. Edwards reports that the results are inconclusive overall for both types of question. The second question is about the effect of world market conditions on the interaction of exports and growth. A common strategy has been to estimate the equations separately for the periods before and after the first oil shock of 1973, since the industrial world then entered into an extended period of slower growth. Again the results are inconclusive, but have 'provided strong indications that world business cycles play some role in the way the external sector interacts with aggregate GDP' (Edwards 1993, p. 1385).

A third question addresses the validity of the equation specification used by Feder and others: have some crucial variables been omitted? For instance, in a two-gap setting, export expansion could promote growth by relaxing foreign exchange constraints that limit the import of intermediate goods. Esfahani (1991) has found that when intermediate inputs are included, the coefficient on Feder's export expansion term falls and becomes insignificant in some periods. There is also evidence that the link between GDP and export growth is not linear but subject to diminishing returns.

Edwards argues that econometric studies linking exports to GDP growth implicitly or explicitly posit a two-stage approach: it is assumed that more liberalized economies experience faster export growth; then, they test for correlation between export and output growth. A positive result is interpreted as providing proof of the underlying proposition. This approach was popular on account of the difficulty of quantifying trade policy and trade orientation (discussed below). Finally there are questions about the direction of causality between exports and growth. There is sufficient a priori justification to think that rapidly growing economies would also expand exports faster. Some researchers have attempted to test for this, but the results are inconclusive.

Edwards (1993, p. 1389) concludes his summary by stating that 'much of the cross-country regression based studies have been plagued by empirical and conceptual shortcomings. The theoretical frameworks used have been increasingly simplistic, failing to address important questions such as the exact mechanism through which exports expansion affects GDP growth, and ignoring important determinants of growth such as educational attainment.' He adds that many papers have also treated endogeneity and measurement issues in cavalier fashion. Edwards sees new growth theory as offering a sounder conceptual framework for further analysis.[1]

## 4.2  TRADE ORIENTATION AND OUTPUT GROWTH

Multi-country studies of trade orientation and economic performance begin with the projects of Little et al. (1970) and Balassa (1971). These used a measure of the effective rate of protection (ERP) which was defined as the ratio of the differential between domestic value added in a given industry (i.e. at domestic prices) and world value added (at world market prices) to world value added. Aggregate ERP measures are then computed based on the input-output structure of each industry. The essence of the approach was to take account of tariffs on intermediate inputs as well as the tariffs on final goods.

These studies found that the degree of effective protection granted to manufacturing value added was significantly higher than that indicated by the nominal rate of protection. Little et al. concluded that for most developing countries in the post-war era, industrialization had been excessively

---

[1] Edwards (1993) argues that export or import ratios depend significantly on the economy's structure, including the country's size; thus independent of trade barriers, larger countries exhibit lower export ratios.

encouraged at the cost of curtailing incentives for agriculture and exports. These protectionist policies led to worsening income distribution, lower savings rates, increased unemployment and lower rates of capacity utilization. The ensuing policy recommendation was to greatly reduce protection by opening up the economy to international competition. A number of measurement difficulties were encountered in these studies and no attempt was made to track the evolution of ERPs with time; in particular no attempt was made to analyse liberalization episodes (Edwards 1993). These studies, of course, struck the first major blow for more liberalized trade but did not significantly influence the development establishment.

The NBER Krueger-Bhagwati study of 1978 (Krueger 1978) proposed the first systematic attempt at classifying trade regimes. Trade orientation was measured by the extent to which the protective and incentive structure in a country was biased against exports. The formal index used was the ratio of the exchange rate effectively paid by importers to the rate effectively faced by exporters. If the ratio is one, then the trade regime was defined as neutral, but if greater than one, it was said to be biased against exports; if the ratio was less than one, then the country was following an export promotion strategy. This index could be applied on an individual industry basis or as a weighted average for the entire economy.

As originally applied, a liberalization episode was one that reduced the anti-export bias which was prevalent at that time. A country could have high tariffs and still maintain a neutral trade regime. Edwards notes that with time, the term liberalization evolved to mean an absolute elimination of tariffs. Since in many countries non-tariff barriers have constituted the more important form of trade restrictions, the NBER study used a theoretically derived equivalent tariff or 'premium' for each quantitative restriction. This exercise was of course fraught with serious difficulties. Krueger and Bhagwati then combined the concepts of premium and bias to define five phases in the evolution of trade regimes ranging from blanket protectionism to full liberalization.

Krueger (1978) found that non-traditional exports were positively affected by a more depreciated real exchange rate for exports, whereas traditional exports were not. The move to a more liberalized regime also had a positive effect on exports, but to a much lesser extent. This led her to conclude that it was bias reduction rather than liberalization which elicited the export response. Krueger also found that higher exports raised GNP growth; she argued that liberalization did not directly affect output growth but only indirectly through exports. The conclusion that trade regimes had no direct effect on growth was disputed by Balassa (1982). Using an alternative four-way classification of trade regimes, he found that protectionism adversely affected export expansion.

In a later team study directed by Krueger (1981), they examined the relationship between trade orientation and employment in the long run for a sample of 10 developing countries in which the labour markets were highly distorted. They found that industries with Heckscher-Ohlin export potential tended to be more intensive in labour, particularly unskilled labour, than import-competing ones. The conclusion was that trade had largely followed the direction indicated by the predictions of the Heckscher-Ohlin formulation. They also found that employment grows faster in outward-oriented economies and that removal of factor market distortions and trade restrictions benefit employment creation in the long run (Edwards 1993).

In many studies the index of trade orientation is constructed quite subjectively, such as in the 1987 World Development Report. Edwards remarks that because of this, South Korea is used as an example of an outward-oriented liberalized economy by one school and also as a prime example of a country that has benefited by avoiding abrupt liberalization by an opposing school. To overcome this limitation Edwards uses six objective indices of openness proposed by Leamer to regress growth against trade orientation for two sets of developing countries (one set of 30 and the other 51); these indices measure both openness and intervention. He finds a strong and robust relationship between trade orientation and growth; countries with more open and less distorted external sectors grew faster. He also identifies a catch-up effect; i.e. countries with lower initial income per capita grow faster. Physical and human capital accumulation are found to be important contributors to growth.

Dollar (1992) also reports results of a regression of per capita GDP growth against an objective index of outward orientation. This index is based on a computation of real exchange rate distortion using price data from the Heston-Summers set of 121 countries. In fact he combines a real exchange rate distortion measure with a variability measure to get a better outward orientation index, since this reduces anomalies. He finds that this outward orientation measure is highly correlated with per capita GDP growth in a large sample of 95 developing countries for the period 1976–85. The results show that 'trade liberalization, devaluation of the real exchange rate and maintenance of a stable real exchange rate could dramatically improve growth performance in many poor countries' (Dollar 1992, p. 540). Asian economies have low price levels and African economies have extremely high price levels indicating high levels of protection. Latin American economies have moderately high price levels.

## 4.3   NEW LINES OF RESEARCH

The awareness has grown in recent years that previous research has not satisfactorily established a clear-cut connection between trade policy and economic growth. The new growth theories have certainly formalized and thereby provided some intellectual support for the growth-promoting effects of openness. But in the final analysis, it is empirical results that establish the validity of a theoretical proposition; at least that is the way it should be in any legitimate science.

Levine and Renelt (1992) re-examine the robustness of many previous regression results using a variant of Leamer's extreme bounds analysis. Their data is drawn from many sources and covers 119 countries. They find that many results are not robust to small variations in explanatory variables. But they do find positive and robust correlation between average growth rates and the average share of investment in GDP. They also find a similar relationship between the share of investment in GDP and the average share of trade in GDP. Exactly the same relationship is obtained if export/GDP or imports/GDP were substituted for the trade share. Finally, they find that other likely determinants such as measures of trade policy are not robust when investment/GDP is included in the regression. These results are disturbing and have been quoted widely in the literature.

A major problem faced is that correlation between various measures of openness is quite low. To get around this problem, Sachs and Warner (1995) construct a zero-one measure of openness, which takes the value zero if one or more of the following conditions are met, and one if not.

1.  Non-tariff barriers cover 40% or more of trade.
2.  Average tariff rates are 40% or more.
3.  The black market exchange rate is depreciated by 20% or more relative to the official rate, on average for the 1970s and 1980s.
4.  The country has a socialist economic system.
5.  The state holds a monopoly of major exports.

When inserted into growth regressions, this index turns out to be highly significant and robust after controlling for other determinants of growth, such as investment in human and physical capital. The data for the study are taken from Summers-Heston 5.5 and 5.6 and other sources.

Sachs and Warner find very few developing countries continuously open from independence: these are Singapore, Malaysia, Cyprus, Mauritius, Hong Kong and Barbados. Some that were initially closed following inward-oriented policies opened up later: Taiwan in 1963; South Korea in 1968 and

Indonesia in 1970. They find a strong and robust link between their index of openness and per capita growth for the 1970–89 period for both developing and developed countries. Within developing economies, the open group grew at 4.49% per annum and the closed group at a mere 0.69% per annum. Open developed economies grew at 2.29% whereas the closed group grew at the much lower rate of 0.74% per annum.

Sachs and Warner find that while there is no convergence for the group as a whole, there is strong convergence within the group of open economies. Additionally, the open economies adjust more rapidly from the status of primary-intensive to manufactures-intensive exporters, thus contradicting Prebisch-Singer expectations (see section 5.1 for details). They admit that their trade policy index serves as a proxy for an entire array of policy actions which goes somewhat beyond the usual meaning of trade policy.

Rodriguez and Rodrik (1999) repeat the Sachs-Warner analysis with the same data and find that almost all the explanatory power of their index is concentrated in the black market premium (BMP) and the state monopoly of major exports (SMME), or the indicators 3 and 4 as listed. They point out that the SMME indicator is virtually indistinguishable from a sub-Saharan Africa dummy on account of a double selection bias deriving from the use of data exclusively for African countries that were undergoing structural adjustment under World Bank guidance. Countries not in this sample of 29 in Africa and elsewhere escape scrutiny.

In addition, Rodriguez and Rodrik point out that the BMP indicator of a 20% or higher black market premium is indicative of sustained macroeconomic imbalances. Such high imbalances emerge mostly when countries are afflicted by political conflict, top level mismanagement of macroeconomic policy, inefficient and corrupt bureaucracies and lower capacity to enforce the rule of law. A high black market premium on the exchange rate is clearly indicative of poor trade policy. But the fundamental determinant is not trade policy at all, but the deeper maladies which are likely to adversely affect growth performance and lead to external sector distortions.

Edwards (1998a) regresses calculated total factor productivity growth (TFPG) against nine alternative indices of openness, along with initial income and a measure of schooling, for a data set of 93 countries. His results show a statistically significant relationship between TFPG and openness robust to alternative specifications of the latter. He finds though that openness is less important as a predictor of TFPG than initial income and human capital. He also finds that the coefficients on the original variables are not affected by new regressors related to institutional strength and macroeconomic instability.

Rodriguez and Rodrik (1999) point out that Edwards' results are heavily dependent on the regression procedure using weighted least squares. The weights used are 1985 GDP per capita, which means, for example, that the USA contributes about 7.7 times more than Ethiopia to the final results. Repeating the regressions with the log of GDP per capita as weights, Rodriguez and Rodrik find that the original clear-cut relationship between openness and TFPG loses robustness. They also find other methodological and data problems which further reduce the validity of the original results.

Rodriguez and Rodrik survey many other recent studies and reach the conclusion that the link between trade policy and growth has not been established conclusively. They argue that the very proliferation of studies and various indices of trade restrictiveness indicate some sort of conceptual cul-de-sac. Rather than seeking a purely deterministic link between trade policy and growth performance, they suggest that research should focus on micro-level data drawn from plant, firm and industry studies, the role of FDI, export-processing zones and international business linkages. They also suggest that firm-level studies indicate that efficient producers self-select into exporting activity, so that causality often goes from productivity growth to exports, rather than the other way round.

# 5.    East Asia in the evolution of development thinking

The debate over trade and development strategy is one that shows no signs of winding down. From arguments about the superiority of 'export-led' development over 'inward-oriented' import-substituting industrialization (ISI), the terms of reference have broadened to include the role of the state, the effectiveness of industrial policy and the best strategy for integrating with the world economy. In the aftermath of the financial crises in Asia, the recently implemented measures of financial liberalization and economic reform have come under renewed scrutiny, generating differing views within the ranks of economists and between the Bank and the Fund.

The continuing strength of the debate is entirely justifiable: it raises fundamental issues about development policy and the role of integration with the global economy. In recent times, particularly from around 1987 to 1997, 'outward-oriented' openness to the influences of the global market became accepted as the best possible development strategy by academic economists and policy-makers. The extraordinary success of the strongly export-oriented EA-NIEs and the failure of ISI strategies in most other developing nations provided the experiential backdrop to the emergence of the remarkable 'Washington consensus' as it was called.[1] Despite the continuing vitality of the debate, there is now wider agreement about the policies and institutions that promote sustained growth.

The presently available country-specific studies, cross-country regressions and broad surveys on the role of trade and openness in accelerating economic growth, have been summarized in Chapter 4. The resulting insights have also been incorporated to some extent into the new endogenous growth models, thus becoming a part of the stylized formal representation of growth. This chapter briefly summarizes the evolution of thinking on these issues and the extent of consensus. It also delineates the extent of divergence in the mainstream literature by drawing on recent surveys by Edwards (1993), Krueger (1995, 1997) and Rodrik (1996, 1999) and Temple (1999).

---

[1] See sections 5.3 and 5.4, Rodrik (1996, 1999), Stiglitz (1998a, 1998b, 1998c) and Gore (2000) for details and critiques of the 'Washington consensus.'

The chapter concludes by arguing that the evolution of thinking on trade and development strategy is leading to a very fundamental shift in the way the forces driving economic growth are seen to operate. The ideological chasm between structuralists and market fundamentalists is being bridged by a new activist conception of growth. Rather than seeing economic agents as either unresponsive to market incentives or responding perfectly when governments withdraw, the new emphasis is on building social institutions and human and organizational capital, which enable better operation of market forces and progressive removal of the barriers to growth and development. It is a shift from a rather mechanical conception of economic growth to an evolutionary one in which the active involvement of economic agents brings about gains in productivity through adaptation, learning and innovation.

## 5.1    TRADE AS THE ENEMY OF GROWTH

Nurkse (1961) saw trade as the engine of growth in the 19th century, or more accurately as the mechanism of growth transmission from the industrial centres to peripheral areas. The idea goes back at the least to David Hume and Adam Smith who clearly saw that trade – both internal and external – by expanding the effective market leads to specialization which is a major source of productivity growth (Rostow 1990). But along with many other development economists, Nurkse was quite pessimistic about the ability of newly liberated developing countries to grow by exporting to industrial countries or to each other. Hence he advocated an investment strategy of 'balanced growth' in which these developing countries increasingly produce what they need to consume.[2] This idea, of course, leads inevitably to the 'inward-oriented' strategy of industrial growth through progressive import substitution, which then requires selective protection implemented by a strongly interventionist state.

From the early 1950s, development strategy began to incline towards 'import substitution industrialization' (ISI), which calls for protection against competing imports as soon as domestic production in a particular line of products becomes feasible. The ISI model originated in the ideas of Prebisch

---

[2]An important related argument was advanced by Rosenstein-Rodan in 1943. He argued that no single investor would invest unless investment was simultaneously undertaken in a number of related and supporting industries. Hence some planned coordination was vital to ensure success. This argument has reappeared recently in the 'big-push' models. In theory this problem would not arise if the domestic economy was integrated with international markets. But, since new industries find it hard to compete with established producers on quality and price, openness may not be a feasible option for countries setting up industries from scratch.

and Singer.[3] Trade protection was seen as necessary for a limited period within which industrial skills could be accumulated by producing for domestic markets. Without this protection, it made little sense for private investment to go into areas dominated by established producers abroad, nor even for public investment, though such industries could well become viable in the long run through dynamic effects.

This inward-oriented development policy is of course a variant of the much older infant industry argument, advanced by Alexander Hamilton and Friedrich List for the USA and Germany in their respective episodes of early industrial emergence (Freeman 1989). Following on this example, ISI was adopted by most developing countries, but implemented with greater zeal by large countries such as India and Brazil which were politically ambitious for a global role. China, after the 1949 Revolution, can be seen as an extreme example of inward-oriented development, as an attempt to limit market forces to a greater extent than anywhere else. See Sachs and Warner (1995) and Gore (2000) for more detail.

ISI was adopted not merely on account of market failure arguments. Leaders like Nehru, drawing from the early success of the Soviet model and even from the early history of Germany and the USA, saw industrialization, guided and accelerated by strong state intervention, as politically crucial to the task of nation-building.[4] Industry was not only the path to prosperity, but vitally necessary for forging and consolidating the economic and political integrity of countries peopled by many different ethnic and cultural groups. Industry would break-up and modernize societies steeped in traditional ideas sustained by low-productivity agricultural practices inherited from the past.

Intellectual trends presently caught up with the political imperatives: Edwards (1993) states that from the 1950s to the 1970s, a large number of development economists embraced the inward-oriented ISI programme and devoted considerable energy towards the design of planning models for its implementation. In short, free trade began to be seen as the enemy of growth, to the extent that an overly liberal trade policy would inhibit the expansion

---

[3]Prebisch and Singer based their policy on the observed secular decline in the terms of trade of developing countries which were mostly exporters of primary products. They argued that productivity advances in the industrial centres translate into higher wages but advances in the developing 'periphery' merely led to lower export prices. Hence, free trade would lead to a widening gap between rich and poor countries. See Balassa (1989), Edwards (1993), Sachs and Warner (1995), Chenery et al. (1986, ch. 1) and Krueger (1995, 1997) for details.

[4]For Nehru, in particular, the rapid expansion of industry and commerce on a nationwide basis was the economic precondition for modernizing and bonding together the collection of states that constitute modern India; it would secure the secular character of the post-colonial state. In India, as in other countries, the strong support for this Hamilton-style programme offered by financial and industrial interests ensured its adoption (Sachs and Warner 1995).

of domestic industrial capability. It was feared that free trade would lock in comparative advantage towards continued specialization in the production and export of primary products based on low-skilled labour. Manufactures would continue to be imported from metropolitan countries, much as before, and domestic industry would never take off.

The origin and evolution of post-war thinking on trade policy and development, in response to the political and economic realities of the times, is well described by Edwards (1993), Sachs and Warner (1995) and Krueger (1995, 1997). Krueger sees it as an extended learning process involving political leaders, other policy-makers and academic economists. She argues that the field of 'development economics' emerged to provide a better guide to development policy because structural rigidities were assumed to hold back responsiveness to price incentives premised in conventional economics. Krueger expresses surprise at how these new stylized facts were accepted uncritically and devotes considerable space in her 1997 lecture towards explaining this apparent aberration.

What is clear from all accounts, however, is that the theoretical rationale for the policies adopted was derived from the immediate ground reality, albeit from a somewhat limited experience base. It was also consistent with the inherited infant industry wisdom of the past. Export pessimism, now refuted by the export success of the EA-NIEs, was based on low income and price elasticities of demand for primary commodities. The structural rigidities observed in developing countries are now seen as deriving from imperfectly developed markets resulting from the near absence of market institutions.

Since the relationship between the smooth operation of market forces and the evolution of the institutions of a market economy are developed in greater detail in later chapters, this key issue is not pursued here. Krueger is clearly mistaken when she explains 'development economics' in terms of the mere misapplication of good theory or the adoption of dubious stylized facts. She assumes implicitly that theory has not progressed from then to now. In point of fact, there is now a much better understanding of how economic growth and institutional change interact and co-evolve and how trade and openness affect the tempo of change (Stiglitz 1996, 1998a).

To take a single important issue, early liberal theorizing stressed the static gains from trade, which are relatively small. Today, the crucial arguments hinge around the mechanisms by which dynamic comparative advantage works out in practice, as Krueger acknowledges. Some of the peculiarities of developing countries, 'indivisibilities, complementarities, externalities, and economies of scale' were also correctly identified as playing a larger role on account of lower intensity of economic activity than in industrialized nations (Streeten 1984, p. 338). The evolution of thinking is quite apparent in even Krueger's own papers from the 1970s to the present, cited in this book.

Streeten (1984, p. 339) makes the point well: 'the exploration of Southern societies, with different tools of analysis, has often led to new illuminations and discoveries in our own Northern societies, thereby re-establishing the unity of the analysis.' He cites the study of the role of surplus labour, theories of dual labour markets, satisficing behaviour, X-efficiency and structuralist theories of inflation, which were developed in the context of developing economies and subsequently applied to advanced countries of the North. The dichotomous evolution of development and neoclassical economics seem to have originated in the inadequacies of the mainstream theory.[5]

The policies of inward-oriented ISI appeared quite unsustainable in the decade of slowdown and external shocks (1973–83) which followed the two decades of post-war upswing. The conventional wisdom is that the inefficiencies of ISI built up steadily to the point where developing countries could not withstand the post-1973 shocks. Rodrik (1999, ch. 4) shows that the transition was more abrupt and complex. Not only was growth strong in the first two decades, but TFP growth was high as well and did not discriminate unambiguously between the ISI majority and those later found to have followed outward-oriented policies.

As growth rates fell sharply from 1973 in the industrial centres, both GDP/capita growth and TFP growth collapsed in Latin America, the Middle East and sub-Saharan Africa. But East Asia was not affected to a significant extent. South Asia, which followed ISI policies rigidly, actually improved its performance marginally, without any qualitative change in its unsatisfactorily low rate of long-term growth. A number of countries in the first group experienced negative TFP growth and budget and trade deficits widened alarmingly. The issue was finally precipitated by the world debt crisis of 1982 when many of these countries fell into IMF and World Bank receivership and were thereby induced to change policy (Balassa 1989, Edwards 1993, Rodrik 1996, 1999, Gore 2000).

Rodrik argues persuasively that the proximate reason for this failure was the inability of stricken countries to adjust macroeconomic policies to the series of external shocks that pounded them from 1973. These blows led to inflation, rising trade and budget imbalances, debt crises and foreign exchange problems. He traces this weakness to poor fiscal, monetary and exchange rate policies, deriving fundamentally from the inability of governments to manage social conflict associated with stabilization and

---

[5]At that time formal economic analysis proceeded as if markets were complete with perfect information. The role of learning, institutional development, accumulation of skill and business experience, and other dynamic issues, were ignored. The study of developing economies has contributed much to the evolution of theory itself, up to and beyond the 'Washington consensus' (see Stiglitz 1996, 1998a for more detail).

structural adjustment policies. Thus South Korea succeeded in overcoming the crisis quickly, but Turkey and Brazil did not. India experienced no crisis of comparable magnitude, while adhering rigidly to ISI policies, because its links with the global economy were relatively weaker.

## 5.2    TRADE AS THE ENGINE OF GROWTH

The general failure of many countries that followed the ISI strategy opened up space for the philosophy of 'outward orientation.' From early on, a small number of economists had argued that more open, outward-oriented policies would lead to higher growth (Meier and Seers 1984). More recently the idea has been promoted by Krueger, Balassa and others. This new development paradigm came to the fore in the World Bank's 1987 *World Development Report* (hereafter WDR-87). In this report, the trade orientation of a sample of 41 developing countries was tallied against a range of economic indicators for the periods 1963–3 and 1973–85. The conclusion was that the degree of outward orientation was well correlated with performance indices such as growth of income per capita, GNP growth and growth in manufacturing value added.

WDR-87 was very much an expression of the views of Krueger who was chief economist at the World Bank at that time. Drawing ostensibly from the EA-NIE examples, it argued that an undistorted price system and minimal government intervention through tariffs, subsidies and taxes targeted on specific sectors offers the best possible conditions for rapid growth. An outward orientation that is neutral between export and import-competing production and which establishes a liberal trading regime, was advocated.[6]

The argument is not merely that outward orientation mechanically ensures rapid growth through static gains in allocative efficiency. It is that distortion of the incentive structure, subsidized and targeted credit and state investment in industry inhibit competition, promote rent-seeking and thereby lead to inferior growth of output and productivity. The signalling efficiency of a distortion-free price system would enable the state and private producers to correct mistakes and make the best use of local resources. Minimal state intervention would also limit private and public rent-seeking which, Krueger and others (Bhagwati 1989) had pointed out, is a barrier to healthy growth.

---

[6]Outward orientation is not synonymous with *laissez-faire* free trade. It describes a 'neutral' trade regime in which the effective exchange rate for exports is roughly on par with that for imports. The theory was that with rough parity, the market mechanism would shift resources away from heavily protected (inefficient) import substitution sectors towards export sectors, in harmony with comparative advantage, thereby raising allocative efficiency in production.

The creed of outward orientation drew legitimacy from the success of the East Asian economies in the context of general collapse in Latin America and Africa and near stagnation in South Asia. Looking back a decade later Krueger (1997) writes that East Asia dealt the 'final blow to the uncritical acceptance' of the ISI nostrum that 'industrialization could take place only through import substitution.' Not only was rapid growth possible through integration with the international economy, but high and sustainable growth seemed to depend critically on this integration, since growth did not have to be held back by the limited size or lethargy of domestic markets. Export pessimism has decidedly been laid to rest.[7]

The ideas expressed in WDR-87 are perhaps the most extreme statement of neo-liberal, 'free-market' ideas in the development mainstream, outside the neo-liberal think tanks. The positions advocated there were moderated somewhat in the later *World Development Reports* of 1989 and 1991 (Wade 1996, Gore 2000). To a great extent this shift was natural; it represents a careful evaluation of the varied and largely disappointing experience of stabilization and structural adjustment (SSA) of the previous decade. It was also a corrective to the neo-liberal 'policy overshoot' that derived from the collapse of ISI-interventionist strategies. If so, the 1991 WDR represents an overshoot to the left to judge by the more centrist ideas of the Washington consensus, which is where official Bank-Fund thinking seems to have settled in some kind of temporary equilibrium.

The 1991 *World Development Report* (hereafter WDR-91) develops a more detailed and situation-specific approach; alternative perspectives are scrupulously integrated into the presentation. These were derived from a decade of experience of developing countries with different SSA packages and analyses of their impact on socio-economic performance. A more careful accounting of the successes and failures had clarified issues and narrowed differences, moderating the ideological stances of WDR-87. It would be too optimistic to claim that WDR-91 represents a convergence to consensus; the differences in approach between the neoclassical paradigm and the heterodox positions of its critics remains. There is, however, a significant narrowing of issues of contention and closer accord on what the major problems are.

A significant departure for official thinking was the new political economy approach to SSA, endorsed in WDR-91. In a chapter suggestively titled 'Rethinking the state' it called for 'governments to intervene less in certain areas and more in others, for the state to let markets work where they can, and to step in promptly and effectively where they cannot' (WDR-91, p. 128), a view shared by heterodox economists as well. WDR-91 also analyses

---

[7]Rodrik (1999, pp. 38–40) and Hughes (1992). See Rodrigo and Martin (1997) for a general equilibrium study of the feasibility of export expansion by many LDCs together.

the role of culture and social institutions in promoting or stifling economic growth[8]. These include legitimate government, socially accepted property rights, land reform, social peace, modernized, efficient legal and financial institutions and state bureaucracies and curtailment of scope for rent-seeking. The idea that authoritarianism and high income inequality are conducive to economic growth is dismissed, except for East Asia; WDR-91 argues that in general dictatorships have proven disastrous for development and that inequality seems to be associated with slower growth.

The new approach highlights the importance of a host of country-specific institutions or initial conditions rooted in culture, society and history, which go beyond the austere neoclassical framework of the past. Where these do not exist, it is the prime task of the state to create them, such as in Meiji Japan. As expected, rationalization of an overextended public sector is strongly advocated with privatization wherever feasible to promote economic and administrative efficiency; but these ideas are now widely accepted across the spectrum.[9]

Institutions are taken as largely given exogenously; WDR-91 argues that actual policies are determined endogenously within each specific institutional context. The implication is that policy-makers have only very limited control over actual policy instruments. If these instruments are to be deployed more effectively, it would be necessary to change the underlying institutions, which is acknowledged to be a difficult process extended in time under most circumstances. The two-step leap in thinking from WDR-87 to WDR-91 is followed by a one-step retrogression in the analyses and policies of the more orthodox *East Asian Miracle* (1993) which is discussed later in this chapter.

## 5.3   THE WASHINGTON CONSENSUS

Official development thinking quickly settled into a new development paradigm, known as the 'Washington consensus,' which guided IMF and World Bank policy towards developing countries for over a decade. Tracing the evolution of this coalescence of thinking within the economic profession,

---

[8]A short list of indispensable interventions include the maintenance of law and order, the provision of public goods, investment in human capital, the construction and repair of physical infrastructure, and protection of the environment. Infant industry protection, if used, must be short-lived, but is not recommended. Heavy intervention is conducive to corruption which is severely detrimental to efficiency of government and economy. These ideas are not disputed by critics of orthodox theory. WDR-91 refers to the intellectual foundation laid for this integrated approach in the work of Hayek, Hegel, Marx and Weber (WDR-91 p. 134).
[9]Rationalization of the public sector need not always lead to privatization; WDR-91 cites the existence of efficient state enterprises in some developed and developing countries.

Rodrik (1996) points out that it reflected the view that the East Asian miracle could be attributed to sound macroeconomic management, market-oriented trade and investment policies and a reduced role for the government. But a careful study of the evidence indicates that causality seems to operate the other way round: countries that manage to achieve significant economic success tend to reduce trade barriers, starting from the highly protectionist USA of the late 19th century to Western Europe after the second world war (Rodrik 1999, ch. 6). This argument is corroborated by Chenery et al. (1986, ch. 1) who show that overall developing country manufactures exports grew by about 10% a year during the post-war boom and countries such as Brazil, Turkey and Spain shifted towards more neutral trade policies as a result of rising production competence and export success.

Its critics point out that the Washington consensus was cobbled together, not so much from East Asia's experience, but from policy responses to the Latin debt crises of the 1980s. The debate over policy became increasingly ideological and the original ideas of outward orientation were trimmed down into simpler formulae. Along with stress on economic fundamentals, property rights, education, etc., the Washington consensus focused on stabilization, deregulation, privatization and trade liberalization. Many governments in Latin America and elsewhere implemented these policies as best they could, without being able to reproduce anything near the East Asian achievement.

The emphasis on sound economic fundamentals is hardly original or controversial. The value of macroeconomic stability, limiting distortions in the price system, maintaining proper incentives and minimizing rent-seeking activity are widely accepted as conducive to growth. It is clear that in many developing countries outside East Asia, selective state interventions have led to massive rent-seeking, corruption, inferior growth and ultimately failed to even establish economic viability for the targeted industries without state subsidies. But the story for East Asia is not quite consistent with the main thrust of the Washington consensus, as has been established by other studies.

In addition to highly generalized explanations of growth, it is also necessary to look closely at specific trajectories of development and identify special features that contributed to success or failure. In this respect, the literature is vast and still growing. Yet, there are problems that still remain to be resolved, such as the close geographical coherence of all Asian NIEs (Easterly 1994).[10] It is tempting to propose that Japan's experience and the ongoing relationship with Japan played a decisive role in influencing the activist role of the state in East Asia.

---

[10]In fact Easterly and Levine (2000) argue that growth everywhere, across and within nations, is characterized by clustering, coherence within specific regions and divergence across regions and nations. They state that growth exhibits a 'fractal' character in this respect.

The specific conditions of East Asian growth seem to conform very closely to the 'governed market' template enunciated by Wade (1990), except for Hong Kong, where state intervention was limited to the fundamentals. Hong Kong, it seems, stands solitary witness to the growth-generating genius of the invisible hand in East Asia. In other EA-NIEs the state intervened decisively to promote manufactures exports and create the necessary institutional conditions for export-led growth. But Hong Kong benefited from the post-revolutionary influx of a significant portion of Shanghai's textile entrepreneurs, foremen and skilled workers, as already noted in section 3.3. It also contained a large number of British trading and financial houses with a century of commercial experience.[11]

History has played a role in the other EA-NIEs as well. Initial conditions were favourable in South Korea and Taiwan, which benefited from economic transformations carried out under Japanese colonial rule and major land reforms implemented in the early post-war years. China's Kuomintang-dominated administrative class also relocated to Taiwan, but this was at best a mixed blessing. Pack (1988) states that in general for the developing world, there is little prima facie correlation between initial endowment and the relative efficiency of later industrial growth; but he immediately cites South Korea and Taiwan as important exceptions.

Smith (1991) points out that it is wrong to automatically associate export promotion with free trade or to counterpose export promotion to ISI. He argues that many of the major manufactures-exporting NIEs simultaneously protect some infant industries while intervening actively to promote exports in other industries. He shows that virtually all developing countries promoted exports of some kind to finance increased imports needed for growth. Quoting the Chenery et al. (1986) study of industrialization and growth, he argues that periods of significant export expansion are almost always preceded by periods of strong import substitution. Indeed EA-NIEs such as South Korea and Taiwan went through brief phases of ISI with high levels of protection and outright bans on the import of some goods.[12] In fact, Taylor (1988) argues that export success was almost always preceded by a phase of import substitution and required much more than merely getting prices right.

The evidence is also strong that it is the export of manufactures that is closely associated with rapid growth and structural change. Countries specializing in manufactures have consistently outperformed primary

---

[11]Hong Kong conforms most closely to the free market ideal of the 'nightwatchman state.' But even here the government launched a public housing programme, set up labour laws and established many social services (Young 1992, Lall 1994, 1996).
[12]They did, however, limit the period of protection and managed a relatively expeditious transition to exports (Pack and Westphal 1986).

exporters. The terms of trade for the former have also held up very well while those for the latter have exhibited a persistent tendency to decline, since commodity prices are notoriously unstable. A survey by Faini and De Melo (1990) find that manufactures exporters, in East Asian countries and a few others, have adjusted successfully to the turbulent economic climate of the eighties.[13] Taiwan, Korea and Singapore have used industrial policies very effectively to promote selected exports of manufactures on a rising scale of technical sophistication (Amsden 1989, Lall 1990, Wade 1990).

## 5.4 CRITICISMS OF THE WASHINGTON CONSENSUS

The thesis that East Asian success derives from neo-liberal policies as generalized in the Washington consensus has been vigorously contested by many. Every critic has pointed to strong state intervention in Korea, Taiwan, Singapore and indeed in Japan itself, which set up the original blueprint for export-oriented growth. Much of the criticism has been directed at the World Bank's (1993) landmark *East Asian Miracle* study, which was commissioned specifically to bridge the chasm between the Bank's neoclassical conceptions and the reality of successful state interventions in East Asia (Lall 1994). Finally, while Stiglitz functioned as its chief economist, the Bank itself has sought to distance itself from numerous failures brought on by mechanically applied prescriptions (Stiglitz 1996, 1998a).

Lall (1994) brings out the underlying conceptual differences with clarity in his critique of the *East Asian Miracle* (EAM) study. At one pole is the neoclassical view that growth is best promoted by untrammelled markets with incentives neutral between export and domestic markets. This idea comes out of static efficiency considerations in situations of near-perfect competition, information flow, foresight and adjustment of product and factor markets. At the other pole is the view that all of these markets and processes are imperfect

---

[13]In a survey of 83 developing countries since 1965, Faini and De Melo (1990) divide up the sample into manufactures exporters, fuel exporters and a residual category of primary exporters. They find that after adjustment, it is only the manufacturing exporters, mostly the East Asian countries, that have resumed growth at around the pre-crisis rates. They report that the debt service burden for this group is high, but that is because of a few Latin countries in the group. Annual growth in the fuel-exporting group has declined steadily from 6.6% in 1978–81 to 0.9% in the 1986–8 period. Primary exporters have recaptured most of their loss in growth in the same time frame but have suffered a worsening trend in their external debt service. Real non-oil commodity prices have declined by an average of 1.5% per annum from 1948–92; the rate of fall has been even sharper at 2.4% per annum for the 1965–90 period. The terms of trade are calculated here for a basket of 33 non-oil commodities deflated by the export price of manufactures (World Bank 1993, ch. 6; Todaro 1989, pp. 375–7).

in developing countries, because by definition markets and institutions are in their infancy in developing societies. Weak institutions lead to pervasive market failures which, therefore, call for powerful, targeted state intervention if economic growth is to be jump-started.

Lall observes that the EAM study steers a 'market-friendly,' middle-way between standard neoclassical market fundamentalism and the 'revisionist' justification of industrial policy. He lauds the study for clearly admitting the wide extent and scope of state intervention in East Asian economies. 'All intervened functionally, and most intervened selectively: in imports, export promotion, credit allocation, technology flows, firm growth, foreign investment and public ownership ... Japan and Korea led in the scope and detail of interventions, with Taiwan close behind. Among the smaller "Dragons," Singapore intervened pervasively and selectively, but did not protect domestic industry. Hong Kong intervened the least.'

The EAM study accepts the reality of some market failures. Thus, it approves of functional intervention to promote education to build human capital for industrialization. But the need for selective intervention to build skills in particular industrial activities, through learning-by-doing, is not accepted on the assumption that skills are generic and fungible. It also accepts the possibility of market failures in coordinating investment decisions within industry arising from imperfect information, inadequately developed capital markets, economies of scale, investments in interdependent, vertically related activities, externalities in skill creation and learning, and so on.[14]

Lall notes that since many of these failures differ in incidence and intensity across different industries and countries, corrective measures must necessarily be selective. While acknowledging the theoretical case for selective intervention, the EAM study makes no attempt to examine which interventions addressed which failures and the extent to which they remedied the problem. Given the extraordinary richness of the East Asian experience in this respect, it seems the EAM study has missed a golden opportunity to advance development thinking. It dodges the crucial issue of dealing with market failure by concluding that, in any case, such interventions were not really important in East Asia. It falls back on the politically correct homily that in going beyond functional interventions 'governments are likely to do more harm than good.'

But the list of market failures is incomplete and the EAM study does not seriously confront the most important problem of all: technological learning at the micro-level, or the acquisition of technological capability. This being

---

[14]See Stiglitz (1996) for definitions and a fuller explanation of market failures. In many ways Stiglitz's study carries out the task that Lall (1994) faults the EAM study for failing to do.

his speciality, Lall goes into great detail in discussing the different strategies adopted by the four EA-NIEs to address the problem. Since this topic is dealt with comprehensively in subsequent chapters, it is not summarized here. Lall shows that the industrial strategies adopted by each country involved costly learning trajectories, stretched out over decades and successive technologies.

This shortfall is particularly striking as a great deal of detailed work on industrial learning at firm level has been carried out by the Bank's own researchers or under Bank sponsorship. Oblivious to that material, the EAM 'assumes costless and automatic learning and upgrading of industrial technologies.' Lall sees the whole exercise as an attempt to obfuscate the crucial role that industrial policy played in East Asia in deliberately steering market forces to accelerate industrial learning. The conclusion is that, while some attempt is made to confront the real world problems of development in East Asia, in the final analysis the EAM is more an exercise in ideological apologetics than scrupulous science.

Stiglitz's (1996, 1998a) criticisms of the Washington consensus are consistent with Lall's perspectives. Its fundamental weakness, he argues, is that it sees development as a technical-economic problem, much as did the development planners of the earlier school; i.e. if governments get the fundamentals right and then move out of the way, market forces would spring into action and automatically generate rapid growth. He points out that many countries which implemented the 'dictums of liberalization, stabilization, and privatization, the central premises of the so-called Washington consensus' failed to grow at satisfactory rates nonetheless.

This mechanical perspective of growth, Stiglitz argues, is refuted by the experience of East Asia and even more decisively by regional disparities in countries such as Italy, where the North has developed fast while the South stagnates, though there are no trade barriers between them. Even in advanced countries, there are pockets of chronic underdevelopment, which cannot exist in the idealized, mechanical world of the Washington consensus. Stiglitz sees development as a social learning process, a transformation of society from traditional modes of behaviour and thinking into modern ways of doing things. It involves the building-up of institutions which may be specific to particular countries on account of different histories, initial endowments and internal and external constraints.

Stiglitz points out that governments have an indispensable role in all such processes of transformation in recent times, even in the development of the USA, though sometimes mistakes are made in attempting to do too much. Nevertheless, governments have a crucial role to play in supplementing markets and regulating them to ensure efficient operation. For example, the Washington consensus promoted financial liberalization without placing equal emphasis on the regulation of financial markets, which is a job for the state. This one-side approach was partly responsible for the Asian financial crisis of 1997–8, as discussed further in Chapter 8.

Stiglitz is advancing a perspective of growth and development which is essentially evolutionary in conception. It involves the building-up of capability within society, in business organizations and within the ranks of the state bureaucracy and the political structure. It also involves the building up and modernization of institutions. The elements of this perspective are developed in detail in the next two chapters. It represents a fundamental departure from the mechanical conception of economic processes that characterized both the early development planners and the present proponents of the Washington consensus.

The ideas about trade, growth and development covered in this chapter, examine the issues at the level of the nation-state in highly macro-aggregate terms. This approach is reasonable as a starting point and it has advanced understanding of the dynamics of growth some distance. It is clear, however, that the debate has developed to the point where a close look at the micro-level evidence is necessary. Fortunately there already exist a wide range of individual country studies and firm and industry-level analyses to draw on. Chapter 6 looks at insights that can be drawn from firm and industry-level studies about the proximate causes of productivity growth. Chapter 7 examines attempts to reconceptualize such insights into a more satisfactory explanation of how the East Asian NIEs industrialized so rapidly.

# 6. What drives industrial productivity?

Previous chapters have devoted much space to published work that analyses long-term aggregate productivity growth and compares its sources across selected countries. Such studies are undoubtedly important for drawing a balance sheet of growth experience over the second half of the 20th century. But they do not so far give clear guidelines for reformulating development strategies for the future. One comes away with the insight that high sustained investment is closely associated with high long-term growth and with the expansion of trade. But the direction of causality is hard to establish through statistical analysis for a very good reason: much of what we know about economic growth indicates that growth promotes investment and trade as much as the other way round, in a causal loop involving positive feedback. Then the next logical step is to look more closely at sector, industry and firm-level analyses and the industrial strategies of individual countries to build up alternative, micro-level, perspectives on the determinants of growth.

Mainstream theory attributes economic growth to two principal sources. The first of these is the expansion of factor inputs; this is the accumulation component. The second is the rise in efficiency with which inputs are used, measured as TFP growth (see Chapters 2 and 3 for details). This chapter focuses on the second of these determinants, the microeconomic mechanisms and processes by which economic efficiency is raised in developing countries, in particular at the firm and industry level. That evidence is used to examine in more detail the relative merits of the two conflicting views of technical progress, posed in section 3.5.

The equally important division of economic growth into transformation (production) and transaction activities is deferred to Chapter 7, which carries a more comprehensive exposition of the sources of productivity advance.[1]

---

[1]This separation is particularly apropos when analysis is pitched at industry and plant level rather than that of the nation. This is because aggregate, national productivity growth derives from efficiency gains associated with economic transactions as well as from productivity advances in the pure transformation of inputs into outputs, i.e. production per se. North and Wallis (1994) have analysed this important issue *in extenso* and conclude that the transaction sector has grown from 25% to 45% of GNP over the last century in the USA.

There exists now a wide range of industry, firm and plant-level studies that examine the micro-mechanisms of productivity growth; a significant number of these have been carried out in the four EA-NIEs as well.[2] With hardly an exception, such studies emphasize the arduous and uncertainty-ridden processes of technology acquisition involved in the unceasing quest for productivity advance. There is unquestionably a great deal of deliberate and sustained human effort – in learning and adaptation – that is necessary, manifestly fitting the evolutionary model of technical change.

Furthermore, it is entirely possible for a country to get 'locked into' an initially lucrative 'dead-end' technology strategy based on natural resource-intensive technologies. Here, the reduced potential for technological learning can block entry into technological trajectories that generate high productivity in the long run through the process of 'path-dependence.' The ensuing policy conclusions are very significantly different from the standard prescriptions deriving from the neoclassical model of growth.

High growth in the East Asian economies is, of course, associated with high accumulation of physical and human capital. Therefore, some analysts have argued that high growth in East Asia is 'explained' satisfactorily by high investment alone, according to the canons of neoclassical growth decomposition. It is argued in Chapter 3 that accumulation is a necessary accompaniment to growth, but not an exhaustive explanation. In developing countries with poor institutions and low levels of human capital, high growth must necessarily be carried on the back of high investment.

In some special cases, such as Hong Kong, where high growth has been associated with relatively lower levels of investment, there existed other special growth-promoting conditions such as high initial endowments of business-specific human capital. The real miracle, as Nelson, Pack and others have pointed out, is the ability of these Asian economies to have sustained heavy investment over decades without running into diminishing returns.

In opposition to the mainstream view, evolutionary economists argue that the growth momentum derives principally from deliberate decisions of individuals, firms and the government to expand existing economic activity and to initiate new lines of business. A necessary concomitant is investment in physical and human capital, machines, structures and special skills which leverage raw human labour. For successful, sustainable growth, the inputs must be transformed into output on a rising trajectory of efficiency. Since the East Asian NIEs achieved this better than other developing countries, the problem here is to explain the mechanisms which sustained this efficiency.

---

[2]See Mayes (1996), Roberts and Tybout (1996), Caves (1998) and Kim and Nelson (2000). The East Asian NIEs are specifically covered in Amsden (1986, 1989) and Hobday (1995).

This chapter examines three approaches to the dynamics of productivity advance that fall between, or perhaps bridge, the evolutionary-neoclassical divide. The first is the topic of structural change and industry evolution based on empirical studies, on which there has been some work by structuralists. The second is the dynamics of technical efficiency gain through advances in industrial engineering practice. The third is the study of 'industrial learning' at plant and firm level. 'Learning' includes the processes by which technical efficiency is raised, but goes considerably beyond just supply side productivity advance. Until quite recently, the second and third subjects have languished at the periphery of the economics profession, but taken up enthusiastically in the business management literature.

## 6.1  STRUCTURAL CHANGE

The role of structural change in the growth trajectories of the EA-NIEs is very well documented in the literature. The shift from agricultural activities to industry and within industry, movement to higher value-added sectors, are the most palpable aspects of economic growth. The shift of labour and new capital into these paths of expansion are very important contributors to the growth of aggregate labour productivity. Additionally rising efficiency in the agricultural sector, deriving from the increasing use of capital equipment, more efficient techniques, fertilizer, pesticides etc, and higher yielding seed varieties, are undoubtedly significant in the early stages of industrialization.

The well-known contributions of Kuznets, Rostow, Lewis and others are summarized in Tunzelmann (1995) and Rostow (1990). Some of the early theories of development were based on models of structural change which saw development as the shift of productive resources from lower to higher productivity sectors. The best known and most influential studies of patterns of structural change were developed by Chenery and colleagues (Chenery et al. 1986). These studies cover a number of countries including South Korea, Taiwan, Singapore and Hong Kong. They assembled a collection of common patterns or stages of growth and structural change for developing countries, depending on size, average income level or stage of development. The role of international trade in the growth process was also examined.

Chenery et al. find the expected patterns of structural change: industries intensive in lower-skilled labour are displaced by capital and skill-intensive industries; the use of intermediate inputs from domestic sources increase and firms become more closely interlinked. They find that the most important proximate source of growth in developing countries is factor accumulation. The contribution of efficiency or TFP growth is relatively small at around

30%, but larger than the estimates of Young and Collins and Bosworth. They identify three typical patterns of development. The first is the large country 'L' model of Brazil, India and China. The second is the small and primary-oriented 'SP' model of countries that are strongly dependent on primary products. The third is the small and industry-oriented 'SM' model in which manufactures are produced for export.

Larger, L-model countries are able to industrialize faster on the basis of their larger internal markets by exploiting economies of scale and their larger resource bases. Industrialization is accelerated by import-substitution polices which are adopted more easily than export-penetration strategies, which seem to require more concentration of effort, the cultivation of new international business alliances and so on. Industrialization is retarded in the SP model if countries find it easier to stay with primary specialization. In countries of the SM pattern, which have neither large internal markets nor primary exports, the best available option is the aggressive pursuit of manufactures exports. The Chenery schema, based on structural-economic conditions, provide a persuasive explanation of why the resource-poor EA-NIEs took an early turn to export markets.

As is to be expected, there is a substantial increase in the absolute and relative sizes of the manufacturing sector in all countries. Also, countries that followed export expansion strategies grew faster, industrialized sooner and exhibited significantly higher TFP growth, compared to those that followed import-substitution policies. They find that growth variations across countries owe more to variations in economic efficiency than capital accumulation, an issue that is discussed in more detail below. They also find that a country needs to develop a certain minimum industrial base and a threshold level of technical skill before it can successfully embark into the export of manufactured goods. This implies that an initial phase of import substitution may be necessary to launch a growth strategy based on the export of manufactures to competitive world markets.

More recent studies of industry evolution and structural change in a range of countries have built considerably on the early results. Caves (1998) and Roberts and Tybout (1996) emphasize the incessant dynamics of firm entry and exit, the simultaneous expansion and contraction of different units of production in each industry. As more efficient firms expand production and move into higher technologies and less efficient firms scale down or move out, aggregate productivity advances, but not in a smooth or linear fashion. The essentially evolutionary nature of market-driven industrial expansion is brought out very well in the studies included in the latter. While it does not include East Asian countries, the 'micro-patterns of turnover, productivity and market structure' detailed in it are confirmed for the East Asian NIEs by numerous country-specific studies.[3]

Recent works on industrial evolution tend to emphasize the dynamics of technological change, international alliances and such like, rather than the structural change aspect. This is possibly because structural change is seen as a *derivative* aspect of technological and business evolution, dependent on an a priori demarcation of economic activity along arbitrary boundaries, except the shift from agriculture to industry in South Korea and Taiwan and from manufacturing to financial services in Singapore and Hong Kong. The 'East Asian miracles' can be generalized as the 'sustained movement of the workforce from less to more sophisticated products' (Lucas 1993, p. 267).

## 6.2    TECHNICAL EFFICIENCY

While economists have devoted considerable effort to understanding the persistence of dualism in economic phenomena, they tend not to worry too much about dualism in economic theory. A good example of this is the way differences in labour productivity between different plants using the same technology, located in the same or different countries, is explained. Basic micro and trade theory explain such differences as arising out of different labour to capital ratios in the production of output, which in turn derive from different endowments of labour and capital. The observed variation of productive efficiency across plants having the exact same production machinery, both within countries and between different countries, does not appear to have found its way into the body of core microeconomic theory.[4]

Technical inefficiency, or X-inefficiency, to use Leibenstein's more nebulous term, refers to losses accruing from less than optimal organization of production activity with existing factor combinations (machines and workers), i.e. without any change of technology (Torii 1992). Technical efficiency changes derive from variations in individual and organizational learning and even from physical and social infrastructure differentials, as discussed below. Caves and Barton (1990, pp. 1–2) report that 'data on distributions of cost and efficiency levels within industries regularly reveal what seem to be striking amounts of technical inefficiency.' They ask why technical efficiency has received so little attention when in quantitative terms it is so much more important than allocative efficiency in reducing costs.

---

[3]Details of EA-NIE industrial evolution are to be found in Pilat (1994), Song (1990), Wade (1990), Pack (1988), Chen et al. (1991), Young (1992) and World Bank (1993).
[4]This peculiar situation still exists (Grosskopf 1993, Färe et al. 1994), though reference is often made to 'dynamic efficiency gains' and 'learning effects' in the trade literature.

This is an important question since a central argument of the outward orientation school has been that an unbiased trade regime would maximize allocative efficiency by promoting domestic factor choice consistent with relative factor prices. Technical efficiency growth was peripheral to the argument; open regimes were expected to achieve some dynamic efficiency gains from increased competition. A major reason for this neglect, argue Caves and Barton, is the axiomatic contradiction set up in conventional micro theory; an inefficient firm or manager is failing to maximize profits or utility. Caves (1992) remarks 'the hypothesis of profit maximization has mutated into an axiom ever ready to deny any allegation of productive inefficiency.' This bears out the truth of the maxim that theory, after all, is both a framework and a filter for mediating the apprehension of material reality.

Leibenstein insisted that X-efficiency is a wider concept than technical efficiency, since it includes gains extending beyond the knowledge or capability of managers.[5] Throughout this book the term technical efficiency is used, as is common in the literature quoted, and no distinction between the terms is intended. But a clear distinction exists between 'technical efficiency' gains and 'technological advance' as defined below. However, in some of the literature quoted, technological change is referred to as 'major innovation' and technical efficiency advance is included as a part of 'minor innovation.'

Following detailed studies of productive efficiency carried out at firm and plant level, there has been a resurgence of interest in the issue of technical inefficiency, and the mechanisms by which these are overcome to enhance growth. Pack (1987, p. *ix*) remarks that 'economists and industrial engineers had devoted relatively little effort to either measuring or understanding the sources of low productivity in manufacturing in developing countries.' Today technical efficiency is known to be quantitatively far more important than allocative efficiency. There exists a substantial literature on its identification and statistical estimation that has sprung up rapidly over the last decade.

Technical efficiency is defined with respect to the optimal production frontier, which is determined by a production function reflecting the base technological level. A brief review of the associated theory is supplied in the appendix 6.A at the end of this chapter. Consider a distribution of firms in the same industry, in the same country. If all of them realized the full potential inherent in the technology, then their productivities in value added per

---

[5]Leibenstein (1973), whose conceptualization had a significant impact on the economics profession, drew this idea from the experience of management consultants who achieved large productivity gains by better work organization in existing plants. The concept of technical efficiency, however, goes back to Farrell (1957). An analysis of X-efficiency within the institutional framework of transaction cost analysis is given by Thorbecke (1990).

person-hour would fall exactly on the production possibilities frontier reflecting only the varying combinations of capital and labour and be fully explained by the production function. But since most firms do not achieve the optimal level of efficiency, the production function has to be scaled down by a factor which reflects the de facto technical efficiency with respect to the optimum frontier implicit in the technology. A firm on the frontier then achieves a 100% level of technical efficiency and the frontier itself is called the domestic best practice frontier (DBPF). A firm that realized only half of the full productivity has a technical efficiency of 50%.

The DBPF itself is estimated by a statistical procedure. The starting point is the distribution of productive efficiency for individual firms in a particular industry, represented as the input levels required for unit output. The envelope curve hugging the input distribution from below is defined as the DBPF. If some parametric form is assumed for the technical efficiency distribution, the DBPF can be derived by a statistical method which is briefly discussed in the appendix 6.A. Clearly, technical efficiency measured in this way is defined in relation to the performance of the most efficient firms; it is the ratio of the actual productivity of the firm to the DBPF productivity corresponding to the same factor proportions.[6]

A similar argument could be developed for the dispersion of domestic best practice across different nations. For any given nation, the DBPF would in general lie above – in a lower productivity position to – the international best practice frontier (IBPF). The DBPF of the most efficient nation in the group would be the IBPF. The gap between an individual country's DBPF and the IBPF, in a given industry, is generally attributed to major differences in the production technology; but clearly systematic differences in country-specific technical efficiency could also play a significant part. Mainstream economists do not speak of 'technological inefficiency' except perhaps in education and health care, since technology differentials across countries are inevitable in the historical short term at the least.

With regard to estimates of technical efficiency in developing countries, Pack's pioneering work (1972, 1987, 1988) is the starting point. Preceding research on productivity determinants is scant and had focused on inter-country comparisons.[7] Recent studies of technical efficiency in Japan,

---

[6]See Caves and Barton (1990), Caves (1992), Fried et al. (1993) and World Bank (1993).
[7]Pack (1988) notes 'Early post-war research indicated that labor productivity in various sub-sectors of manufacturing was considerably lower in Western Europe and Japan than in the United States.' Hirschman (1958) had suggested that LDCs might exhibit relatively higher productivity in machine-paced capital intensive industries, since the factors depressing productivity in LDCs were less operative here; but no strong evidence of this effect has been found. Clark (1987) finds large productivity differentials in the cotton textile industry around

Britain, Korea and Australia are to be found in Caves (1992). Pack's work began with plant-level studies of manufacturing industry in developing countries such as Kenya and the Philippines. He discusses how and why particular technology choices are made and the numerous ways in which inefficiency (with respect to the DBPF) are generated. Pack states that most developing countries operate well below the IBPF. Productivity advance through technical efficiency gain is realized when inefficiencies are deliberately corrected by better industrial engineering techniques, typically under pressure of competition. Competitive pressure induces firms to move faster towards the DBPF thereby raising aggregate productivity in that sector and reducing the variance of productivity within that particular technology.

Pack found that technical efficiency within the same industry, using the same technology, varied widely. He states that on an aggregate basis the movement to best practice (i.e. elimination of technical inefficiency) would add 25–40% to overall output in Egypt, Ghana and India, but improved allocative efficiency would enhance output by only 7–17%. Caves and Barton (1990) quote previous studies of technical efficiency estimates for various countries; these are 55% for Colombian apparel and footwear industries, 62.5% for Brazilian manufacturing, 62–68% for Indonesia's weaving industry and 71–94% for 10 French manufacturing industries.

In recent years, numerous studies of technical efficiency distribution patterns, covering various countries, have appeared in the literature, and the analytical techniques have been refined as well (Coelli et al. 1999). These mostly employ the stochastic frontier production technique, though DEA analysis is also often employed. These techniques have become increasingly popular as the focus of empirical analysis has shifted from cross-country studies of aggregate productivity to detailed, sector-specific investigation of the sources of heterogeneity in manufacturing industry in individual countries (Roberts and Tybout 1996, Tybout 2000, Temple 1999).

A typical recent example is the analysis of technical efficiency in four major industrial sectors in India, in relation to the domestic best practice frontier for each sector, by Lall and Rodrigo (2000). They find a considerable amount of technical efficiency variation, averaging 50–60% in the machine tools, motor vehicle and electronics industries, with the standard deviation falling in the 11–14% range. In the less technology intensive leather products sector, technical efficiency averages 44% of best practice, with a higher standard deviation of 15%. These results are very similar to those obtained by Pack and later researchers (see above).

They also find that technical efficiency is correlated with a proxy for the

---

1910, between the leader Britain and followers such as Germany, France, India and China.

quality of plant management and the efficiency of energy use. The result is significant across all four sectors, indicating a crucial linkage between plant efficiency and the quality of management. The conclusion is that there exists considerable room for productivity gain through better organization and management of production processes. This could be achieved by internal learning processes without any extra investment in physical plant or equipment, or with the assistance of external management consultants. Both new technology and modern management techniques could also be acquired through business alliances with partners from industrial countries, which seems to be a rising trend in India at the present time. This trend emulates the strategies followed by East Asian firms (see section 7.1). Such developments are likely to accelerate as India liberalizes further and faster in anticipation of reaping East Asian-style economic rewards (Lall 1999).

## 6.3    INDUSTRIAL LEARNING

The discipline of operations management is perennially preoccupied with the task of advancing productive efficiency by deliberate efforts to overcome inefficiencies at various levels of the organization. By contrast, economists have tended to conceptualize economic processes as machine-like input-output systems, with 'rational agents' making choices within well-defined sets of alternatives. The mechanical metaphor, of course, has its uses; but it has held back the economics profession from appreciating and modelling real-world economic behaviour and individual and organizational learning, until recent times at least. Gurus of business management, on the other hand, have always placed conscious human activism, with the possibility of errors of judgement, at centre stage in their theories of growth and change.

It is clear from the foregoing discussion that a considerable part of the productivity gains achieved in both industrial and developing countries is realized through the deliberate raising of technical efficiency. Such actions constitute industrial learning of different types and at different levels of the organization. Learning effects and the 'learning curve' have therefore figured prominently in the thinking of management consultants and in the syllabi of schools of business management. The fact that management consulting inputs often tilt the balance between success and failure in a wide range of business organizations must surely refute the argument that productivity advance is automatic, costless or determined by capital investments alone.

One popular strategy in business strategic planning is to enter into new technologies early to capture dividends from learning (because production costs decline with accumulated experience in a new activity). The objective is to acquire and maintain a dynamic cost and quality advantage over one's competitors. By the same logic, it can be argued that an infant industry in a follower country needs a protected growing-up phase in which to master the technological skill needed to compete with the international leader.

'Learning-by-doing' is not a topic that is new in economics.[8] But the issue is more widely discussed in the business literature, since modern industries exhibit a pronounced learning curve. Learning takes place when unit variable cost in production declines with cumulative output as workers, supervisors and managers build up skills around a specific production process. It is not sufficient for unit total cost to decline, since that would happen in any case as fixed costs are spread out over a larger volume of output. The skill accumulation process works not only in direct production activities such as fabrication, machining and assembly, but also in supporting activities such as inventory control, scheduling and production planning in general and supply chain management.

Potential for skill accumulation by learning is different for different activities. Important insights into the economic significance of learning effects in East Asia and other developing countries have been detailed by Amsden (1986, 1989), Pack (1972, 1987, 1988), Hobday (1995) and Pack and Westphal (1986). Amsden argues that learning effects are greatest in 'skill-intensive' industries, less so in capital-intensive industries and least in unskilled labour-intensive assembly operations. Skills are built up through varying combinations of formal education (though not always) and on-the-job experience. Such learning is accelerated by competitive pressures.

A detailed account of learning dynamics and efficiency gains in the different constituent activities of spinning and weaving is given by Pack (1987). He shows that task-level efficiency in Kenya and the Philippines can often be high in comparison with textile industry practice in Britain. But overall efficiency is low because higher-level aggregate activity is performed at lower levels of efficiency. The critical weakness is often in the area of production management. The crucial lesson here is that even relatively unskilled workers in developing countries can reach international norms of task-efficiency quite quickly through learning-by-doing. But, *management skills are much less amenable to informal learning*; these have to be painstakingly acquired by some combination of formal vocational training and on-the-job apprenticeship with experienced managers.

This is an important issue since it highlights a significant lacuna in the conventional theory, which sees East Asian export success as depending merely on selection of industries intensive in unskilled labour, in accordance

---

[8]Arrow's (1962) famous article is often quoted in the economics literature.

with allocative efficiency considerations. Pack (1987, 1988), Amsden (1986, 1989) and Pack and Westphal (1986) have argued that the skills of foremen and supervisors played an important role even in labour-intensive processes in East Asia.[9] These critical managerial skills in turn were inherited from the period of Japanese occupation and then built up further.

A detailed account of the skill accumulation process in South Korea is given in Amsden's book (1989) on Korean industrialization. She describes not only skill accumulation at various levels of production activity, but also in the political leadership and bureaucracy, in short in the entire social infrastructure of production. The conclusion is inescapable that without the 'social accumulation,' more industry-specific accumulations of skill would have had a lower impact on aggregate productivity. This is a crucial insight that falls out of all studies of East Asian economies (such as Wade 1990).

The crucial role of production-specific skill accumulation in a nation's economic progress is analysed cogently by Amsden (1986, p. 265). She argues that it is a delusion to think that these can be purchased because one operates in a market economy; these skills have to be acquired in the course of production and cannot be imported unlike physical capital. Thus 'such skills and knowledge are necessary to import foreign technology successfully, to produce more efficiently, or to graduate to production processes requiring still more skill and knowledge. They complement but *cannot be replaced* by skill and knowledge acquired off the job, in research and training institutes, or via imports. They arise largely because *technology can never be entirely explicit or codifiable*, which is what neoclassical theory assumes when it takes technology to be universally available in blueprints' (emphasis added). She also argues that 'because technology is more tacit the more skill intensive the production process, learning effects are greatest in such sectors.'

Perhaps the best example of the critical importance of initial human capital endowment is Hong Kong. As discussed earlier, the precipitate migration of Shanghai's textile industrialists, along with their foremen and skilled workers, to Hong Kong following the 1949 Chinese Revolution, was a major factor in the colony's subsequent success (also see Amsden 1999). Since historical determinants are absent in the 'Washington-consensus' view of economic success (Gore 2000), the ensuing policy lessons are seriously

---

[9]Pack (1988) states that the role of skill growth has not been carefully explored even for East Asia. The exceptions cited are Saxonhouse (1978) and Izumi (1980) who analyse the generation of industrial skills, rather than formal education, in the early Japanese cotton textile industry and Leff (1968) who carefully analyses the growth of labour skills in the Brazilian engineering sector. Pack also shows that the two most important studies of Korea and Taiwan to date, Mason et al. (1980) and Galenson (1979), respectively, do not consider the accumulation of industrial skills nor the acquisition of production technology.

misleading for developing countries that do not enjoy similar historical endowments. However, the less-than-stellar performance of India (Lall 1987), which did have a similar colonial inheritance, shows that other economic conditions are important as well, in particular the nature of the trade regime and the degree of internal business competition.

The ways in which a more open trade regime promotes productivity growth through learning effects are described by Amsden (1986, p. 265): 'learning effects don't depend upon increased production from trade per se, although trade may uniquely expose firms to new technological environments and consequently help them broaden their technological knowledge.' By opening up a channel to the world market, trade also serves to promote specialization and sustain production tempos of goods in which learning effects are embodied; if constrained by domestic market size alone along with associated domestic business cycle uncertainty of demand, firms would be less willing to make the investments needed to capture gains from learning.

The interaction of learning effects and trade policy has given rise to the strategic trade policy literature that has developed recently. These exercises provide theoretical underpinning, and therefore academic respectability in the current context, to industrial policy and infant industry arguments. Since this issue is not of central importance to the arguments developed here, it is not pursued any further; the essential insights are summarized by Grossman (1990) and Krugman (1990). These insights are generally more applicable to industrial countries than to developing ones. The related issue of how to model learning effects, which is common to both strategic trade theory and the analysis of East Asian growth, is considered further in appendix 6.B.

Starting from the business management approach to the formalization of experience effects, Amsden (1986, p. 267) derives useful insights: 'The division of labour is ... greater the more elaborate the production process, i.e., the greater the application of capital and skills. Therefore, learning will be greater the more skill and capital-intensive the operation.' She reasons that this is because skilled jobs consist of a larger number of tasks than unskilled jobs and separately and together require more effort to master.

These ideas corroborate the observation about the distinction between task efficiency and production management expertise made earlier. Amsden proposes a definition of skilled activity and a categorization of different skill classes. She supplements the conventional definition of skilled labour as raw labour enhanced by training and experience by proposing that 'skill' is a *production factor that cannot yet be replaced by a machine within the margin of profitability*. The progress of technology is hypothesized as successive stages in the automation of labour, starting from the low skill end. She notes that capital and skills are better treated as complements rather than substitutes in each stage in the short term. Progressive substitution is a long-term effect.

Amsden defines skilled sectors as those which employ large numbers of skilled people. She considers these sectors to be conceptually and empirically distinct from sectors which employ large numbers of skilled people and large amounts of capital, large amounts of capital and few skilled workers and little capital along with few skilled workers.

Productivity advance derives not only from individual learning by workers, skilled and otherwise. Amsden identifies learning achieved by organizations and also by the economy as a whole, all of which raise plant-level productivity. This is an important insight developed further in various writings on technological capability, which are discussed in Chapter 7; the idea derives from the literature on technological change and institutional economics. Organizational learning is a very well-documented phenomenon; it manifests itself as a concatenation of small, incremental improvements in technology or procedures which occur in the course of production.

Such incremental technological changes can be represented as downward shifts of the learning curve. It is generally greater, the more skill-intensive the production process (Amsden 1986, Pack and Westphal 1986, Lall 1990). Amsden argues that such adaptations and the learning effort elicited are greatest where the technology is least 'explicit,' i.e. where it is not fully codified, not fully understood nor available in blueprint form. This seems to be where the greatest leeway for 'operational innovation' exists. She gives examples of process plants in NIEs where imported turnkey technology is incrementally adapted, by informal methods, to perform better with local raw materials, costs and conditions. Further, while such effects occur to a limited extent in process industries, these are even more common in discrete batch or job-shop production processes.[10]

Amsden's overarching point is as follows: the setting-up and promotion, in NIE-type developing countries, of industries that are intensive in skill and/or capital, has the important effect of building production-specific human capital. It is not the unmitigated disaster seen by neoclassical economists who argue that capital or skill-intensive exports run counter to Heckscher-Ohlin logic which implies that developing countries should export only products intensive in unskilled labour, its manifestly abundant resource. This conside-ration is especially important when the producer country can export capital goods to other developing countries. South-South exports of skill-intensive goods can help to raise the stock of technological knowledge and skill levels in the exporting country. By contrast, resource-based South-North exports embody only a rent effect with little useful learning.

---

[10]The purely technical aspects of manufacturing engineering and technology are covered in Kalpakjian and Schmid (2001). Pack (1987) provides a detailed account of the interaction between technique and productivity for the textile industry in developing countries.

## 6.4    LEARNING AS CAPABILITY ACCUMULATION

Some major sources of productivity advance in developing countries have been discussed above. For Japan and the EA-NIEs, reallocation from low-productive agriculture to high-productive industry had been substantially exhausted in the first one or two decades after the Second World War, but there was successive reallocation from lower to higher-productivity industrial sectors. In South Korea and Taiwan, early export success clearly accelerated structural change. These patterns are similar to those observed in industrial countries in similar stages of growth.[11] In the foregoing analysis structural change is subsumed under considerations of technological change in general.

An important source of growth for rapidly industrializing countries is the 'catch-up bonus' deriving from technology developed elsewhere. It is clear that follower countries typically experience faster productivity growth than the technology leader in the catch-up phase, since already developed technologies and techniques are more easily acquired. Japan followed by the EA-NIEs have benefited tremendously from such technology-gap effects. The 'catch-up bonus,' however, is far from automatic and accrues only to nations such as the EA-NIEs that have strongly promoted competitive economic environments and sustained export growth.

In the industrial economy of a country, Pack (1987) sees three main sources of productivity growth: rising technical efficiency as firms move towards the domestic best practice frontier (DBPF) through learning; gains in allocative efficiency as firms make new investment decisions more in line with market signals; technological advance mediated through new equipment (usually imported) as firms move towards the international BPF (IBPF). Gains from technical efficiency dominate over allocative efficiency gains since many firms in developing regions operate well below their own DBPF, as discussed in section 6.2 above.

To organize these insight into a tractable conceptual framework, Pack proposes an augmented aggregate production function $Q = Q (K, L, T, O)$, where capital $K$ and labour $L$ are augmented by the level of technical and organizational 'knowledge' $T$ and $O$ respectively. Here $T$ and $O$ are treated as supplementary forms of capital, which raise the productivity of labour in the same way as physical capital $K$, and need to be invoked to explain output growth comprehensively.

This construct brings on board the positive role of 'technical' and 'organizational' capital as important sources of growth within a capital accumulation framework. The accumulation of these intangible 'knowledge

---

[11]See Pack (1988, 1992), Chenery et al. (1986) and Maddison (1987) for detailed coverage.

capital' forms take place through the various learning processes described above.[12] Pack's framework is an advance on the neoclassical production function. It does not, however, account explicitly for the level of physical infrastructure and the effectiveness or level of development of the country's formal and informal business institutions. One could also argue that the vitality of a nation's entrepreneurs, or the 'entrepreneurial temperature,' is a significant determinant of overall productivity, an issue taken up later.

Important characteristics of industrial learning processes are brought out by Alwyn Young (1991) in his model of bounded learning-by-doing. He begins from two empirical observations: the first is that innovations exhibit considerable spillover across firms and industries; the second is that beyond a certain threshold, learning curves plateau out so that productivity advance through learning is essentially bounded. He notes that even Arrow (1962) in his seminal paper used cumulative investment rather than cumulative output as the index of experience, because in the absence of major changes in the productive environment, learning-by-doing is bounded. He argues as follows.

> Perhaps learning by doing can be conceived of as the exploration and actualization of the productive potential of new technologies; if you will, a series of minor technical innovations that are learned from a major technical breakthrough. Thus the development of new productive technologies, perhaps as the result of R&D efforts, and their use in the production of existing or new goods, initially leads to rapid learning by doing. After some time, however, the productive capability of these new technologies is exhausted, and learning by doing slows and perhaps ultimately stops. In the absence of the introduction of new technical processes, it is likely that learning by doing cannot be sustained (Young 1991, p. 372).

Young develops a model of unbounded growth based on learning-by-doing with spillovers across goods. The quantity and variety of goods produced increase continuously over time; learning-by-doing gains are exhausted in each subset of goods, but continues in the successor, thereby maintaining the growth momentum indefinitely. Trade also plays a role in the model, accelerating technical progress and growth under certain conditions. The model embodies many of the empirical features of the growth process.

What is of principal interest in this analysis is the conceptualization of bounded learning-by-doing in successive technologies. An adaption of this idea is presented Figure 6.1. Here, learning-by-doing proceeds, unevenly, in relatively small steps, along the technology 1 curve. At some point there is a shift to a superior technology with a greater potential for productivity gain. A similar learning-by-doing process continues along the technology 2 curve.

---

[12]Pack's approach here bears out an insightful observation made by Nelson (1981). 'Sensible empirical researchers often will add variables that the formal theoretical models do not contain and, more generally, interpret the background theory very flexibly.'

At the point of transition, the operational productivity may drop below the previous value as in the transition from technology 2 to technology 3. But the shift is undertaken because of the expectation of longer-term gain deriving from the inherent superiority of the successor technology.

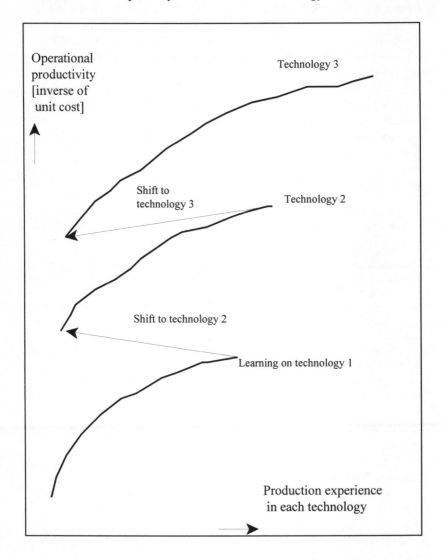

*Figure 6.1  Labour productivity advance through bounded learning and major technological change.*

Some important issues are raised here. In countries where markets are characterized by sharp competition, technology transitions are made well before reaching a productivity plateau, as firms strive to gain competitive advantage over each other. With shorter technology cycle times, the pace of innovation and, more importantly, the associated rate of learning and productivity growth is higher. It is important to emphasize that competition accelerates two related productivity-enhancing processes: the first is faster technological change; the second is the rate of advance of technical efficiency which is faster in the initial phase of the learning curve for all technologies.

One of the central arguments made in this book is that learning and productivity growth are dual aspects of a single phenomenon. This yields a new perspective on economic growth: i.e. growth is fastest in periods of rapid technological change because of the enhanced learning potential offered. Furthermore, competitive struggle between firms is essential for sustaining the momentum of the growth process through the drive for productivity advantage. Young argues that in the pre-modern era, even intense economic activity did not lead to sustained economic growth because of the slow pace of technical change which generated little scope for learning activity.

This model of learning-driven productivity growth supplies a rationale for the association between equipment investment and TFPG. Since major technological change necessitates new machines, it is clear that enhanced learning opportunities would be correlated with investment in equipment capital. It is also clear that the derived benefits would continue to accrue over a longer time span than the period in which the seminal investment was made, nor are they automatic. Furthermore, not all investment has the same learning/productivity potential. This, of course, makes the modelling of the process more difficult. Many of these points have been cogently explained by Nelson (1981) in his comprehensive review of productivity growth.

## APPENDIX 6.A    MODELLING TECHNICAL EFFICIENCY

Though developed in 1957 by Farrell, technical efficiency saw little empirical application until the technique of stochastic frontier production function (SFPF) estimation was developed by Aigner et al. (1977). The general principle underlying the procedure has been described in section 6.2 in relation to the identification of the domestic best practice frontier which is treated as the theoretical ideal. The modified production function for statistical estimation is formulated as in equation 6.A.1.

$$Q \;=\; F(z).\exp(v + u) \qquad (6.A.1)$$

$Q$ is output, $F(z)$ is the deterministic core of the frontier production function which could be Cobb-Douglas, CES or translog; $z$ is a vector representing inputs and $v$ is some symmetrically distributed random error. Variability of technical efficiency for firms in the sample is represented by a one-sided error term $u$ (i.e. $u$ is negative or zero). With some assumption about the form of the distributions, the relevant parameters can be estimated by corrected least squares or maximum likelihood techniques and the technical efficiency component separated. More detail of the theory and estimation procedure are given in Lall and Rodrigo (2000). With additional information about factor prices, it is also possible to estimate allocative efficiency.[13]

The above functional form neatly separates out the contribution of factor accumulation from the effects of technical and technological change. With logarithmic differentiation, the growth rate of output can be similarly decomposed into a factor accumulation component and a TFP residual as discussed in Chapter 2. A variant of equation 6.A.1 with the symmetric error term dropped, used by Pack and Page (1994) in their analysis of growth in high-performing economies (Chapter 3), is given in equation 6.A.2.[14]

$$Q = F[z(t),t].\exp[u(t)] \qquad (6.A.2)$$

Logarithmic differentiation of 6.A.2 with respect to time $t$ decomposes the fractional growth rate of output $Q$ into three components, as indicated by equation 6.A.3 below. Here the $\wedge$ symbol indicates the rate of growth of the qualified variable as in Chapter 2. The vector $F_z$ represents output elasticity of $F(z,t)$ with respect to the inputs $z$; $\hat{z} = \dot{z}/z$ is the vector of factor input change rates and $F_t$ is the output elasticity of $F(z,t)$ with respect to time $t$. The dotted variables indicate time derivatives.

$$\hat{Q} = F_z.\hat{z} + F_t + \dot{u} \qquad (6.A.3)$$

Here factor growth is represented by the first term, the rate of progress of the best practice frontier by the second term and the rate of advance of technical efficiency by the third. When TFPG is computed in the usual way as the growth residual of output growth less weighted input growth, it decomposes into technological progress measured at the frontier and the rate of change of

---

[13]See Caves and Barton (1990), Caves (1992), Coelli et al. (1999) and Lall and Rodrigo (2000), for details. A more comprehensive approach, covering both parametric and non-parametric techniques, is given by Grosskopf (1993) but it raises no extra conceptual issues.
[14]This recent study builds on previous work by John Page, in particular Nishimizu and Page (1982) which was a pioneering attempt to separate technical efficiency from technological change in total factor productivity estimates. More detail is given in World Bank (1993).

technical efficiency as indicated in equation 6.A.4 below. The subscript *i* is introduced to signify each individual unit of production at the level of nation, firm or plant as the case may be; at each level the advance of the best practice frontier is assumed to be common to the whole set.

$$TFPG_i \;\; = \;\; F_{it} \;\; + \;\; \dot{u}_i \hspace{3cm} (6.A.4)$$

The above formulation provides a framework for linking the estimation of technical efficiency to productivity growth analysis. It is intended to be applicable at the level of an industry, a single nation or a set of nations.[15] This framework is particularly useful for explaining the source of extraordinary growth in East Asian type countries, which is the objective of the Pack and Page (1994) paper; the arguments are further developed in World Bank (1993). Negative TFPG is also explained more elegantly by this model: if technical efficiency change is negative and larger than the contribution of technological progress, then their sum is negative.

In their analysis, Pack and Page make the simplifying assumption that advanced countries employ international best practice; hence their TFPG is determined by the first term alone, representing technological progress. This is, of course, not necessarily true even for the majority of firms or for most periods. In the estimation they also assume that the second term representing advance of the best practice frontier is common to all countries; this is also not a realistic assumption since the ability to absorb technology is likely to vary from country to country, as discussed earlier in this chapter.

## APPENDIX 6.B    MODELLING THE LEARNING CURVE

The business management approach to the modelling of learning curves is summed up in Teplitz (1991) and much more succinctly in Argote and Epple (1990). The theory is also  summarized in Amsden (1986). Empirical work began with the observation in 1936 that unit labour costs in air-frame production declined with cumulative output. Subsequent case studies have confirmed the existence of learning or experience effects in many industries and in a range of economic activities. Indeed the evidence is that the potential for learning, and inevitably the costs of learning, rise fast with increasing technological complexity. Learning associated with rising technical efficiency in a given technology is distinct from learning to use new technologies.

---

[15]There is an aggregation problem here relating to sources of productivity growth. It is not clear how gains from inter-sectoral reallocation of productive resources, which are quite large for developing countries, can be separated from technical efficiency (Pack 1988).

Learning is also not automatic, but strongly contingent on various enabling conditions. In general learning is faster the more competitive the market environment, though it would logically seem that diminishing returns must set in at some point. It is also well known that knowledge accumulated in learning depreciates, just like physical capital. The rate of accumulation also depends on the frequency of employee turnover. Increasing exploitation of economies of scale seem to enhance learning, to some extent at least, but again there must be obvious limits; in any case the actual parameters are industry and technology-specific. At the present time, there is insufficient basic research to make any definitive conclusions. Often scale effects are misconstrued as learning effects though the two are conceptually distinct (Argote and Epple 1990, Teplitz 1991).

Perhaps the most useful feature of learning is its potential for diffusion; learning transfers across product lines, organizational units and firms, albeit with distinct time lags; i.e. it induces economies of scope. This is the source not just of internal economies, but also of the various non-pecuniary externalities that are central to the new growth economics. The representation of the learning-experience effect is quite straightforward. If $y_i$ is the average labour time required to produce $i$ units, $y_1$ is the labour time required to produce the first unit, the Wright form of the learning curve is as follows.

$$y_i \;=\; y_1 . \, i^{-b} \tag{6.B.1}$$

Here the progress elasticity $b$ is a positive constant in the range 0.1–0.2. The more frequently used Crawford model relates the marginal cost of the $i$-th unit $x_i$ to $y_1$. The two forms are not entirely equivalent.

$$x_i \;=\; y_1 . \, i^{-b} \tag{6.B.2}$$

The cost functions are typically modelled as straight lines on log-log scales. Learning curves are characterized by the 'progress ratio' which is the percentage to which the marginal cost falls when production is doubled; thus if $b = 0.234$, the doubling of output makes $x_{2.i}/x_i \;=\; 2^{-b} \;=\; 0.85$, yielding an 85% progress ratio. Teplitz also details various modifications made to the basic form to better model particular situations, the 'plateau,' 'sigmoid' and 'Cochran's S-curve' formulations.

# 7.    The acquisition of technological capability by firms and nations in East Asia

This chapter takes up the broader issue of how the East Asian economies and their industrial companies acquired 'technological capability.' The concept of technological capability is necessary to explain why market forces do not work as hypothesized in the standard theory. It appears to have emerged from the expression 'social absorptive capability,' which was coined to explain and measure the ability of a developing country to absorb already developed technologies (Dahlman and Nelson 1991, Pavitt and Bell 1992, Temple and Johnson 1998). It was assumed that the challenge for a developing country was to catch-up[1] with the industrial world by mastering technologies already developed in the latter, a task that should prima facie be easier than advancing at the technological frontier.

However, 'follower' strategies turned out to be extraordinarily difficult. It seems that market forces in developing countries manifestly do not work as in industrial countries. It was soon realized that a great deal of institutional change and investment in human and social capabilities were necessary to advance along even well-trodden technological pathways. Some of these problems at least were realized at the very beginning by some economists (Meier and Seers 1984). But the rarity of East Asian-style success indicates that the extent of difficulty involved in building up technological capability was not widely appreciated by key policy-makers in developing countries.

The previous chapter examined some of the ways in which productivity growth is realized through learning processes. This chapter develops a generalized account of how such learning leads to the building of firm (level) technological capability (FTC) and 'national technological capability' (NTC), and relates it to the East Asian experience. It is generally recognized that the East Asian NIEs (EA-NIEs) have done this successfully, perhaps uniquely –

---

[1]The concept of 'catch-up' is developed more comprehensively in Chapter 1. The goal is to acquire world class competence in a selected set of technologies (Porter 1990), sufficient to ensure institutional structures and living standards characteristic of an advanced country. Larger countries would naturally be able to target a broader set, or afford the heavier R&D investments necessary in leading edge technologies.

as a group – among developing nations in the post-Second World War era. While they have some features in common, as discussed in previous chapters, it is also clear that the individual strategies were distinctly different.

National technological capability is most palpably carried, or developed, by a nation's industrial firms. But the extent to which capability can be developed depends crucially on the general educational and cultural levels of the active population. NTC also depends on the role of government organizations concerned with industry, education, health, research and infrastructure development. Additionally, NTC is a function of the country's economic and social institutions, both formal and informal, that promote or retard business activity. In short, NTC is not just the sum of the capabilities of individual firm FTCs. 'It comprises the nonmarket system of inter-firm networking and linkages, ways of doing business, and the web of supporting institutions' (Lall 2000, p. 14). The objective here is to analyse NTC in terms of these broad determinants by drawing on the East Asian experience.

In section 1.4, NTC was separated into a 'hardware' component and a 'software' component. The former carries technology hard-coded in physical investment, i.e. machines, equipment and physical infrastructure. The latter, identified as 'social capability,' consists of all the non-physical accumulations needed to realize the productivity latent in the hardware. In other words, the productive potential of the economy depends on these two components working together in harmony. In early development thinking NTC was seen as determined mainly by the hardware of physical capital; so the challenge of development was seen as primarily the problem of accumulating physical capital as fast as possible.

That view has now changed radically: in recent years a number of studies have emerged that develop the concept of social capability and discuss how it can be proxied or measured (Temple and Johnson 1998, Knack and Keefer 1997). It appears that economists and other social scientists are now quite comfortable in discussing the effect of social factors including institutions on economic growth; however, the older term social capability has been broadened into the more widely used 'social capital' (Burki and Perry 1998). The two terms are used interchangeably here.

The exposition developed in this chapter sees the accumulation of social capability as the real key to the building of NTC; hence the discussion that follows is focused almost entirely on the accumulation of the non-physical capabilities. This capability can only be built up through intense economic activity involving investment, production, sales, exports and so on. The non-physical must be carried on the back of physical investment – the hardware part of FTC and NTC– which must be seen as a necessary concomitant to the accumulation of crucial non-physical capability. This view is consistent with the conclusions drawn from the research work summarized in section 3.5.

## 7.1    TECHNOLOGICAL CAPABILITY OF FIRMS

This section develops an account of essential firm (level) technological capability (FTC), i.e. what is needed to remain viable in competitive markets. The next section summarizes and evaluates the extent of the FTC building experience in the EA-NIEs. Some aspects of the uncertainty-fraught processes of firm-level adaptation and learning have already been described in the previous chapter, especially in section 6.3. In general though, FTC involves many more activities, which are broadly described in the literature as 'industrial innovation.' The understanding is that critical elements of the activities undertaken are clearly 'new to the firm' though not new to the world or even to the country. It is also understood that innovation includes organizational, marketing and other advances, not merely those in the technical-engineering area (Lall 1990, 2000).

Lall (1990) distinguishes three aspects of FTC, in line with general thinking in the technology literature. First, 'technological mastery' refers to the skills and competence needed to operate an installed technology efficiently. Second, the capability to effect 'minor innovations' describe successive adaptations and improvements that raise the productivity of installed technology, as described in section 6.3. Third, the ability to manage 'major innovation' refers to the introduction of entirely new products and processes, usually through new capital investment and the deployment of new or upgraded technical skills. All three types of capability are necessary for an industrial firm to maintain viability in a dynamic competitive environment.

Technological progress calls for advance in all three of the above areas and involve considerable learning effort, at every level of the process, which is manifested as productivity growth. Rosenberg (1976, 1982) has shown that every major innovation is followed by numerous minor innovations after introduction, which consolidate the viability of the former. Minor innovations are shown as short upward movement of productivity above the trend line, along each technology curve in Figure 6.1. However, the innovation process is industry-wide and interactive across firms, not confined to individual firms.

Such minor innovations and advances in technical efficiency are the sources of year-by-year productivity growth which reflect the degree of dynamism of the firm. The introduction of a major innovation is represented in Figure 6.1 as a one-time shift from one technology curve to the next higher one. Major innovation may initially lower productivity but eventually leads to substantial gains over the displaced older technology. It should be noted that both types of innovation involve advances in quality as well as productivity and the introduction of new products and processes, though only productivity is shown in the graph of Figure 6.1.

Lall (1990, 2000) presents a detailed analysis of the diverse technological tasks involved at the firm level, organized in a time sequence ranging from the investment phase to the production phase. Perhaps the most important is that learning, which is important for every aspect of FTC development, is a skill that itself has to be learnt (Stiglitz 1987). The learning processes are also highly technology-specific: simple technologies require investment/learning in straightforward technology mastery; complex technologies require minor innovation capability and formal R&D units. A textile firm would not require a distinct R&D function, but a firm making advanced information technology products, such as disk drives for example, clearly does. Some technologies, especially process technologies, tend to be embodied in the equipment, while others involve greater tacit aspects requiring more intense learning effort.

The three components of technological capability are in general common to both developing and developed countries, though of course their relative roles would differ. R&D activity devoted to the development of new products and processes is clearly more important in developed industrial economies. Conventional theory assumes that developing country industries merely copy existing designs at little cost, save that incurred for licensing. Lall shows that this is far removed from reality: considerable effort is needed to successfully internalize a capability for a particular technology. A firm needs to have developed skills and knowledge up to one or two steps below that of the target technology for it to be successfully undertaken.

The same point is made by Nelson (1990a, p. 45) in the context of Asia: 'the learning of technology to the point of reasonable mastery is a highly active process, not a passive one. It is sometimes said that it is easy to "buy" technology from abroad ... [t]echnology is not like a tennis racket which one can simply pick up at a store, pay for, and take home. Rather, acquiring a technology is much more like acquiring the skills of playing tennis. One can buy "tennis lessons", and that may help, but that is a far thing from actually buying the skills to play tennis well.' Nelson (1981, 1990b) makes the same argument in the context of technology transfer from one firm to another in the US economy itself. He shows that it is necessary for an imitator firm to build up its capability in a particular technology near to the level of an innovating firm before an innovation can be successfully taken on board. Greenwood (1999) estimates that the cost of adopting a new technology over the entire economy exceeds invention costs (in the innovator firm) by a factor of 20:1.

The above argument is crucial to understanding why most developing countries have failed to progress rapidly along technological pathways already charted out in the advanced industrial economies. Obviously the more complex the technology, the more time, effort and investment, needed to indigenize the technology. Amsden has shown that there has to be a necessary sequence or a specific logic of progression determined by carry-over linkages from one technology to the next higher one; details are given in section 6.3. The role played by learning under competitive pressure, in the stage-wise upgrading of skills and knowledge required to build technological capability in East Asian firms, is related in great detail by Hobday (1995).

Latecomer firms do not, of course, innovate at the international frontier as regards the development of entirely new products or processes, as do technology 'leaders' in industrial countries. Leader innovation is naturally characterized by a high degree of uncertainty and is undertaken only by a small number of leader firms in industrial economies. Such firms have very substantial R&D departments which enable them to stay at the forefront of technological innovation. Technology 'followers' in advanced industrial economies are also quite distinct from NIE latecomer firms. Such followers also have substantial R&D capacity which enables them to quickly imitate leader innovations and sometimes out-compete the leader. Both leaders and followers have the great advantage that they are directly 'plugged in' to advanced markets and operate within the highly developed institutional framework of such market economies.

Latecomer firms are technologically weak, remote from advanced users and operate in environments characterized by poor institutions and weak or absent markets for key inputs. They are also burdened with imperfect or fuzzy knowledge of the technologies they use and the range of technical alternatives that exist globally. As a result, their technological progress is hazard-prone and costly: there is a great deal of costly innovation, i.e. experimentation and learning involved in finding strategies to circumvent the many market failures that exist in developing countries, particularly in the early stages of industrial take-off. Some of these are supply side problems such as mastering new technology and manufacturing processes and building up workforce skills, when latecomer firms are far removed from the centres of technology.

Lall (1990, p. 24) considers the particular obstacles to FTC development arising from imperfect product and factor markets in developing countries, which are quite often prone to market failure. 'Labour and capital markets generally suffer from lack of information and problems of moral hazard; technology markets are notoriously imperfect; inter-industry transactions suffer also from moral hazard and asymmetric information; and so on.' All of these lead to inadequate investment in FTC or, alternatively, to investment in capabilities not conducive to economic growth. Details of how these problems were overcome in East Asia are given in Stiglitz (1996).

These pervasive market failures often stimulate a political demand for state intervention, such as in most developing countries in their ISI phases. In the relatively successful EA-NIEs, three distinct strategies are seen, in addition to strong public intervention. The first is the formation of large conglomerates, the chaebol, in Korea, which partially compensate for weak markets. The second is the bringing-in of MNCs on a large scale as in Singapore. The third is the formation of international business alliances with foreign business partners. The way such alliances partially compensated for market failures is discussed in detail by Mody (1989), Egan and Mody (1992) and Hobday (2000). Of course, all of the EA-NIEs used a mix of strategies.

In his comparative study of the electronics industry in South Korea and Taiwan, Mody (1990) draws out the role of industry structure and firm size in promoting rapid economic development in accordance with Williamson's arguments. Thus the conglomerate provides an internal capital market to substitute for the imperfect external market which is unable to efficiently assess risk and the feasibility of new projects. Mody argues that by means of the chaebol strategy, Korea has now moved technologically ahead of Taiwan, though the latter had the initial advantage.

Similar studies by Levy (1991) and Levy and Kuo (1991) comparing the footwear and personal computer assembly industries in Korea and Taiwan also brings out the relevance of industry structure and transaction costs in shaping the different trajectories of development. Mody sees state intervention as critical, especially where the institutional support of a powerful industrial combine is lacking. He argues that Taiwanese firms have little incentives to upgrade quality individually because they do not have strong company/brand identities. Seeing the chaebol model as superior, Mody expects convergence towards Korean-type structures in Taiwan. However, the economic crises of the late 1990s has brought out the greater resilience of the less centralized Taiwanese model with its proliferation of small and medium companies and greater reliance on market forces (Chapter 8).

There are, however, other important components of FTC, beyond the issue of technological learning.[2] Wide capabilities are needed by any mature industrial firm in managerial and entrepreneurial competence. The first refers to the ability to manage physical and human resources, i.e. to organize and manage business operations, financial control, marketing, personnel issues and so on. The second involves the identification and selection of new projects and the marshalling of resources, both financial and human, needed to implement them. These skills too are critical for economic success and need to be built up with great care. They are as important as technological competence and also have to be built up the same way through formal education and successful business activity (Nelson 1981, Lall 1990).

---

[2]There is a problem here with the terminology used by Lall. Thus entrepreneurial and managerial competence are included along with technological ability within the wider rubric of firm-level 'technological' capability. Clearly the word is overused and a better term would perhaps be 'industrial capability.' The former term is more widely used at the present time.

## 7.2   EDUCATIONAL LEVELS AND HUMAN CAPITAL

One important issue on which orthodox and heterodox economists are in clear agreement is the value, indeed the absolute necessity, of human capital accumulation for economic growth. The problem is that some neoclassical analysts equate human capital with the level of formal educational. While formal education is most surely a necessary condition for growth, it does not automatically lead to growth, as exemplified by the experience of Sri Lanka, the Philippines and the Kerala state in India (Sen 1999, ch. 2).

Lucas (1993), however, articulates a view that is entirely consistent with the description of non-physical capital accumulation developed in this book. He examines the 'miracle growth' of the East Asian economies by comparing the very different growth experiences of South Korea and the Philippines, which start from roughly the same economic situation in 1960. He argues that a 'successful theory of economic miracles ... should ... offer the possibility of rapid growth episodes, but should not imply their occurrence as a simple consequence of relative backwardness' (Lucas 1993, p. 269).

> The main engine of growth is the accumulation of human capital – of knowledge – and the main source of differences in living standards among nations is differences in human capital. Physical accumulation plays an essential but decidedly subsidiary role. Human capital accumulation takes place in schools, in research organizations, and in the course of producing goods and engaging in trade. Little is known about the relative importance of these different modes of accumulation, but for understanding periods of very rapid growth in a single economy, learning on the job seems to be by far the most central (Lucas 1993, p. 270).

Lucas's concept of human capital needs to be expanded to 'social capability' as defined here in the preamble to this chapter, to cover the entirety of non-physical accumulations. That is what determines the realization of the growth potential latent in the physical factors, in the non-mechanistic fashion that is required by Lucas. This crucial idea is developed further in Chapter 9.

Numerous studies show that education, training and other forms of skill formation are critically important to industrial competence and productivity (Nordhaug 1993). Basic literacy and numeracy are essential for the entire workforce in all modern industry. Vocational and technical training are necessary for technical personnel and for skilled workers in more advanced industries. The complexity of technical training rises with the level of technical sophistication of the production processes employed.

In addition to technical training, on-the-job training is needed for supervisors and junior managers and often supplemented by more formal management training in-house or in outside institutions. Lall (1990) touches only lightly on managerial skills and training, often seeing it merely as a part of 'technical' skill. This appears to be a blind spot in his otherwise comprehensive analysis. It is clear that a range of educational institutions, from technical and vocational schools to engineering departments and management schools in universities, are necessary to supply the demand for formal education. Managerial and business skills, even more than technical skills, are the scarcest productive resource in many developing countries. As the technologies employed reach international frontiers, such as in Korea and Taiwan, pure science capability also becomes important (Kim 2000).

Lall makes a number of points in relation to the supply and demand for the above skills. First, as technologies change rapidly, intensive in-firm training becomes necessary to create new skills continuously. Second, for the efficient diffusion of skills through the industrial structure by migration of personnel, these skills need to be sharply demarcated, recognized and, not least, certified accurately. Third, the quality of technical education is as important as its quantity and fourth, the distribution of technical skills supplied must match the specific requirements of the industrial economy.

This last point applies more generally to all productive resources: 'It is the productive deployment of capabilities that we are concerned with, not with the potential existing in, say, stocks of underutilised capital, engineering manpower or academic knowledge' (Lall 1990, p. 26). Despite common assumptions to the contrary, there is a high degree of complementarity between skills and physical resources; thus investment in education can be wasted if it is not geared to the evolution of industry. For this reason, wastage associated with superfluous resources are much less likely in market-driven systems where investment in resources is guided by expected returns. The problem is, in fact, the reverse: there is insufficient investment in human resource development because the returns cannot be completely appropriated by the firm. Consequently, public investment has to play a large role in the development of human capital to correct this market failure.

From the arguments developed in Chapter 6, it is clear that skill/ competence and firm-level training acquired through production and other economic activity constitute a very important part of the total human capital that bears directly on productive efficiency. Formal education is an *enabling condition* for the accumulation of 'experience capital.' With regard to human capital Lall (1990, p. 29) states: 'A large part of this is measurable, but some is not: the experience and firm training component is almost impossible to measure in a comparable way, as is the quality of formal education. In addition, human capital is conditioned by the socio-cultural legacy and past experience of commerce and industry – again these are difficult to measure precisely and have to be ignored.'

## 7.3   NATIONAL TECHNOLOGICAL CAPABILITY (NTC)

There is general agreement that the appropriate unit of analysis for studying the building up of technological capability is the nation and not just the firm. This is because national technological capability (NTC) is not merely the aggregation of a nation's FTCs. It includes the synergistic interaction between different FTCs mediated through market and non-market linkages, within the institutional structure of the nation. Since these features are unique to each nation, the nation is the natural unit of analysis for studying variation in technological capability, despite the undoubted and increasing importance of international linkages.

Lall (2000, p. 14) defines national technological capability as 'the complex of skills, experience, and effort that enables a country's enterprises to efficiently buy, use, adapt, improve and create technologies.' The acquisition of national technological capability by individual nations has recently been examined under the rubric of 'national innovation systems' (Lundvall 1992, Nelson 1993). Such studies, however, are more concerned with the setting up of effective innovation systems in advanced industrial nations.[3] The basic idea underlying both types of studies is the well-established fact that technology evolution in all countries is ridden with externalities, path-dependence and market failures that lie outside the idealized world of neo-classical micro-theory with perfect markets and information (Stiglitz 1996).

For example, Rosenberg (1982) has shown that there is substantial spillover of innovation and other production-specific knowledge across firms and industries. Innovation stimulates other related innovation in downstream technologies. In short, there is cumulative learning and path-dependence in the way many technologies diffuse and in the way they evolve within firms. Numerous studies of industrial innovation in advanced countries alone establish the key role of linkages and externalities between firms, between industries and the state and between domestic industry and international markets. The complex interaction of these many features generate the unique character of the innovation systems of advanced industrial nations (Dodgson and Rothwell 1994, Freeman and Soete 1997, Carlsson 1997).

The metaphor that most appropriately describes this dynamic jumble of interactions is the concept of an integrated and evolving *economic ecosystem.*

---

[3]The distinction is generally one of emphasis, since both kinds of studies examine the institutional framework promoting technology acquisition as well as strategies for mastering particular technologies. Studies that focus more on particular industries are Freeman and Soete (1997) and Carlsson (1997). Porter's (1990) monumental study examines country and technology strategies from a business management perspective.

Growth leads to increasing complexity and specialization which raise the efficiency of economic transformations (i.e. production) and exchange transactions, in the sense of North and Wallis (1994). These gains appear at the aggregate level as productivity growth and other measures of economic success. The nature and efficiency of the linkages determine the evolution of both NTC and individual FTCs, since they are often responses to market failure. They cover the transfer and diffusion of technological, managerial and entrepreneurial skills and capability across the entire industrial sector of the economy. It is also true that increasing global interdependence leads to some convergence of institutional structures across developed economies.

Lall (1990) discusses linkage capabilities associated with the transfer of technology across firms, among buyers, suppliers and competitors, from service firms to manufacturers and from the science and technology infrastructure to industry. Conventional theory assumes that such transactions are characterized by efficient markets. Research shows that in developing countries 'Inter-firm and inter-industry transactions of this sort are often marked by market failure; markets are narrow and fragmented, incapable of providing the kind of information participants need to design, manufacture or invest' (Lall 1990, p. 23). He continues, 'all such markets, regardless of level of development, are consequently characterized by very high levels of extra-market linkages, whereby firms provide each other with information, assistance, forecasts and even finance and materials.' In other words, the progress of NTC shares many of the features that characterize the advance of individual FTCs. The role of forward and backward linkages in East Asia and their relationship to FDI are discussed in Battat et al. (1996).

One solution to imperfect markets is to increase firm size so as to internalize transactions that are costly on the open market. The firm, after all, is a social organization designed partly to shield internal transactions from the external environment. The specific location of the boundary depends on whether particular transactions are more advantageously carried out within the shielded region or through external market transactions, taking due account of scale and learning curve efficiencies. However, firm size does not automatically expand and contract to evolving market opportunities. In both advanced and developing countries, top management is loath to spin-off or divest uneconomic business units, except in the throes of a wrenching crisis.

This is particularly true of Korea which has pursued the large-firm strategy the furthest by deliberately promoting the formation of the giant 'chaebol' conglomerates. The inherent tendency of large firms towards inefficiency has been counterpoised to some extent, in Korea, by compelling them to compete in export markets. Other solutions are also possible through different institutions that minimize risk and facilitate transactions, such as in Taiwan with its proliferation of small and medium-sized firms.

## 7.4    INSTITUTIONS AND NTC

Firms, of course, are only the most palpable entities on the broad economic landscape. In every country economic transactions and transformations (i.e. production activities) take place within a network of institutions that are set up over fairly long periods of time and constitute an important component of NTC. North defines institutions as rules, enforcement characteristics of rules, and norms of behaviour that structure repeated human interaction. When particular sets of economic transactions are repeated frequently because they benefit all participants, the pattern of transaction solidifies into an 'institution' much as a sustained flow of water will cut a channel on the ground, thus making easier the subsequent passage of water.[4]

Institutions come into being through natural economic evolution or are deliberately set up. Their positive economic role is threefold. First, they significantly reduce the uncertainty associated with repeated economic activity; second, they reduce transaction costs associated with negotiation of the terms of exchange; third, they substitute for absent or undeveloped markets. Institutions are a vital part of NTC. They fall into two broad categories: formal and informal institutions; both types grow and develop along with the progress of economic activity. Formal institutions include business and professional associations, training centres, technical colleges, universities, standards institutes, legal bodies and many financial institutions such as banks and stock markets. Informal institutions cover business practices, codes of behaviour, networks of business contacts and a host of inherited nation-specific business-cultural norms and practices.

Institutions can also become dysfunctional when their evolution lags behind the evolution of the economy as a whole, such as the Korean chaebol conglomerates in the context of present-day Korea. Thus institutions that play a positive role at their inception can become a major obstacle to further development, as has happened periodically in Europe and North America. But institutions are difficult to reform or replace because of habituated inertia in human agents and social groups. The setting-up of modern, efficient business institutions, however, is enormously important for the building-up of NTC. Indeed healthy social institutions are difficult to set up and involve considerable social investment in social learning.[5]

---

[4]The nature and role of institutions, as described here, are summarized from North (1989, 1990, 1993) and Thorbecke (1990). See also Temple and Johnson (1998).

[5]It could be argued that market forces – through its avatar of crises, i.e. disequilibrium events – tend to identify dysfunctional institutions and call for their regeneration to forms more in accord with contemporary needs. This is surely as much a part of Schumpeterian 'creative destruction' as is the displacement of inefficient firms and outmoded technologies by their

Institutional development need not, indeed should not, follow the same path in all countries. It is now well understood that institutional innovation or adaptation can serve to bypass imperfect or non-existent markets or improve the functionality of weak markets.[6] In fact research has established that pre-capitalist institutions, such as Chinese clan networks, have been effectively pressed into service to make up for the absence of modern financial institutions in East Asia. Thus institutions can also substitute for government intervention in correcting the imperfect nature of weakly developed markets, at least on a temporary basis.

While efficient institutions are crucial for the functioning of the entire business sector, a vital part of institutional efficiency depends on the free flow of information about all kinds of business activity (Chapter 8). A major reason why the US economy is highly attractive to foreign investors is the transparency of business activity and the availability of detailed business information about companies, banks and regulatory policies. By contrast, a major reason why 'emerging markets' are less attractive to foreign investors, despite higher rates of return, is the absence of reliable business information.

Wallis and North (1987) and North and Wallis (1994) separate out all economic activity into the transformation of inputs into outputs (production) and (narrow-sense) transactions involving exchanges of inputs and outputs. They show that technological change on the production side – which reduce the costs of transformation – induce changes in institutions that control pure transactions as well. While transformation activities take place within firms, transaction activities take place within and outside the boundaries of the firm. In fact transactions and transformations are closely interwoven and technical improvements in one sector can reduce costs in other sectors; thus progress in transport and communications reduce transaction costs in all sectors.

They argue that technology, organizations and institutions evolve not so much to reduce transformation costs and transaction costs separately, but jointly, since it is total cost reduction that is the objective of firms. They find that as industrial structure and interactions become more complex the size of the purely transactional side of the economy expands as well; they estimate that the transaction sector in the USA has grown from 25% to 45% of GDP over 1870–1970. Thus while transaction costs may well trend downward at the elemental level, the size of the transaction sector as a whole grows.

---

successors? If so, then the relentless logic of the market is a necessary counterpoise to social inertia. This argument is developed further in Chapter 8 in the context of the analysis of economic crises in East Asia.

[6]Lall (1990) quotes a number of publications to document the scope and diversity of institutional structures analysed in developing countries. See also Burki and Perry (1998).

While estimates of the extent of the transaction sector are not available for most other economies, the chances are that it would grow in the long-term as NIEs become more market-oriented. It is an empirical question whether modernization of the economy would increase or reduce overall transaction costs in the first phase of reform for developing economies such as India.

## 7.5    THE NTC SYNTHESIS AND OTHER APPROACHES

The NTC synthesis appears to comprehensively cover many of the specific economic problems encountered in East Asia and also explain its relative success compared to other developing countries. As stated at the beginning of this chapter, the NTC approach starts from the existence of pervasive market failures. The evolution of FTC and NTC are then seen as strategies designed to overcome these market failures along trajectories specific to each country. Needless to say, this evolutionary approach throws up a different perspective on economic development to conceptions deriving from orthodox perspectives, ranging from neoclassical fundamentalism to the Washington consensus (see Chapter 5). These issues are taken up in Chapter 9.

The heterodox NTC synthesis is consistent with the findings of all field-based research in East Asia, including the work of Amsden, Wade, Hobday and others quoted in Chapters 6 and 7. The sticking point is the heterodox conclusion that deliberate, state intervention was necessary to promote rapid growth, including selective distortion of incentive structures. This is based on the recognition that technological learning processes are riddled with all kinds of market failures, which are more acute and prevalent in developing countries. Yet its advocates recognize that with the exception of a small number of countries in East Asia, state promotion of industry has a pretty dismal record. This is because governments themselves face information and incentive problems and have misunderstood the importance of maintaining proper incentive structures while addressing problems of market failure.

Summarizing the different approaches to East Asian growth, Bradford (1994) shows that the theoretical literature has gone through several phases of explanation. The first phase, based on the experience to 1973, emphasized outward orientation. In the 1980s a second strand of thought developed, drawing mainly on the experience of the EA-NIEs in promoting exports and accelerating industrialization through industrial policy. This approach was consistent with the strategic trade theory of Helpman and Krugman and the business school perspectives exemplified by Porter (1990). In the late 1980s and the 1990s, a third strand of literature emerged emphasizing technological change and human resource development as key elements of an industrial catch-up strategy. This third strand, exemplified by Lall (1990) and previous OECD work, takes a more systemic approach to the problem of development.

Bradford sees the third strand as transcending the older dichotomy between inward-looking interventionist import substitution and the open economy, market-oriented outward orientation. He argues that the first strand focused on markets, the second on the interaction of the public and private sector and the third on the diffusion of technological innovation throughout the economy. In practice, the economic evolution of East Asia drew on all three of these processes, in different proportions at different times, along a continuously rising path of industrial progression.

Porter's (1990) analysis of the 'competitive advantage of nations' is clearly more consistent with Lall's systemic approach, but is more industry-specific and prescriptive.[7] It is also couched in management school idiom and illustrated with detailed case studies. Porter's conceptual framework is evolutionary and departs explicitly from general equilibrium analysis without apology: 'As Schumpeter emphasized many decades ago, competition is profoundly dynamic in character. The nature of economic competition is not "equilibrium" but a perpetual state of change' (Porter 1990, p. 70).

Porter groups the determinants of 'competitive advantage' into four components arranged in a diamond to emphasize mutual interaction between nodes. The four elements are also influenced by two sets of exogenous influences: these are 'chance,' covering historical events and cultural endowments and government policy. A crucial feature of Porter's schema is the qualitative distinction he draws between 'basic factors' and 'advanced factors.' The former include physical resources such as capital, infrastructure, natural resources and unskilled labour. The latter include highly trained personnel with application-specific human capital and knowledge resources such as public and private research institutes, leading universities and industry associations. To oversimplify somewhat, the proximate determinant of long-term industrial competitiveness is identified as the creation of the advanced factors. The other nodes of the diamond play supporting roles.

The basic factors are inherited or developed with relatively modest investment. In an internationally competitive environment, the value of these diminish with widening accessibility. For developing nations striving to catch-up with the advanced industrial world, advanced factors are the key to competitive advantage. These are scarcer and require sustained, intelligently directed, investment in both human and physical capital. Porter (1990, pp.

---

[7]In an excellent review of Porter, Smith (1993) states that 'It is the first serious attempt to develop a really original grand theory of national economic development processes since the early years of Postwar development economics, and represents one of the most original ways of thinking about development policy in years.'

77–8) argues thus. 'The institutions required to create truly advanced factors (such as educational programs) themselves require sophisticated human resources and/or technology.' His stress on advanced factors, which are 'more difficult to procure in global markets or tap from afar via foreign subsidiaries,' echoes the insights of Amsden (1986) and Lall (1990).

An explicit evolutionary perspective governs much of Porter's insights. Thus selective disadvantage in basic factors is seen as a hidden advantage because, in a competitive environment, this forces innovation in advanced factors, an insight accurate for the resource-poor EA-NIEs and Japan. Fierce domestic competition between rival firms is also extolled because this stimulates dynamic efficiency, i.e. the faster upgrading of technology and productivity and forestalls rent-seeking by monopolies. As regards export markets, Porter favours larger numbers of independent buyers because captive buyers will undermine long-term strength by reducing the pressure to raise productivity and innovate. Though he is not writing specifically about the EA-NIEs, his analysis fits their success stories with remarkable accuracy.

Porter also discusses the positive effects deriving from the economies of scope and scale, from industrial 'clustering' which generates Marshallian externalities, international marketing alliances and multi-national firms. Clustering of firms in cohesive industrial districts is seen as very important. Clusters promote the rapid development of business institutions that reduce transaction costs and facilitate the diffusion of ideas, technology and personnel. Porter sees domestic rivalry as more important than foreign competition. Multi-nationals should be cultivated only as an ancillary strand in a complex national strategy and only to the extent they are ready to go beyond exploiting the countries' basic factors towards the development of advanced factors. Porter also proposes a four-stage sequence of development. These are summarized below from Smith's (1993) review of Porter.

1. The basic factor-driven stage in which basic factors are the essential source of advantage.
2. The investment-driven stage in which the beginnings of advanced factor creation can be seen, size and growth of domestic demand become an advantage, domestic rivalry is very intense and motivation is high.
3. The innovation-driven stage in which firms develop a global strategy, domestic demand sophistication becomes an advantage, related and supporting industries develop, advanced and specialized factors develop and selective factor disadvantages can lead to the building of advantage (Porter 1990, pp. 81–82).
4. The wealth-driven stage similar to that of advanced industrial countries.

Porter sees Korea and Taiwan as being on the threshold of entry into the third innovation-driven stage (back in 1990). Of course there is nothing automatic about progression through the stages and much depends on specific political and cultural factors. Import substitution as a long-term strategy is excoriated as dysfunctional, but he accepts infant industry protection as a necessary short-term measure. Needless to say, the role and responsibility of the state (i.e. public policy) looms large in the Porter conception (Porter 1990, ch. 12).

In fact the role of government is crucial in enhancing competition, regulating capital markets and promoting the growth of advanced factors through education, infrastructure development and through its position as a major buyer. Porter sums up the long-term task of government thus.[8]

> The central task facing developing countries is to *escape from the strait-jacket of factor-driven national advantage* (emphasis added) ... where natural resources, cheap labour, locational factors, and other basic factor advantages provide a fragile and often fleeting ability to export. Dependence on such industries, where exports are invariably sensitive to price, leaves the nation vulnerable to exchange rate and factor cost swings ... Creation of advanced factors is perhaps the first priority. Education, local technical capability, an information base, and modern infrastructure are prerequisites. The investment-driven stage provides an approach to accelerating development that has been successful in Japan and Korea (Porter 1990, pp. 675–6).

Porter's monumental study validates the findings and insights detailed in Chapters 6 and 7. It also supplies specific empirical detail and operational prescriptions to the general conclusions by means of extensive case studies.

## 7.6   ASSESSING THE EAST ASIAN ACHIEVEMENT

Nelson (1993) surveys technical innovation systems in a number of countries including Korea and Taiwan. He shows that though differences exist in the particular strategies adopted, some strong similarities show up between these countries. First, they both have broad and deep industrial structures unlike most other developing countries. Second, the industrial drive was partly at least motivated by the desire to develop military capability. Third, the strong emphasis on education was crucial in providing the educated workforce necessary to support the transition to products of increasing complexity.

As regards technological capability, it seems that Korea and Taiwan are at the apex of achievement in the developing world. Nelson remarks that they are models for emulation for LDCs, and quite deservedly so. Indeed, these

---

[8]Porter's guidelines are at odds with conventional wisdom based on old trade theory. It, however, accords with new trade theory which accepts the possibility of trade based on comparative advantage created de novo through specialization (Krugman 1990).

countries serve as a bridge or a region of articulation between the advanced industrial nations and the developing countries, providing a feasible path of progress. Their economic trajectories and strategies of technology acquisition even bear some broad similarity with the development paths of the USA and Germany in the late 19th and early 20th century period when these countries took over technologies developed earlier in Britain (Nelson 1993).

There are other ways in which we can establish the level of technical advance in the EA-NIE four. First, a cursory perusal of the coverage of East Asian technological progress in business and technical journals reveal a story of achievement that is dramatically different from the sombre picture painted by Krugman (1994). The technological achievements of East Asia inclusive of Japan were covered in great detail in the *IEEE Spectrum* (1991), which is the flagship journal of the Institute of Electrical and Electronic Engineers, USA. The survey found that Korea, Taiwan, Singapore and Hong Kong, had made tremendous technological progress in many areas. The most obvious is consumer electronics in which their prowess is displayed in myriad retail outlets around the world. Also covered were computers, integrated circuits, automotive products, automation in manufacturing, aerospace and military, telecommunications, medical electronics, power, energy and transportation.

By 1991, they had shifted well beyond the mere assembly of components to high value-added, high-technology manufactures, such as ICs (integrated circuits etched on semiconductor wafers). Each EA-NIE had forged a niche in some aspects of information technology manufacturing. South Korea is reported to have astounded the world in growing from a minor supplier of discrete semiconductor devices to establishing a major presence in the world IC market. It had also started production of numerically controlled machine tools. Taiwan too has developed its own indigenous IC industry; electronics has been its principal industry since 1984. Singapore's dominance in disk drives is well known and even Hong Kong has specialized in areas such as the manufacture of motherboards for personal computers.

The above is only a random selection from the technologies listed in the *IEEE Spectrum*, circa 1991. It is palpably clear to any visitor to the EA-NIEs that their industries are broad and deep, unlike the enclave-like character of most developing country industries. A similar survey of 'Technology in India' (*IEEE Spectrum*, 1994) brings out this difference starkly. It is worth emphasizing at this point that unlike Soviet achievements in science and technology, EA-NIE competence has been built up in the teeth of global competition. The consensus is that the EA-NIEs are more like industrial market economies than developing or planned economies. Living standards are high as a result of high levels of labour productivity. This is a good proxy for technological level in the absence of rich natural resource endowments.

In his highly cited book, Hobday (1995) develops a detailed account of how latecomer firms in the four EA-NIEs built up technological capability in the electronics industry. Hobday catalogues not only the various technologies mastered for each of the four countries, but described the institutional framework and business alliances through which the step-wise ascent up the technology ladder was realized. He includes many case studies, but since the focus of the study is electronics, other achievements in areas such as steel, automobiles, shipbuilding, etc. are not included. Hobday finds it necessary to warn that EA-NIE strength lies in low-cost, high-quality production engineering, rather than software or R&D.

A strong aspect of Hobday's work is that he documents the painstaking and cumulative process of technological learning through which firms operating in East Asia climbed up the technology ladder. In general, EA-NIE firms entered the international value chain as OEM (original equipment manufacturers), assembling goods for advanced country MNCs according to design specifications provided by the latter. The MNC partners marketed the OEM products under their own brand labels. Some OEM producers evolved into ODM (own-design manufacturers) able to develop their own innovative designs. In the 1990s, some local firms were marketing their 'own-brand manufactures' (OBM) with mixed success in global markets (Hobday 2000).

Hobday (1995, p. 200) does not find evidence of leapfrogging: 'much latecomer learning took place in a field which could be described as pre-electronic: mechanical, electro-mechanical and precision engineering activities, for example. Competencies tended to build upon each other incrementally, leading to advanced engineering and software.' Technological learning is slow and costly, eliciting vast investment of public and private resources.

More detailed accounts of technological advances made by firms in the EA-NIEs, in the 1990s in particular, are given in Kim and Nelson (2000). In Chapter 6 of this book, Lee examines technological learning in the capital goods sector in Korea; though largely oriented to the domestic market, significant exports are being realized in the 1990s. Duysters and Hagedoorn (in Chapter 7) and Dodgson (Chapter 8) discuss the hesitant beginnings of high technology R&D, largely through collaboration between EA-NIE firms and firms in the USA, Europe and Japan. These international alliances, with technology leaders, such as Intel, IBM, Motorola and NEC, have enabled some of the best Korean and Taiwanese companies such as Samsung and Acer to build up impressive capabilities in leading edge technologies.

The strategic industries targeted by firms in Korea, Taiwan and Singapore for the future, include biotechnology, chemicals, advanced engineering, aerospace, semiconductors and information technology (Kim and Nelson 2000, Chapters 7 and 8). A comprehensive account of the origins and impressive progress of the semiconductor industry in the EA-NIEs and Malaysia, is provided by Mathews and Cho (2000). This book provides extensive detail regarding the international commercial alliances, public investment and technological learning that made this achievement possible. Mathews and Cho also discuss the three distinct strategies exemplified by Korea with its reliance on the large chaebol, Taiwan, through small and medium enterprises and Singapore and Malaysia, by harnessing the first world expertise of MNCs. They point out that China is following all three models at the same time. Singapore's undoubted technological strength resides mostly in domestic subsidiaries of MNCs; but that is hardly an issue in a globalizing world.

In Chapter 11 of Kim and Nelson (2000), Linsu Kim summarizes the major problems faced by Korea's firms, and its national system of innovation in general, as the country faces up to the challenge of consolidating itself as a first world industrial power. At the firm level these include authoritarian management practices, other structural weaknesses of the unwieldy chaebol and excessive debt levels. At the national level, he identifies an inadequate education system and technology infrastructure, a weak financial system and debilitating levels of political patronage and corruption that hold back Korea's transition to a modern economy. These institutional problems are, of course, common to all developing countries; they have been tabled on the immediate social agenda precisely because Korea's rapid economic progress has brought it so close to the status of an advanced industrial power.

Finally, we can look at educational levels in the East Asian countries in relation to standards in the main industrial nations. Maddison (1995, Table 3–12) shows that average years of education per person aged 15–64 for Korea and Taiwan are well within the upper range for OECD countries like Japan, the Netherlands and the UK. Figures for Singapore and Hong Kong are not given, but are generally believed to be higher. Perhaps a better indicator than schooling data are the results of the Third International Mathematics and Science Study. Released in February 1998 (*IEEE Spectrum*, 1998), Korea, Singapore, Japan and Hong Kong are placed at the top of the rankings in mathematics and science for the 4th grade and 8th grade. Additional data on educational standards in the EA-NIEs are given in Collins and Bosworth (1996) and Lall (2000), which further confirm their stellar ranking.

The overall synthesis developed here hopefully presents a coherent and consistent generalization of the East Asian experience, grounded in empirical research and the best insights of East Asian specialists.[9] Despite presently

---

[9]In addition to the literature cited, many ideas presented in this book have been drawn from discussions with economists, business and industry leaders and engineers in Korea, Taiwan, Hong Kong, Singapore and Indonesia (see Acknowledgements).

revealed weaknesses, the consensus is that the EA-NIEs are well ahead of most other developing nations as regards the acquisition of technological capability and are on the threshold of integration with the advanced industrial world. Since by all accounts they started at the bottom, as also indicated by Figures 1.1 and 1.2, their present state must represent sustained technological progress in any meaningful sense of the term. This reality is not reflected in TFPG estimates because TFPG is not an adequate measure of technical progress, as argued in Chapter 3.[10]

## APPENDIX 7   ASPECTS OF EVOLUTIONARY CHANGE

This study, like most other analyses in the field of economics, concentrates on drawing out general patterns abstracted from the concrete evolution of economic activity and institutions. This approach misses, or understates, some specific aspects of learning and adaptation that characterize economic trajectories in East Asia. This appendix attempts to correct for this bias by focusing very briefly on the evolution of economic policy and the role of small and medium enterprises (SMEs) in East Asia.

Analysing the evolution of development trajectories and policy in East Asia, Kagami (1995) shows that policy shifts were responses to external shocks, tightening labour markets, domestic crises or bottlenecks that came about unexpectedly. These adaptive changes were 'structural adjustments' undertaken voluntarily to restore strength and vitality to the economy. Over the long-term they constituted an *adaptive evolution* towards more liberal, market-oriented policies and more conservative macro-management practice. As major trading nations, a crucial aspect of macro-policy was the maintenance of a realistic exchange rate to sustain international competitiveness.

Thus when South Korea and Taiwan faced foreign exchange constraints in the first stage of import substitution, they started to promote the export of light-industry products. Kagami shows that these countries followed a dual strategy for a period, promoting import substitution in capital-intensive industries with strong forward linkages and labour-intensive export industries with strong backward linkages. He argues that these two strategies were complementary and subsequent liberalization was made possible only after industrial momentum and export potential was built up by state intervention, i.e. by selective promotion, as explained above.

---

[10]Ironically, the consensus is that technical advance is least in Hong Kong, the very place that exhibits the highest TFP growth among the EA-NIEs in Young's (1994a) ranking. Other countries that match or exceed Hong Kong's TFPG, Malta, the Congo, Botswana, Pakistan, Egypt and Syria are not commonly held up as paragons of technological excellence.

Kagami argues that policy adapted pragmatically to actual events and problems. Thus targeting and promotion of key industries was crucial to success and made necessary by market failure involving externalities. Along the same lines, there is repeated emphasis on the 'virtuous circle' linkage between high investment and high growth, which is a key feature of East Asian growth. To maintain export competitiveness despite rising wages, it is necessary to raise productivity and quality by means of sustained investments in new machines and equipment. This is possible because fast growth itself leads to high investment levels thereby completing the feedback loop. Costs are also reduced through economies of scale made possible by large export markets. These important phenomenon are often ignored or underplayed in orthodox analyses, perhaps partly because it provides justification for industrial policy in the initial phase. See Stiglitz (1996), Lall (1990) and Kim and Lee (1996) for other interesting perspectives on these processes.

Kagami also discusses the role of foreign direct investment (FDI) in promoting NTC building. FDI flows are seen not as an independent determinant, but as a natural response to changing factor prices leading to the setting up of international supply chains. The key attraction for FDI was the availability of high-quality labour at lower wage rates. FDI is identified as the main vehicle for the introduction of modern management techniques and production technology which then diffuse throughout the economy. But FDI was restricted in Taiwan and South Korea which as a result have gone on to spawn internationally viable companies. In South Korea, where FDI was severely constrained, the domestic companies are considered the strongest.

In addition to linkages with advanced country MNCs, the intra-region linkages within East Asia inclusive of Japan are explicitly described. These include the role of Japan in supplying capital goods and high-technology intermediate goods to EA-NIE industry. The EA-NIEs are seen as pulling in technology-intensive R&D-type industries from advanced countries and pushing out labour intensive industries to SEA-NIEs and China. The cross-flow of investment within the region is well documented, showing that the greater part of FDI in SEA-NIEs and China originates within East Asia. This point is brought out in other studies as well, in particular Lall (1991).

Kagami (1995) devotes a great deal of attention to the evolution of industrial structure, how supply chains consisting of SMEs developed out of initially vertically integrated production units. Efficient parts and component subcontractors, it is argued, are crucial to maintain export competitiveness through a cooperative relationship between prime firms and subcontractors through the sharing of information, expertise and profits. Such cooperative knowledge-sharing is seen as crucial to technology acquisition which is presented as the main driving force behind rapid productivity advance. There is detailed discussion of how technology acquisition can be accelerated by state policy with regard to education and the setting-up of science and industry parks to incubate innovative firms, induce technology spillover and other 'silicon valley' clustering effects. The concentration or agglomeration of SMEs are necessary to realize such Marshallian externalities.

Even here, Kagami argues that such efficient SME supply chains did not evolve naturally but required state intervention, especially in South Korea. In 1964, particular sectors were demarcated and reserved for SMEs in South Korea; however, Kim and Lee (1996) point out that this policy did not work all that well in practice on account of the porous nature of technological boundaries and also as a consequence of the political power of the chaebol. Drawing on Japan's experience, Kagami argues that networks of firms can respond faster to market and technology changes than large vertically integrated firms. Though such efficiency-promoting structural change can take place relatively rapidly in highly developed markets, such as say the computer industry in the USA, it appears that state intervention is necessary to realize similar decentralization in NIEs.

The argument about the crucial role of SMEs and supply chains is taken further by Kagami, through a consideration of the Japanese subcontracting system. The evolution of SME supply chains, starting from the wartime needs of the Japanese economy, are traced with much useful and interesting detail. The 'Far Eastern Method' (FEM) of work organization based on a fuzzy division of tasks is contrasted with the 'Western Method' (WM) of Taylor and Ford based on the rigid division of tasks. FEM also involves cooperation between workers and managers and prime firms and subcontractors.

The superiority of FEM over WM is attributed to the realization of enhanced learning or accumulation of production-specific knowledge; this results from the fact that in WM information only flows vertically, whereas in FEM there is substantial flow of information horizontally across different tasks leading to greater responsibility among all workers for raising quality and reducing costs. Kagami points out that after the FEM system was tried out in a GM-Toyota joint venture in 1983, it was adopted throughout the USA.

Other interesting issues are taken up. It is shown for instance that SMEs can be more profitable than large enterprises, even though value added per employee is typically about three times as much in the latter. Therefore Kagami argues that there is no exploitation of SMEs. But he ignores wage differentials between large and small enterprises in Japan, which are well known to be very large; so the argument is not complete to say the least. Again, he argues that government protection of SMEs was necessary in the initial phases in Japan to set up efficient supply chains and promote rapid technological change through the sharing of information and the establishment of standards.

# 8.     The East Asian crises of 1997–8

Crises are an integral part of the evolution of market economies. All major industrial economies of the world have gone through periodic financial crises which from time to time turned into more generalized economic crises. Yet the 'Asian crisis of 1997–8,' as it was called, came as a surprise to mandarins of global finance as it did to economists specializing in international finance and East Asia. Radelet and Sachs (1998) discuss this problem at length and conclude that financial markets failed to signal alarm or understand the real nature of the crisis until it broke out in mid-1997. Yet signs of impending trouble were clearly there, a few years in advance at the least, and were read quite correctly by at least one analyst.[1]

The conclusion here is that the markets were lulled into complacence by the long record of hyper-growth in Asia. Beginning with Japan from around 1950, and the EA-NIEs a decade later, hyper-growth had spread from around 1980 to South-East Asia and China with what seemed like an unstoppable momentum. Taken as a whole, this phenomenon was unprecedented on account of the strength, persistence and geographical coherence of the growth impulse. For most of this period, growth was financed largely out of domestic savings which were very high by historical standards (see Figure 3.1). But in the 1990s, the region began to attract inflows of portfolio and short-term capital which reversed at short notice to precipitate the crises (Park 1996).

This book is concerned mainly with the problem of building technological capability in latecomer nations and the lessons that can be drawn from the superlative success of the East Asian four in this respect. The recent crises do not change that assessment, any more than the extended 'great depression' of the 1930s negated the rising potential of the USA to become the dominant industrial power in the world. On the contrary, it was this very success that

---

[1]In a remarkably prescient Brookings paper Yung Chul Park (1996) warned that the East Asian countries had become 'highly vulnerable' on account of financial market liberalization which unleashed an investment boom, weakening trade competitiveness in the face of China's ascendency and their own internal weaknesses. He located the incipient financial crisis in the general context of investment booms and speculative bubbles in East Asia. Later work has little to add to this remarkable 'ex ante' analysis.

stimulated the flood of finance into the region, thereby exposing policy errors and structural flaws that had been glossed over for long periods.

This particular dynamic plays out every time financial markets scent an opportunity for superior returns. Short-term capital cascades in and the boom turns into an euphoric bubble which ends in the inevitable crash as overblown expectations are shattered. At the first sign of trouble there is a panic-stricken reversal of short-term capital flows and the region as a whole is driven into breakdown, a reaction much in excess of what would be warranted by its real weaknesses. The basic mechanics of this 'boom-bubble-bust' cycle is well described by Krugman (1998a) in a *Slate* magazine article appropriately titled 'Paradigms of Panic.' In it, he compares the Asian crises to the crash of 1873 in the USA when it was emerging as the fastest growing region in the world.

But while wreaking havoc on the productive forces of the economy, crises play a less-noticed positive role as well. The role of crises in the evolution of market economies is described by Galbraith (1999, p. 3) with characteristic pithiness: 'capitalism is inherently unstable and it is especially unstable in early youth ... financial crisis cleans up incompetence in the banking system, in the industrial system, and, to some extent, in government.' This is the essence of the evolutionary perspective, adopted here and elaborated in section 1.1. Thus, episodic crises are seen as a *potentially* self-regenerating mechanism by which structural and institutional flaws that need correction are pushed forward on to the immediate agenda.

It is necessary, then, to identify the longer-term domestic causes that generated vulnerability to economic instability and the short-term factors that triggered the breakdown. In addition to analysing the roots of the crises, this chapter attempts to discuss how the crises relate to the primary concern of this study. The important issues of how best to resolve the crises, through domestic reforms linked to concurrent restructuring of the global financial architecture, are touched on only very briefly. While the rest of this book deals only with the four EA-NIEs of South Korea, Taiwan, Hong Kong and Singapore, the 'Asian crisis' is a phenomenon that engulfed the entire region, including the South East Asian countries of Indonesia, Malaysia and Thailand and then travelled further into Russia and Brazil as well. Since only South Korea, among the four EA-NIEs, was seriously affected, its internal problems alone are taken up here, in addition to the systemic problems common to all and some of Thailand's problems for purposes of illustration. The internal problems of other affected countries are not dealt with in this book.

The singular expression, 'Asian crisis,' is widely used in the literature to describe the onset and progression of the regional phenomenon as a whole. The plural term 'East Asian crises' is preferred here to refer to the experience of all of the East Asian and South-East Asian countries affected, because in fact there are individual differences. As regards their undoubted collective coherence, this was shared by Brazil and Russia, but not by India, Pakistan and China, though China played a major role in the crises. Hence the latter term seems somewhat more geographically accurate. Further, since it is widely accepted that this was the regional manifestation of a pattern of global crises (Radelet and Sachs 1998, Corsetti et al. 1999, Mishkin 1999, Caprio and Honohan 1999), it seems incorrect to define its character as purely Asian.

The domestic weaknesses in East Asia revealed by the crises were real and serious, not only in the financial systems and their governance, but also in the way the industrial companies were set up, financed and governed and even in the broader institutional framework of the countries affected. South Korea had built up impressive strengths in the deployment of its technolog-ical capabilities. But its banking system and chaebol conglomerates were becoming increasingly anachronistic in an industrially advanced market economy. Taiwan's structural flaws are fewer and hence it weathered the crisis better. But along with well-administered Hong Kong and Singapore, which did not have domestic weaknesses on anything like that scale, Taiwan was tumbled into the maelstrom by the 'contagion' effect.

'Contagion' kicks in when international creditors pull their money out of an entire region on account of insufficient knowledge about specific countries or industrial sectors. Contagion is then primarily an information failure at the centres of global finance. It operates through powerful feedback linkages between panic-driven perceptions and the collapse of entire sectors in the stricken countries as short-term financing is withdrawn. Radelet and Sachs (1998) describe how several powerful positive feedback mechanisms generated a cascade of credit withdrawals throughout the financial sectors of the region. The mechanism of positive feedback itself, which is pervasive in economic processes, is defined and described in the appendix to this chapter.

It is argued in section 1.1 that necessary reform and regeneration are not at all automatic, since these depend on the mobilization of the necessary political will and consensus. Japan has now gone through almost a decade of low-level persistent crisis without building up political momentum for major change, until Spring 2001 at the least. Since South Korea has recovered its growth momentum rather quickly, the chaebol are now in a stronger position to resist pressures for reform (Krause 2000). Clearly industrial prowess can prop up a great deal of weakness in other areas of the economy as in the past.

The above arguments are developed in more detail below starting with a review of the global economic background to the crises. This is followed by a discussion of the domestic weaknesses and policy errors that contributed to the severity of the crises. The progression of the crises is also touched on along with general issues relating to the phenomenon of financial crises. The chapter concludes with some comments on the reforms proposed for curing domestic weaknesses and flaws in the international financial architecture.

## 8.1    THE GLOBAL ASPECT OF RECENT CRISES

Contemporary analysts identify the 'Asian crisis' as the latest round in a series of recurring instabilities in the international financial system.[2] They are seen as manifestations of the volatility of global finance operating in a highly liberalized and integrated world economy. Since the collapse of the Bretton Woods system in 1971–3, the world has seen one major financial crisis and two relatively moderate ones (Cline 1995) until the Asian crises of 1997–8. These crises have generated a great deal of alarm and attention because the globalization of finance ensures that instabilities precipitated by problems in emerging economies are rapidly transmitted back to the banking centres of the advanced industrial world (Kho et al. 2000, Soros 1998).

The first major Latin debt crisis, which began in Mexico in 1982 and spread to other Latin countries, was finally brought to heel around 1993 with the 1989 Brady Plan. Cline (1995) charges that the international banks were totally unprepared (i.e. with no provisions for bad loans on this scale) as was the IMF. He describes how close the international financial system came to breakdown and how delicately a soft landing was managed. By comparison, the second Latin crisis of 1994–5 was a 'moderate after-shock,' in the words of Cline, more in the nature of a liquidity crisis, compared to the 'earthquake' of 1982. The third fairly moderate crisis was the collapse of the European Monetary System in 1992.

Scholes (2000, p. 17) traces the crises of 1997–8 as a single shockwave shuddering through the financial system. 'It started in Southeast Asia, moved through Latin America, and then visited Russia and returned again to South America. The financial crisis also infected Europe and the United States, especially during August-October 1998.' This was when the collapse of the Long-Term Capital Management (LTCM) hedge fund was narrowly averted with extraordinary intervention from the Federal Reserve Bank. These global crises are the result of the emergence of a single, seamless global capital market from around 1980 as major industrial countries began to dismantle exchange controls (Bosworth and Collins 1999). Since this market operates largely outside the control of national government, it has attracted increasing quantities of relatively short-term funds.

In the late 1980s and the early 1990s, the rapid growth observed in the EA-NIE four was seen to be spreading to China and the SEA-NIEs of Indonesia, Thailand and Malaysia. Under IMF tutelage, these economies, with the exception of China , had begun to deregulate their financial systems and open up capital markets to external funds. As a result they became attractive

---

[2]Mishkin (1999), Radelet and Sachs (1998), Corsetti et al. (1999).

destinations for both long and short-term capital flows. With Latin America seen to be endemically stricken with economic difficulties during the 1980s, East Asia, along with China, became the destination of choice. Summers (2000, p. 20) writes: 'the flow of private capital from industrial to developing countries has mushroomed from $174 billion in the 1980s to $1.3 trillion during the 1990s.' About half of these went to East Asia (Park 1996).

Why does finance capital seek out risky investments in developing countries? As high return investments are exhausted in their own countries, the competition between finance providers induces some to look for higher returns in outside markets. Rates of return are higher in emerging markets, because here capital is relatively scarce and productivity growth is stronger. Once pioneer banks do well with foreign investments, the perceived risk diminishes and other banks begin lending in foreign markets. This process builds up momentum until finally there is a stampede to lend abroad.[3]

From the standpoint of emerging economies the above process opened access to a global capital market in which large quantities of funds could be borrowed without signing on to IMF conditionality or World Bank supervision. Previously, the flow of capital to developing countries had been mostly aid from official sources. Once private flows were set in motion, the natural competitive logic of the process impelled banks to seek out more and more borrowers. When safe projects are exhausted, capital invariably moves on to riskier ones until the onset of a major crisis reverses the momentum. The generalized crisis of the 1980s was generated by just such a debt build-up.

The problem is similar to that encountered in financial panics in domestic intermediation, with a few added complications such as depreciation of the exchange rate and trade effects. If there is a suspicion of inability to service the debt, everyone scrambles to pull their money out fast before it is too late, and to withhold further credit. This then precipitates a crisis. In global capital markets a credit crunch works in the same way as with purely domestic intermediation. But here, a reversal of capital flow also forces through a rapid depreciation of the currency as the balance of payments is adversely affected.

If the economy is basically solvent, then all that the country needs is a short-term loan to bridge the liquidity shortfall until the markets recover from

---

[3]Park (1996, p. 361) describes it thus. 'When foreign investors see an opportunity to earn handsome returns, they will rush into a local market as a herd. As a result the volume of their aggregate lending can be excessive, in that it is greater than the host country can absorb in the short run. Many of these foreign investors are likely to be noise traders, however, and will not understand or care about the possible consequences of their lending, but there is no mechanism to coordinate their behavior. Local borrowers, for their part, will be encouraged to borrow as much as they can by the positive interest rate differentials between local and international financial markets.' Similar warnings are issued by George Soros (1997, 1998).

the panic. This was the case with the Mexican bail-out of 1994 when Mexico paid back the loan ahead of schedule when the crisis subsided. This is an example of a 'liquidity crises' when the underlying economy, the so-called 'fundamentals,' are sound.

But sometimes as the result of a major shock, or because of economic problems built up over a long period, a country loses its underlying ability to service its foreign debt. A situation like this is a 'solvency crisis.' At this point stabilization loans are not of much use. A writing-down of the debt is necessary. In the Latin debt crisis of 1982–93, debt-to-equity swaps were used to write down the debt of a number of major countries including Mexico and Brazil. In 1982, banks which had lent to Latin America were persuaded to act collectively and extend fresh credit. This enabled the debtor countries to service their debt. The banks suffered some losses in the long run and Latin America lost a decade of growth, says Soros (1997) rather sorrowfully.

## 8.2    SPECIFICS OF THE CRISES IN EAST ASIA

The sequence of events and causes that set off the crises in East Asia are well documented in the literature (Radelet and Sachs 1998, Corsetti et al. 1999, World Bank 1998, Goldstein 1998). The short-term unfolding of the crises began with the build-up of unhedged, short-term debt, which exposed the vulnerability of Thailand, Indonesia, South Korea, the Philippines and Malaysia, leading to a sudden collapse of confidence. At a certain point when companies and banks started to fail, there was a panic-stricken reassessment of the state of all Asian economies. This led to indiscriminate withdrawal of short-term credit which plunged other banks and companies into a crisis.

As the crises progressed, capital outflow, depreciating currencies and falling asset prices drove many companies into insolvency. The global market did not have enough information to distinguish good firms from bad ones, hence even healthy firms were adversely affected. Here we see the 'vicious cycle' of self-fulfilling crises, driven by positive feedback linkages. As explained above, a cascade of credit restrictions then slowed down the real economy, which led to further bankruptcies in a descending spiral.

It is important to point out that some features of the East Asian crises are very different from characteristics of previous crises in Latin America and elsewhere, particularly those of the 1982–95 period. In East Asia, bad loans were made to the private sector, to banks and firms. East Asian governments had run budget surpluses or small deficits unlike the cohort of previous debt-ridden developing countries which suffered from excessive public debt. The economic fundamentals in most of East Asia continued to be strong, with high sustained savings and growth rates, low inflation, and a broad and deep skills base for industrial activity, especially in South Korea and Taiwan. The fundamentals in Latin countries were very weak by contrast (IMF 1997).

A feature that East Asia – excluding Singapore and Hong Kong – shares with Mexico and other Latin countries is the existence of cronyism, nepotism and other forms of corruption. It is well known that these are widespread, though not on the same scale as in Mexico. The special privileges enjoyed by the Suharto family with its extensive business interests, became a major issue in the fall of his regime, with his successor Habibie promising to restore some of the public money diverted into family coffers. However, this is a common feature of most emerging market economies in their formative stages.

Radelet and Sachs (1998) argue that the Asian crisis can be understood as a 'crisis of success' caused by a boom in international lending followed by a sudden withdrawal of funds once panic set in. 'One ironic similarity between the 1995 Mexican and 1997 Korean crises is that both countries joined the OECD on the eve of their respective financial catastrophes.' They point out that this is much more than a bizarre coincidence. 'Both countries collapsed after a prolonged period of market euphoria.' Apparently, its OECD membership lulled many German banks into extending heavy loans to Korea without looking too closely at the over extended nature of the debt structure of many chaebol. Most of them were excessively leveraged with very high debt to equity ratios and a number of them were bankrupt even before the currency crisis hit in late 1997 (Corsetti et al.1999).

The rapid rise of China as a major exporter of labour-intensive manufactured goods contributed to the decline of export competitiveness in other East Asian economies.[4] East Asia's increasing dependence on China and its integration with the world economy is the major challenge faced by all the smaller economies of the region (Park 1996). At the beginning of 1994, China devalued its currency bringing it to around 50% of its official value prior to 1990. This increased competitive pressure on other East Asian economies, especially Thailand and Indonesia, whose labour-intensive exports were in competition with China's (IMF 1997, World Bank 1998).[5]

---

[4]China's entry into global markets has particularly affected Thailand and Indonesia which failed to move quickly beyond low technology, labour-intensive manufactures. For example, in June 1997, the author interviewed a distraught Bangkok shoe manufacturer, who complained that smuggled high-quality China-made Nike shoes were selling on the streets for half the price of his own equivalent designs which additionally did not have a global brand name. Extensive detail on China's interaction with East Asia in the international markets is to be found in World Bank (1998), IMF (1997), Park (1996) and Loungani (2000).

[5]The extent to which China's devaluation affected the other East Asian economies is disputed by some analysts (Loungani 2000, World Bank 1998, p. 24), since China had a dual exchange rate system, which was merely rationalized by the 1994 devaluation.

The adverse effects of China's devaluation were temporarily ameliorated by a weakening dollar, in 1994 and early 1995, which led to depreciation of East Asian currencies linked to the dollar, in trade-weighted terms and gave them an added advantage. But in mid-1995 the dollar recovered sharply, taking away this temporary cushion. A few months later in 1996, global export market growth began to slow: Korea, Malaysia, Singapore, Thailand and China experienced a dramatic slowdown of export growth. The causes of the 1996 export slowdown are analysed in World Bank (1998, ch. 2).

The other external problem that weakened most East Asian economies was the persistence of recession in Japan throughout the 1990s. Japan's long stagnation significantly dampened the growth of exports of its Asian trading partners. This was compounded by sector-specific shocks such as the 1996 fall in demand for semiconductors (see Corsetti et al. 1999, Goldstein 1998 and Radelet and Sachs 1998 for details).

Most analysts of the East Asian crises have identified the appreciation of real exchange rates in the 1990s as a significant contributor to the declining trade competitiveness of the region. All developing countries are vulnerable to this particular phenomenon. It was clearly exacerbated by the inflow of short-term funds in the 1990s. Corsetti et al. (1999) investigate this problem in detail. They conclude that the degree of real appreciation differed widely across the region and, therefore, the evidence is somewhat mixed. However, the maintenance of fixed or quasi-fixed parities against the dollar was clearly a mistake.

Financial vulnerability was generated by misguided exchange rate and monetary policies and the premature liberalization of capital markets, which allowed the free flow of short-term capital from outside. Thailand maintained a fixed rate against the dollar and all East Asian countries maintained tight monetary policies with high domestic interest rates. This encouraged local banks to obtain lower interest credit from abroad and channel it to property developers. Foreign lenders were lulled by implicit government guarantees, though of course they should have known better. In effect the implicit guarantees generated 'moral hazard' problems where borrowers and lenders were encouraged to undertake excessive risk.

Stiglitz (1998b, 1998c) argues forcefully that the policy error at the core of the problem was the excessively hasty liberalization of the financial system, under pressure from the IMF and World Bank, without first putting into place an adequate system of regulation and supervision. This led to rising financial instability and a slowing-down of growth, though the intention was to improve the flow of finance to productive enterprises. Beyond East Asia, he sees the rising frequency and severity of financial crises in other developing and transitional economies as deriving from this fundamental error.

In the last decade Thailand has reduced reserve requirements, eased the rules governing non-bank financial institutions, expanded the scope of permissible capital market activities (such as allowing banks to finance equity purchases on margin), and increased access to off-shore borrowing. Beginning somewhat earlier, Korea eliminated many interest rate controls, removed restrictions on corporate debt financing and cross-border flows, and permitted intensified competition in financial services. While the advantages of these changes were lauded, the necessary increase in safeguards was not adequately emphasized ...Thailand, for instance, used to restrict bank lending for real estate, both because it realized the danger of such lending and because it wanted to direct credit to what it viewed as more growth-enhancing investments. But again, partly under pressure from those who claimed that such restrictions interfered with economic efficiency, it liberalized, eliminating the restrictions with the predictable consequences we have seen (Stiglitz 1998b).

There was misallocation of investment, particularly into the commercial real estate sector; overbuilding was obvious in many East Asian cities. But Stiglitz (1998b) has pointed out that commercial vacancy rates in Jakarta and Bangkok were around 15% and were projected to rise to 20%, which was comparable to contemporary vacancy rates in Dallas and Houston in Texas, but well below the vacancy rates of 30% or higher seen in many major US cities in the 1980s. However, the risk to banks posed by these vacancy rates in East Asia were much higher.

Many of the investments made in East Asia were misguided, especially those made in highly speculative property development. These could only have been the product of an extensive 'crony' system linking bankers, politicians and developers. Furthermore, it was sheer business incompetence to fund long-term investments with short-term debt taken out in international markets. Not only was there a mismatch of maturities, which violates a cardinal principle of finance, but there was a mismatch of denominations: hard-currency debt was linked to pay-off in domestic currency, thereby introducing exchange rate risk into investment returns. Of course, lenders and borrowers believed that the exchange rate peg to the dollar would hold. In retrospect, the dollar peg itself was too rigid an arrangement.

There certainly was lack of transparency which made it difficult for the international market to discriminate between solvent firms and insolvent ones; it amplified the withdrawal of credit when the initial failures occurred. But this is obviously not the critical cause of crises, since financial crises have occurred recently in Norway, Sweden and Finland which have highly transparent economic systems and advanced institutional infrastructures (Stiglitz 1998c, Caprio and Honahan 1999).

In short, the crises revealed serious weaknesses in the institutions mediating the flow of finance in all of the countries affected. Perhaps the most important institutional factor responsible is poorly managed financial liberalization including the opening of the capital account. It is well known that China too suffers from corruption and has possibly the worst-stricken banking system of all major economies in Asia, with about 50% of all state-owned enterprises, its main customers, effectively bankrupt. But China was not affected by the East Asian contagion because capital flows are controlled by the state. It is important to emphasize that financial volatility arises not from the inflow of external capital in general, but largely from the inflow of short-term 'hot-money' which can reverse at short notice (Park 1996).

**Capital Flows to East Asia**

The flow of capital to the Asian economies over the 1993–7 period, just prior to the crises, is shown in the Table 8.1. The flows are broken down into the following categories: 'net private capital flows' is the total of the other three categories, 'net direct investment,' 'net portfolio investment,' and 'other net investment'. Net official flows are also included in the total figure, but are not shown separately, since they are relatively small. The adjective 'net' is used because these are all differences between inflow and outflow; but outflows are very small except for Taiwan and Korea.

The last category of 'other net investment' is mostly short-term credit flow that is of greatest interest for understanding the financial crises. Net direct investments are investments in plant and machinery made by foreign companies, which obviously cannot be withdrawn at short notice; they are a stabilizing factor that strengthens the domestic economy. Portfolio investments are purchases of local stock by foreign capital and also have limited effect. So volatility is associated with 'other net investment' flows.

From Table 8.1, it is clear that China has been drawing very large capital flows into its economy from abroad, of the order of 5% of GDP, every year since 1993. However, the vast bulk of this is in the form of foreign direct investment (FDI) in factories and machinery and do not constitute a source of financial instability. Taiwan, at the other extreme, is a net source of capital for the rest of the world with much of it going into mainland China.

Indonesia has also attracted heavy inflows of capital, about half of it in FDI. But in recent times (1994–6) the inflow of short-term credit has risen sharply to around 3% of GDP. A similar dependence on short-term credit had developed in Korea, but Thailand is the worst case of all. Net capital flow had largely come from short-term credit markets rising up to around 7–10% of GDP. The Thai baht's fixed link to the dollar with implicit government guarantees for private borrowers was obviously a major factor in the readiness of lenders to pump in these vast quantities of hot money. The above figures show that Thailand was clearly the weakest link in the chain, the obvious place for the crisis to break out. More detailed statistics for all these countries are provided by Corsetti et al. (1999) and Radelet and Sachs (1998).

*Table 8.1*  *Capital flows to selected East Asian economies during 1993–7 (expressed as a percentage of GDP)*

| Country | 1993 | 1994 | 1995 | 1996 | 1997 |
|---|---|---|---|---|---|
| China |  |  |  |  |  |
| NPCF | 4.5 | 5.6 | 5.2 | 4.7 | 3.7 |
| NDI | 5.3 | 5.9 | 4.8 | 4.6 | 4.3 |
| NPI | 0.7 | 0.7 | 0.1 | 0.3 | 0.2 |
| ONI | −1.5 | −0.9 | 0.2 | −0.3 | −0.8 |
| Taiwan |  |  |  |  |  |
| NPCF | −2.1 | −0.6 | −3.6 | −3.2 | −3.8 |
| NDI | −0.7 | −0.5 | −0.4 | −0.7 | −0.6 |
| NPI | 0.5 | 0.4 | 0.2 | −0.4 | −0.6 |
| ONI | −1.9 | −0.5 | −3.3 | −2.1 | −2.6 |
| South Korea |  |  |  |  |  |
| NPCF | 1.6 | 3.1 | 3.9 | 4.9 | 2.8 |
| NDI | −0.2 | −0.3 | −0.4 | −0.4 | −0.2 |
| NPI | 3.2 | 1.8 | 1.9 | 2.3 | −0.3 |
| ONI | −1.5 | 1.7 | 2.5 | 3.0 | 3.4 |
| Indonesia |  |  |  |  |  |
| NPCF | 3.1 | 3.9 | 6.2 | 6.3 | 1.6 |
| NDI | 1.2 | 1.4 | 2.3 | 2.8 | 2.0 |
| NPI | 1.1 | 0.6 | 0.7 | 0.8 | −0.4 |
| ONI | 0.7 | 1.9 | 3.1 | 2.7 | 0.1 |
| Thailand |  |  |  |  |  |
| NPCF | 8.4 | 8.6 | 12.7 | 9.3 | −10.9 |
| NDI | 1.1 | 0.7 | 0.7 | 0.9 | 1.3 |
| NPI | 3.2 | 0.9 | 1.9 | 0.6 | 0.4 |
| ONI | 4.1 | 7.0 | 10.0 | 7.7 | −12.6 |

*Codes*:  NPCF = net private capital flows comprising NDI, NPI, ONI and net official flows, which are not shown. NDI = net direct investment; NPI = net portfolio investment; ONI = other net investment which comprise mostly short-term capital flows.

*Source*:  IMF *World Economic Outlook* (December 1997, p. 6).

## The Chaebol, High Debt and Crony Capitalism

The chaebol, the large Korean conglomerates, were heavily dependent on debt rather than equity financing. While debt/equity ratios are kept under 1.0 in the USA in accordance with prudent practice, they were around 2.5 for all listed companies in Korea during 1991–6 and around 4.0 for the top 30 chaebol (Hahm and Mishkin 2000). Back in the 1970s and 1980s, debt/equity ratios of 0.5 were considered high for most US businesses, but since then companies have got used to carrying more debt. Though debt is cheaper to the company than equity financing when times are good, it becomes a serious burden when profits are down, since debt imposes an invariable contractual obligation to service the debt. Equity capital, on the other hand, does not have to be returned or paid dividends when times are bad.

An interesting, but flawed, argument is brought by Wade and Veneroso (1998a). They argue that the Korean system is particularly suitable for Korea's specific conditions, given the high rate of domestic savings, the weak state of equity markets and general aversion to risk where most savers prefer to put their money into secure bank-type deposits than stocks. The Korean system also requires coordination of foreign borrowing by the government and cooperation between banks, firms and the state. They argue that this system is mistakenly seen as 'crony capitalism' in the USA. The radical financial deregulation undertaken by Korea to meet the criteria for OECD entry and pressure from Western sources destroyed the stability of this high debt mode. Wade and Veneroso develop their argument as follows:

> High household savings, plus high corporate debt/equity ratios, plus bank-firm-state collaboration, plus national industrial strategy, plus investment incentives conditional on international competitiveness, equals the 'developmental state.' For all the white elephants and corruption (inevitable when a third of national income is being intermediated), the system that allows firms to borrow multiples of their equity has yielded a quantum leap up the world hierarchy in technology and scale, and rates of improvement in living conditions that surpass virtually all other countries ... Domestic corporate borrowers discovered that they could borrow abroad half as cheaply as they could borrow at home. Foreign debt escalated, most of it private and short-term (maturing in 12 months or less). In Korea, foreign debt incurred by its banks and the companies that borrowed from them exploded from very little in the early 1990s to roughly $160 billion by late 1997(Wade and Veneroso 1998a, pp. 7–8).

This change is reflected in the current account deficit, which fell from zero in 1993 to about 5% of GDP in 1997, to balance the capital inflow, over half of which was short-term debt (IMF 1997). In Korea the collapse of Hanbo steel, the first bankruptcy of a leading chaebol in a decade, was probably the triggering event that reversed market sentiment. But the trigger is not that important. If there is a sufficient number of firms in serious difficulty, one of them is going to fail soon enough and by the self-reinforcing feedback processes described in the appendix, it brings down the others as well.

Wade and Veneroso's arguments are persuasive for what sustained Korea in the past. But with Korean companies investing heavily abroad and seeking even closer integration with global capital markets, the old equilibrium which they extol obviously could not be expected to last. It is unlikely that the old relationships could have persisted without change, after Korea had crossed the threshold leading to a modern industrial economy, signed and sealed by OECD entry. They seem to be saying that the quirks of Korea's industrial adolescence must be preserved indefinitely into the future, an argument that is clearly at odds with an evolutionary perspective of economic change.

## 8.3    ASSESSING THE ASIAN CRISES

Mishkin (1999) has argued that the swings of GDP growth over the course of the East Asian crises are of the same order of magnitude as those which took place during the Great Depression in the USA. This raises questions about the existence of long repetitive patterns of growth in the evolution of the world economy, which cannot, however, be taken up here. The practical problem is to draw lessons about what would reduce the severity of future crises, assuming that these are likely to recur over the indefinite future.

It is clear that the major international banks bear much responsibility for the severity of the crises in East Asia. Most primary investors clearly do not have the ability to monitor the financial strength of companies and banks and even governments in distant countries. Banks and other financial institutions exist to bridge these information asymmetries and deal with the problem of adverse selection where the least creditworthy borrowers become the keenest supplicants for credit. These problems are re-examined in the context of recent crises by Mishkin (1999). Stiglitz (1998b) illustrates the problems of small emerging economies with the following graphic metaphor and argues that international banks should be held to a higher standard of accountability than domestic banks which channelled funds to risky domestic investments.

> But even with the best economic management, small open economies remain vulnerable. They are like small rowboats on a wild and open sea. Although we may not be able to predict it, the chances of eventually being broadsided by a large wave are significant no matter how well the boat is steered. Though to be sure, bad steering probably increases the chances of a disaster, and a leaky boat makes it inevitable, even on a relatively calm day ... If domestic banks were foolish in lending to, say, Indonesian corporations, so too were the foreign banks. Indeed, the foreign lenders in many cases should be viewed as the marginal lenders. If they – presumably models of good banking practice – were willing to lend to these sometimes heavily indebted corporations, why should we be surprised that domestic banks were willing to lend as well? (Stiglitz 1998b).

From the material assembled here, it should be clear that the East Asian crisis resulted from the explosive conjunction of serious internal flaws masked by lack of transparency, interacting with the natural volatility of global financial markets. Hardly anyone accepts the extreme argument that the markets and the IMF are mostly to blame, since domestic problems such as collapsing property markets and excessive debt were real and growing. Given the worsening internal problems, the sharp reversal of sentiment in the financial markets was surely inevitable. The only issue was what particular shock would trigger the panic reaction of the market and precipitate a full-blown crisis. The consensus among independent analysts, however, is that the initial interventions of the IMF amplified the severity of the crises (see section 8.5).

Stiglitz's analogy does not reflect the full complexity of the situation. The volatility of oceans or the incidence of earthquakes[6] cannot be controlled. But the excessive volatility of speculative short-term capital flows can be moderated. Stiglitz and other economists have proposed such controls. Chile had controls on short-term flows which insulated it from the worst aspects of the Latin crises. However, Wall street, the US Treasury and the IMF are strongly opposed to all such controls (Wade and Veneroso 1998a).

The synthesis put together here is based on the idea that capitalist market systems go through periodic crises, interspersed by episodes of relatively crisis-free growth. Crises are always associated with political conflict and calls for reform. Sometimes these crises are severe and are followed by decades of economic and political conflict. But on a very broad historical scale, market systems build up towards greater flexibility and increased resilience towards systemic shock.

In East Asia as well, if the institutional reforms planned are put in place, then these countries will generally move in the same direction. The general argument has already been stated clearly in section 1.1 and does not need to be repeated. What this chapter has attempted to do is to spell out the evolution of the Asian crises, in both their global and local dimensions, to illustrate the dynamics of change postulated there.

Crises seem to represent another aspect of 'creative destruction' within capitalism in addition to technological innovation (Schumpeter 1936, 1942). They temporarily weaken the system but also clear the ground for recovery and transition to a stronger, more productive, arrangement of the economy. The weak and inefficient companies are eliminated and the state is forced to reform its institutions for greater resilience. This is exactly what happened in the USA and in Japan over the historical long-term, and what is likely happen in Korea unless there is systemic breakdown. This is a feature of what are now commonly called 'self-organizing' systems.

---

[6]Another metaphor that illustrates the linkage between the international and domestic determinants of crisis and reform, within an evolutionary framework, can be drawn from the experience of Japan, a country subject to frequent earthquakes. Houses built too rigidly tend to crumble when earth tremors reach a certain intensity. Learning from experience, the Japanese design houses that ride the shocks and survive moderate stress at least. In similar fashion, the Asian crisis is forcing countries to reform their institutions for greater resilience.

During the crisis, one or more weak institution or practice is exposed and reformed. It does not happen all at once. The major institutional reforms brought in after crises in the USA, such as banking regulations, the Federal Reserve system, the FDIC, the SEC and a host of other institutions, were put in place over the time span of a century or more. These have made the system more resilient and capable of responding more effectively to diffuse the scope and power of crisis. However, as argued in more detail in section 1.1, there is nothing automatic about reform: if the necessary political consensus is not mobilized, reform is delayed or watered down. If that happens, then typically the crises recur with increasing severity. That could well happen in East Asia.

## 8.4   AGENDA FOR DOMESTIC REFORM

There is a great deal of agreement among agencies and analysts on the institutional reforms needed *within countries* to address domestic sources of crises. These are summarized immediately below and developed further in this section. These institutional reforms 'prevent crises,' of course, only in the sense that they are designed to reduce the likelihood of future crises (Eichengreen 1999). There is less agreement about the specifics of systemic reform at the level of the international financial architecture. Some of the systemic reforms highlighted by the experience of the recent crises are discussed in the next section, though not exhaustively.

1.  The internal problems of emerging economies need to be addressed: excessive debt/equity ratios of corporations and banks must be reduced; adequate regulation and oversight of financial markets and institutions must be put into place; cronyism, political pay-offs and so on, must be curbed by strong regulatory bodies.
2.  Transparency and efficiency of business activity must be built up with the putting in place of internationally recognized accounting and auditing practices, creditor rights, bankruptcy procedures and investor protection.
3.  Exchange rate regimes must be made flexible to enable better adjustment capability towards adverse trade and capital movements.

Modern financial reporting procedures need to be set up to create a good information base to establish transparency. This can be done relatively easily. But it is vital that debt/equity ratios be reduced as well. This will take time, since domestic investors are not likely to favour equity over debt in the immediate aftermath of a crisis-ridden period. The governments can change the policies that favoured high debt/equity ratios and the search for external financing. But since institutions are built out of habit, it will take time for attitudes and institutions to change.

Companies and the relationship between major companies and political leaders need to be brought into a transparent setting as well. Corruption and nepotism are not conducive to healthy business activity, at least in modern industrial economies. This will not be changed immediately, for sure. As the East Asian region recovered rapidly from the crises of 1997–8, the pressure for reform has subsided. But with Japan still deeply enmeshed in its crisis and the US economy slowing down in early 2001, the economic climate has changed again in East Asia. Just as in earlier crises in industrial countries, there is no reason to think that reforms will not be eventually carried out.

Major structural reforms have been put into place in Korea and Thailand in the 1998–9 period; these two economies have recovered considerably. In Indonesia, the political situation is still very fluid – circa Spring 2001– so it is not possible to begin serious reforms. New laws and regulations that address the above weaknesses have already been passed. The banking systems are being restructured with the weakest banks closed, non-performing loans written off and the remainder consolidated under proper financial oversight. All of these countries have now moved towards flexible exchange rate policies which are more resilient against shocks.[7]

Korea has made the most progress in this respect. Corporate leverage has also been reduced significantly there. However, the restructuring of the chaebol has hardly begun, even though a small number have collapsed under the weight of excessive debt. Strengthened by unexpectedly strong growth in 1999 and supported by labour unions fearful of job losses, the chaebol have managed to block major reform for the present (Krause 2000). But the social trauma of the 1997–8 crisis has set into motion some new developments. A recent study found that 9% of Korean adults are now employed by new, start-up firms supported by a venture capital market created by investors anxious to sidestep the chaebol and troubled Korean banks. Other institutional and operational changes have been initiated by younger business people impatient with the slow pace of change.[8]

A detailed discussion of the reforms being undertaken in the region cannot be attempted here. In any case reforms have proceeded for only about two years in what is surely a process that will take five years or more. The Asian crises and the reforms show, however, that even in the most successful market economies of the newly industrializing world, which the four EA-NIEs undoubtedly are, 'market forces' do not magically bring about balanced, crisis-free advance. They do not automatically correct inherited weaknesses

---

[7]*Economist*, April 15, 2001, pp. 76–8.
[8]*Economist*, January 13, 2001, p. 60 and April 15, 2001, pp. 76–8.

or ensure the consolidation of the institutions of a modern economy. Instead, high growth may exacerbate problems over time and often generate acute disequilibria. Countries dependent on the extraction of rich natural resources are particularly prone to such destabilisation, as exemplified by Indonesia.[9]

The general impression among East Asian specialists is that by the year 2000 the reform process had stalled somewhat, in South Korea in particular. The main reason for this has been faster than expected recovery in the region. However, East Asia's troubles are far from over. As a result of the recent slowing down of the US economy, East Asian countries are again experiencing a slowing down of exports, depreciating currencies, weakening stock markets and corporate defaults. From strong growth in 1999 and 2000, these economies are again experiencing much slower growth. However, the major weaknesses of the pre-1997 period are absent: none are dependent on short-term loans, they all run current account surpluses and the exchange rates are flexible except in China, Hong Kong and Malaysia.[10]

It may well be that East Asia is headed for another period of crises; as before, the positive aspect of this is that it may push the region into another round of reform. The East Asian crises appear to have had a significant effect on China's leaders, however, since they are reported to be keen to reform their institutions in line with best practice in advanced industrial economies. A McKinsey consultant based in Beijing is quoted as saying that 'the main effect of the crisis in South-East Asia and South Korea may have been that it scared China into getting its priorities right' (*Economist* 2001, p. 4).

## 8.5    ISSUES RELATING TO SYSTEMIC REFORM

There is a lively ongoing debate on how the crises in Asia and elsewhere were handled by the IMF and affected country governments. There is no dispute about the disastrous social effects of the crises and the need to avoid them where possible. Many economists and even political personalities have entered the debate to ask how the incidence of financial instabilities leading to breakdown can be reduced by coordinated public policy across the major market economies (*Economist* 1999). In addition to domestic reforms advocated for countries stricken by crises, there is now widespread discussion about the pressing need to reform and redesign the structures and guidelines regulating global financial flows and the IMF itself. These arguments are analysed in detail by Goldstein (1998) and Eichengreen (1999).

---

[9]The best option seems to be proactive, anticipatory interventions that address problems in their early stages, as has been practised most effectively in Singapore (Goh 1995, Lee 2000).
[10]*Economist*, May 19, 2001, p. 41.

The IMF itself, or at least its policy-making bodies, have come under a great deal of criticism, not least from Stiglitz (1998c). First, they are held responsible for urging premature financial liberalization on Asian countries, which contributed very significantly to the crises. Second, once the crises erupted, they imposed prefabricated policies, such as high interest rates, which instead of alleviating the impending contraction of demand, actually deepened the slump (Krugman 1998b). The IMF took measures developed in the context of typical Latin American crises and mechanically applied these remedies to the Asian countries without regard to the very different conditions prevailing there.

Latin crises have been characterized by large public sector fiscal deficits, excessive demand and strong inflationary tendencies. In that context, IMF-style austerity measures, involving high interest rates, reduced government spending and devaluations designed to reduce domestic absorption, at least have the merit of justification on the basis of conventional economic theory. 'But the East Asian economies were in rough macroeconomic balance,' protests Stiglitz (1998c) 'as evidenced by their low and in some cases, falling inflation rates.' But without regard to the very different context, the IMF demanded contractionary measures which then led to a severe slump.

Edwards (1998b) argues that the IMF in its present form cannot meet the needs of the global economy. He suggests that it be broken up into three separate, specialized institutions. The first would provide timely and uncensored information on the financial health of countries, or if information was insufficient, would say so, thereby providing countries with a strong incentive to adopt modern accounting practices. The second institution would provide contingent credit lines to countries that face temporary liquidity problems though fundamentally solvent, provided they meet minimum standards of disclosure and transparency. This body would play a proactive role in preempting crises, rather than the reactive role preferred by the IMF. The third institution would assist countries that get into serious crises to recover and restructure their debts and extend funds subject to conditionality. Edwards argues that this separation of functions would reduce crises and minimize moral hazard problems.

Eichengreen (1999, pp. 102–3) counters that while Edwards' proposal would cleanly delineate the separate functions, its implementation would involve increased international funding and create some serious coordination problems as well. It should be asked, however, whether these coordination problems may not be easier to resolve than the conflicting demands presently encountered by the IMF, as identified by Edwards. Further, the extra cost need to be assessed against the very large costs incurred when economies fail and rescue efforts need to be funded.

The argument that the IMF deepened the crisis has been stated more forcefully by Wade and Veneroso (1998a, 1998b). They claim that the time has come to set up a separate Asian Monetary Fund (AMF) to handle Asian economies. They state that an AMF was proposed by Japan in August 1997 to deal with the Asian crises, with the support of China, Taiwan, Hong Kong and Singapore. But 'The United States Treasury pulled out all the stops to kill the proposal, and it died.' It will be difficult to suppress this idea in the longer-term, given the general awareness of IMF failure. Many people seem to think that competition from an AMF is just what the IMF needs.

Wade and Veneroso highlight an East Asian strength downplayed in the West. 'Asia is the world's great savings-surplus region. Its governments' foreign exchange reserves of almost $800 billion dwarf those of all other regions.' Virtually all of those reserves are parked in US Treasury bills and to a lesser extent in Europe. 'The private sectors of Japan, Taiwan, and Singapore are also large net lenders to the West. How ironic that a region with such massive savings surplus and net foreign assets should be plunged into crisis by the flight of capital belonging to institutions that reside for the most part in the United States, a massive net debtor with a savings deficit.'

The most severely affected countries in Asia, Korea, Thailand, Malaysia and Indonesia had a gross external debt of $400 billion, of which about $100 billion have long-term maturities and are therefore not in need of refinancing. Even if the entirety of the remainder is to be refinanced, which is an unlikely extreme, at $300 billion, it is a small part of the aggregate net creditor position of the region. Clearly this is an absurd situation. Currently Asian reserves in the USA and Europe earn much less than what Asian borrowers have to pay. The setting up of an AMF would mobilize Asian funds to easily resolve the debt crises of Asia. Further, the AMF could lend to Asia at a small margin above cost, thereby saving an enormous amount in excess interest payments now accruing to the West (Wade and Veneroso 1998b).

The question is raised whether external capital is needed at all in East Asian countries that have high savings rates in excess of 30%. Taiwan, for instance, is a large exporter of capital. Korea has invested heavily abroad, far and wide, so it has needed to draw in external finance as well. The fact is that investment opportunities in these countries were attractive and returns high.

One of the more radical ideas that has gained currency as a result of the recent crises is the proposal to control the flows of short-term capital. In earlier times the need to allow the free play of market forces, especially in the area of global finance, was almost an article of faith in the Western world, or perhaps more precisely, in the Anglo-Saxon world. From the late 1970s the global capital market had established its autonomous existence riding rough shod over the attempts of even the strongest governments to control it.

After the crises, a rising chorus of influential voices, among them Soros, Krugman and Bhagwati have suggested that short-term capital flows be dampened by means of a Chilean-style tax on capital inflows (*Economist* 1999). Wade and Veneroso expand on this idea as follows.

> The great lesson of the Asian crisis is that the desirability of free movements of short-term capital has to be put in question. We have tended to lump together trade liberalization with capital liberalization, and discuss them as though what applies to one also applies, more or less, to the other. Bhagwati's point is their effects are fundamentally different. He argues for trade liberalization without capital account liberalization (Wade and Veneroso 1998a, p. 21).

This issue of capital controls is discussed in detail by Eichengreen (1999). He considers the related idea of a small tax on all foreign exchange transactions, the famous 'Tobin tax,' originally proposed by James Tobin in 1978. The purpose of the tax is to dampen speculative foreign exchange transactions which introduce a great deal of volatility to currency markets. Eichengreen dismisses the Tobin tax as infeasible, but supports a Chilean-style tax to restrict short-term borrowing, not just by banks, but by all domestic entities.

An impeccable argument, based on mainstream theory, can be advanced to the effect that the excessive volatility of short-term capital flows is market failure on a gargantuan scale, an inevitable result of information asymmetries associated with the international intermediation of funds (Eichengreen 1999, ch. 4). Since crises are induced or exacerbated by overly volatile finance, there exist strong practical and theoretical arguments for institutional reform. Given that some banks in emerging market economies are likely to be badly managed and inadequately regulated for some time to come, Eichengreen sees such controls as essential in an era of liberalized international capital movement. He also shows that Chile dropped the controls in 1998 only when excessive inflows ceased, much like folding an umbrella when the rain stops.

The other relatively radical reform gathering support is the call to 'bail in' the private sector. This means that banks and other private entities making risky investments in emerging markets should be compelled to bear some of the losses in the event of default. In the past, the main thrust of rescue packages has been to 'bail out' creditors with public funds to avoid systemic risk. Eichengreen describes the problem thus:

> In Mexico in 1995, South Korea in 1997 and Russia in 1998, official funds were used to repurchase and retire short-term debts. Having benefited from high interest rates while their money was in place, creditors were protected from losses when it came time to sell. The moral hazard thereby created provided an obvious incentive to engage in even less prudent lending, setting the stage for still larger crises and still larger bailouts. It would be better from a public-policy standpoint were international investors and banks in particular forced to "take a hit" (Eichengreen 1999, p. 59).

Other reforms have been proposed such as the tightening up of operating standards on transparency for banks, which is uncontroversial; the Basle committee is already working on these. An exhaustive summary and analysis of all these proposals is to be found in the sources cited (*Economist* 1999, Eichengreen 1999). Reform is clearly necessary to ensure the stable operation of market forces with the same proactive logic that advanced industrial societies have learned to use to harness natural forces through the conscious promotion of technological change.

Just as laissez-faire capitalism has been replaced by regulated capitalism in major industrial nations, we now seem to be on the threshold of a transition from an essentially laissez-faire system of global finance to one that is regulated internationally. Some also argue that the international system of production and exchange should not be put in jeopardy to safeguard the 'rights' of hedge funds and suchlike to rake in speculative profits when times are good and then be bailed-out with public funds when things go wrong.

## APPENDIX 8   POSITIVE FEEDBACK IN FINANCIAL MARKETS

The strength and weakness of market systems is that investment is driven by expectation of profit. When profits are actually realized, bullish expectations are reinforced and investment is increased. This is an example of a self-reinforcing mechanism that is called positive feedback. If expected profits are not realized, investors turn bearish and withdraw or withhold further investment. This reaction is also an example of positive feedback. Positive feedback tends to amplify the initial impulse and is therefore inclined to generate instability. But it is positive feedback that gives capitalism such a strong forward thrust when investment conditions are good. Soros (1998) has argued that financial markets are inherently unstable because of the existence of positive feedback or 'self-reinforcing mechanisms.' The role of positive feedback in financial markets is described in detail in Shiller (2000).

The problem with modelling[11] such phenomena is that expectations (of significant groups of economic agents) enter into the process of investment and asset price determination. The peculiar thing about expectations is that the inertia associated with them can evaporate suddenly; in other words expectations can be unchanging or conservative for a long period and then suddenly change very rapidly and even reverse completely. Expectations, like

---

[11]See Arthur (1994) and other papers posted on his website (http://www.santafe.edu/arthur/) for details on the modelling of positive feedback processes.

political consciousness, can precipitously shed inertia. Since such highly volatile expectations enter crucially into investment and asset price determinations, economic processes display a volatility and unpredictability that is not commonly displayed by processes in physical science. Chaotic physical processes display some of these characteristics and have even been used to model economic phenomena. But expectations anticipate future events imperfectly on account of information failures and human weaknesses.

The problem is that expectations are often not rational at all. But even when ill founded, beliefs can actually bring about the very conditions they anticipate, or exacerbate an incipient crisis as explained earlier on. The panic-stricken reversal of hot money flows can often tip a country into a full-blown financial crisis, even when this was not justified by the fundamentals. Such self-fulfilling expectations generate instabilities which then push the entire system into a non-linear region of chaotic breakdown. Since most everyday thinking is implicitly based on linear dynamics, the instability generated by non-linear phenomena are hard to grasp.[12]

The theoretical argument for regulating global finance, at least regarding the volatility of short-term flows, is linked to the need to control 'positive feedback' in global financial markets. Aficionados of high fidelity music are aware that 'negative feedback' is used to stabilize solid-state amplifiers against instabilities arising out of temperature variations and suchlike. Positive feedback has the opposite effect: it leads to unstable ratcheting-up of final output, pushing a system into non-linearity. It is positive feedback that generates instability in public address systems, when sound from the speakers is picked up by the microphone, amplified and fed back to the speakers; the sound rises until the system is driven to non-linear breakdown.

The history of numerous asset price bubbles, from the Tulip Mania of 17th century Holland to 20th century stock market and property bubbles, show very clearly how pervasive are such phenomena. In the scramble to realize extra gains during the period of euphoria, excess funds flow in, thereby feeding the bubble. After the collapse, funds drain away and the country or region is starved of finance and goes into a slump. Wade and Veneroso (1998a, 1998b) argue that few economies could have withstood a reversal of capital flows on the scale that actually took place in the afflicted East Asian economies. The volatility of the capital markets exacerbated the problems that undoubtedly existed, and made eventual recovery much more difficult and prolonged.

---

[12] The hedge fund LTCM discovered, the costly way, that models based on relatively normal operation break down when pushed into non-linear regions of operation (see section 8.1).

# 9.    East Asia and development policy

The central issue raised in this book is the question of how the development experience of the four East Asian economies can be translated into guidelines for development policy. The prescription deriving from the neoclassical model is that investments in human and physical capital are good for growth. The model is silent about the how physical and human capital accumulation relate to each other and to technological change. The neoclassical model is a simple, open-ended, input-output system in which the real driver of growth – technological advance – is treated as an exogenous determinant. The failure of the old neoclassical model has induced leading mainstream theorists such as Romer and Lucas to look for alternatives in which growth is endogenized. Such models are better, but do not take into account the multi-level and complex learning processes observed in developing and assimilating technology, in either developed or developing countries (Nelson 1998).

The neoclassical approach of analysing economic performance in terms of total factor productivity advance has been examined in detail in Chapters 2 and 3. The conclusion is that TFP analysis is useful as an engineering rule of thumb for comparing the economic efficiencies of similar economies over comparable periods. The idea that it is a measure of technological change has been fairly well laid to rest by studies carried out over the last decade or so. In section 3.5 it was shown that, even when starting from the assumptions of the neoclassical model, the greater part of measured accumulation is actually 'induced' by technological change and misattributed to the former.

The current state of understanding is that high growth is almost always associated with high accumulation,[1] as it must be in any theory of growth. High savings and investment, and superior accumulation of human and social capital, are found to be induced consequences of high growth, as even recent econometric analyses seem to indicate (see Easterly and Levine 2000 and Temple 1999 for detailed surveys). These new findings generate problems for policy analysts used to working with 'open-loop' models of causation, since the various growth-inducing accumulations now appear as 'cause' and

---

[1]Anomalous cases such as Hong Kong have peculiarities that point to other reasonable explanations for high growth with moderate levels of investment (see Chapter 3).

'consequence' on both sides of the black box. These can, however, be handled by closed-loop dynamic models which involve feedback from output to input, giving rise to the famous 'virtuous circles' and 'vicious circles' of the classical economists.[2]

Economic theorists such as Nelson (1998) and Stiglitz (1996, 1998a) have risen to the challenge with more complex models of real-world economic processes, which deal with feedback, path-dependence, externalities and other departures from the highly restrictive neoclassical framework. Stiglitz in particular starts from well-known departures from the implicit assumptions supporting the standard Arrow-Debreu framework about information and technology. His work, over several decades with many collaborators, has established that imperfect information and incomplete markets give rise to market failures that can be addressed under certain conditions by government intervention (Stiglitz 1996, p. 156). On the basis of this theoretical work Stiglitz and others have built up an impressive theory of the economics of the public sector, of the indispensable role that public goods production plays in sustaining the social and economic vitality of modern industrial societies (Stiglitz 2000). Not least, is the crucial role that public investment plays in sustaining the processes of industrial innovation, in even the USA.

The mainstream of the economics profession has not yet bought into the more complex conceptions of the innovative theorists, who offer dynamic, evolutionary models. This is partly because there is as yet no compelling alternative to neoclassical models.[3] Economic theory and, at its heart the theory of economic growth, still appears to await an evolutionary synthesis. In the wider economically literate public, increasing awareness of the great importance of economic matters appears to have led to a fundamentalist regression in Britain and the USA over the last two decades. Here 'free markets' unshackled from state interference, reduced tax rates and hoary prescriptions like the gold standard are often touted as panaceas for major problems, by gurus and politicians who should know better. However, market fundamentalism may even be a step forward if it is seen as the initial reaction to the recognition of the complexity of real economic processes.[4]

---

[2]Feedback processes are discussed in the appendix to Chapter 8. Dynamic models involving feedback, path-dependence, hysteresis and other complex dynamics have been developed in electrical engineering and used in a range of practical devices. Recently they have been pressed into use in explaining economic phenomena (Arthur 1994). Shiller (2000) provides a scholarly, but accessible, introduction to the role of positive feedback in financial markets.
[3]Stiglitz (1996, p. 151), in generalizing the lessons of the East Asian miracle, says he offers only a list of ingredients rather than a formula or recipe, indicating that loose ends remain.
[4]Perhaps all fundamentalism, from East to West, is the first intellectual response to sudden, unprepared exposure to real world complexity. If so, it is the first stage of rising awareness.

This book has attempted to pull together insights deriving from various studies of growth phenomena in a heterodox, evolutionary tradition. This alternative approach has been developed mainly in Chapters 6 and 7, building on the work of Nelson, Amsden, Hobday, Lall and a number of other well-known analysts of technological change and economic growth. Their ideas are rich in the ability to provide a comprehensive description of growth and technological capability acquisition. The essence of that synthesis is drawn out here and examined with regard to its implications for economic theory and development policy. Its drawback is that the analysis is couched in terms of a verbal appreciative theory (section 1.4) of evolutionary change. This 'weakness' is shared with all attempts to build formal models of evolutionary economic processes; the task is still very much a 'work-in-progress.'

The argument developed here is that it is necessary to analyse technological advance in terms of the broader concept of technological capability, covering both physical and non-physical accumulations, which determine overall productivity and the nation's capacity to innovate. The primary task of development is to raise national technological capability (NTC), or more strictly its non-physical component which is often called 'social capability,' to higher levels within the global economic context, so as to generate greater economic output. The clear experiential backdrop to the synthesis developed here is the set of similar, but distinct, strategies of development pursued by the East Asian nations of Singapore, Hong Kong, Taiwan and South Korea.

The above conception is largely consistent with the alternative, more prescription oriented, approach to promoting rapid growth developed by Porter (1990), which has been summarized in section 7.5. By contrast, the emphasis in this book is on drawing out the general lessons for the promotion of rapid growth within the context of the evolution of economic theory. The main idea common to both approaches is that public policy intervention is vital to the realization of high, sustained growth, going well beyond the limited role assigned for the state in orthodox development policy.

The problem is that non-physical accumulations must be built up through long and costly learning processes along well-chosen technological trajectories as argued in Chapter 7. Because these processes are path-dependent, early choices can lock a country into a dynamically inferior path of capability building.[5] In particular, excessive dependence on low wage unskilled labour, natural resource endowments or inherited low-technology industries can

---

[5]Indonesia seems a prime example of this: on the one hand its businesses have concentrated excessively on primary resource-based products; on the other, it has embarked on the production of aircraft before building up an adequate technological infrastructure from which to launch this exacting enterprise.

block or retard entry into higher-productivity activities conducive to superior growth. Hence strategies built exclusively on the exploitation of neoclassical comparative advantage can be seriously detrimental in the long run. A more activist conception of growth is called for. This chapter attempts to develop an integrated account of the alternative approach implicit in the various analyses laid out in previous chapters. It then goes on to examine the feasibility of public (industrial) policy intervention to promote growth along East Asian lines in other developing countries.

## 9.1    THE THEORETICAL CHALLENGE

The social capability or national technological capability (NTC) model is able to deal with the usual neoclassical sources of growth, and also the evolution of technology, institutions and organizations. It is also able to take account of the commonly encountered departures from ideal market conditions. This feature is important since economic growth is often characterized by messy disequilibrium processes with multiple equilibria and path- dependence, even in advanced industrial economies. In developing countries, market failures are pervasive and positive feedback processes give rise to 'poverty traps' or, occasionally as in East Asia, to above-average growth. As already established by mainstream theory, equilibria depend on expectations, which are not always rational but conditioned by institutions. Though some progress has been made, mainstream theory in general is not able to provide models to handle many of these real-world economic phenomena.[6]

Not only is growth characterized by disequilibrium, it is also evolutionary and must be apprehended in the context of time and space: i.e., it must be analysed as historical processes, characterized by discreet stages of expansion and particular patterns of spatial coherence and propagation. Not least,

---

[6]Criticisms of orthodox theory are made by Stiglitz (1995, 1996), Nelson (1998) and more mildly by many other leading economists, including Brad De Long (1996), Paul Krugman (1992) and Kenneth Arrow (1995). Dornbusch (1990) excoriates the IMF model of structural adjustment, where the important questions at issue are solved by assumptions, which manifestly do not hold in practice. While such subversive ideas have often been heard at the periphery of empire, the present period is characterized by dissentient voices raised within Rome itself. Krugman, in particular, speculates that economic theory was driven by an endogenous logic along the path of least mathematical resistance. He argues that formal theory is now acquiring sophistication and flexibility to handle the difficult issues of real-world economics which were raised in *ad hoc* fashion by early development theorists and then abandoned in the drive for rigour. However, fundamental issues of theory have been raised even before, for example in the 'Cambridge Controversies.' But these have not had a significant effect on the evolution of mainstream theory, up to the present time.

growth must be seen in the context of conflict and cooperation between technology leaders and followers striving to catch up (Chapters 1 and 2).[7] An evolutionary theory of economic growth has been proposed by Nelson and Winter (1982), but evolutionary thinking goes back further (Hodgson 1993).

Within the last two decades, there has also been a revival of interest in the role of invention, innovation and technical change in the growth processes of advanced industrial nations as well as NIEs.[8] Mainstream theory itself has developed according to a certain 'endogenous' logic, through endogenous or new growth theory, the new institutional economics, industrial organization theory and game theory including evolutionary game theory. While growth theory and game theory have come up with new models and equilibrium concepts, there does not appear to be any convergence of theory between the mainstream and evolutionary schools.

In fact, it is not clear that there is even any meaningful dialogue between the various schools, engrossed as they are in a Balkanized system of academic discourse. Perhaps this will happen only when evolutionary economists come up with better, more explicit, formal models which can speak across the theoretical divide to engage the attention of neoclassicists.[9]

The theoretical challenge is to develop a comprehensive model of how technological capability is built up and systematically upgraded. In the first instance, capability can be analysed into two main components: the first is application-specific knowledge embodied in machines, physical structures and physical infrastructure, the hardware of NTC; the second is the software component, consisting of human and social capital accumulations. From the beginning of the industrial revolution, human societies have been producing better and more complex machines on an ever-rising scale of technical sophistication. Machines had been in use before, extending far back in history to the primitive tools of neolithic times.

The words 'knowledge' and 'technology' are used in so many different senses that it is necessary to narrow down the exact meaning by attaching qualifying adjectives. Here, these words are used in the senses specified by Rosenberg (1982, p. 143). 'Knowledge' is a broad category that includes scientific knowledge about physical and natural phenomena, and even experiential insights acquired through non-scientific processes. 'Technology' is a narrower body of knowledge about techniques, methods and designs

---

[7]The prime contemporary example is the awkward relationship between China and the USA.
[8]Dosi et al. (1988), Mowery and Rosenberg (1989), Lundvall (1992), Nelson (1993).
[9]This point is disputed by Nelson in a letter to the author commenting on this book. He does not believe that the problem has anything to do with communication through mathematical models. "There are lots of mathematical evolutionary models; I have built a number myself. The problem is the content of the message, rather than the media" (February 27, 2001).

associated with practical activity, i.e. economic and military activity, but mostly economic activity. Rosenberg goes on to say that '[t]echnological knowledge was long acquired in crude empirical ways, with no reliance upon science ... Even today much productive activity is conducted without a deep scientific knowledge of why things perform the way they do.'

Industrial capitalism brings with it a new and ceaseless dynamic: companies strive for competitive advantage over each other and thereby stimulate the invention of new productivity-enhancing machines. The accumulation of physical capital embodied in machine technologies is the manifest source of the explosive growth of labour productivity compared to previous historical standards, up to the information technology age.

But the development of technology has dimensions far transcending the production of machines. As narrowly conceived, technology consists of knowledge, derived from applied science and the experience of production itself, techniques, procedures and blueprints for producing a wide range of services, consumer goods, machines, structures and so on. The quickening pace of technological change has pulled along with it the development of science, first the physical sciences and now increasingly the biological sciences.[10] So, associated with the expansion of technological knowledge is an ever-widening penumbra of insights and investigative techniques about materials, physical processes and the world of living things.

Neoclassical theory had produced a partial answer to the problem of growth. Growth was seen as resulting from the somewhat flexible interfusing of physical capital services and labour. The efficiency of the production process was assumed to be determined by disembodied technological knowledge which was conceived to exist apart from and independent of capital and labour. The production function of neoclassical theory exists in abstract space making no reference to the specific organizational context or milieu of social institutions. While the ensuing models are austerely elegant as in physics, the question has to be raised whether physics is really the best model for economic analysis, rather than say biology, as did Marshall.

Of course many efforts have been made to correct these weaknesses. Technical change has been decomposed, attributed to capital improvement, skill development, education, health, the development of scientific knowledge and so on, especially in the growth accounting literature. There is also the theory of the efficiency of institutions and the transaction costs approach. These undoubtedly represent important developments in broadening the scope of economic explanation (see section 7.4).

---

[10]For an analysis of the relationship between science and technology from an economic perspective see Nelson (1993) and Rosenberg (1982).

Then there is the important economic role of entrepreneurship. Since Schumpeter's (1936, 1942) path-breaking work there has been extraordinarily little work on this important area (Baumol 1993). Some attempts have indeed been made to incorporate Schumpeterian dynamics into some of the new growth models (Grossman and Helpman 1991b), but these hardly amount to a comprehensive theory of entrepreneurship.

This study proposes an integrated approach to the phenomenon of long-term growth. Economic growth must be seen as a human, and particularly a social, activity. People produce in work teams, within organizations and in societies. Further, economic activities are regulated by institutions and take place within an integrated world economy, the various elements of which are in interaction through myriad markets. Firms and formal institutions are invented to support and regulate economic activity. Informal institutions come into being when expectations coalesce and stabilize around the most common economic transactions. Finally, entrepreneurship supplies the *élan vital* in this evolving system, creating new variations and departures, much like mutations in the biological world.

Looked at from this perspective, productive capability takes on a new meaning and a new life. It is not merely an agglomeration of factories and markets whose operation can be captured by general formulae linking output to capital and labour, materials and technology. Production, and even consumption, are profoundly social activities and hence, productive capability must depend on variables that reflect the level of development of social institutions, skill levels, technological capability, degree of specialization and economic organization, the level of 'entrepreneurial temperature' and so on. All these must supplement the standard inputs to the production function.

## 9.2  COMPONENTS OF TECHNOLOGICAL CAPABILITY[11]

To be economically useful technological knowledge has to reside in the skill of human agents or durable physical devices or structures that are used in production or design. At the simplest level, these are referred to as human capital and physical capital (machines), both of which contribute to raising the productivity of labour. However, labour and capital operate within business organizations regulated by particular codes of operation, and

---

[11]This section and parts of section 9.1 are adapted from ideas developed in Rodrigo (2000). These conceptions have some features in common with modern Austrian capital theory as developed in Lewin (1999) and Baetjer (1998), though no direct line of descent is claimed. Baetjer presents an elegant and stimulating analysis of the role of software development which fits in closely with the conception of technology evolution developed in this chapter.

themselves imbued with skills and capabilities that transcend the aggregate skills of employees. Furthermore, business organizations in turn operate within the institutional system of the nation which modulate operational efficiency and capability to develop technology through innovation.

Therefore it becomes necessary to analyse nations in terms of the broader concept national technological capability (NTC) which determine overall productivity and the capacity to innovate. NTC is analysed below into six components, of which only physical capital and infrastructure (defined immediately below) can be acquired relatively easily. The non-physical accumulations, also called social capability, must be built up through long and costly learning processes along well-chosen technological trajectories (Lall 2000). A major objective of the analysis is to establish the largely complementary relationship between the different components and the need to maintain some rough dynamic balance between the different components.

**Physical Capital and Infrastructure**

This is the most tangible form of capital. A piece of capital equipment is a material device designed to perform a particular set of operations with some amount of human intervention. It contributes to the more efficient production of some good or service and may use up energy and other material inputs. It may also be operated by itself or in conjunction with other equipment, as on a farm, factory or high-tech production line. The essential characteristics that make it capital rather than simply a physical input are the following:

a)  physical capital enhances the productivity of labour;
b)  it is used over a relatively long time span, over many production cycles;
c)  the logic of operation is hard-coded into the physical design.

Overall, physical capital consists of technology embodied in machines, devices, automatic control systems, software, physical structures[12] and physical infrastructure such as transportation and communication systems. All this can be seen as economically useful knowledge hard-coded into durable physical constructs or 'soft-coded' in automatic control systems and software. Both types consist of application-specific knowledge, accumulated through various research and development processes and embodied in long-lasting devices or routines that deliver the benefits of higher productivity without users having to develop the embodied knowledge from scratch.

---

[12]Gort et al. (1999) show that progress in technology embodied in physical structures is a significant contributor to overall technological progress.

Note that in this conception computer software is included along with physical capital as 'embodied knowledge.' Software, control systems and machines are ways of disseminating 'application-specific knowledge' to a multiplicity of users in prepackaged form. It is important to realize that embodied (knowledge) capital can be a substitute for human (knowledge) capital, at relatively low and medium levels of economic development. At high levels of economic development, it is more often complementary to the advance of human capital. In skill-intensive activities such as design, capital embodied in machines is secondary to human ingenuity and resourcefulness. This is the capital-skill complementarity hypothesis (Greenwood 1999, p. 6).

The discussion of physical capital, and its identification as an important carrier of technology, is not complete without a consideration of physical infrastructure. Physical capital consists of physical infrastructure and machines, equipment and structures in production plants and service providing organizations. Together, these can be considered as the 'hardware' of economic growth (Nelson and Romer, 1996). Such capital is appropriately identified as hardware because, once in place, the technology implicit in the machines and other fixed structures rigidly determines particular patterns of activity, which cannot be reconfigured without physically replacing the machines or structures.

It is important to note that the general pattern of technological change in the industrial world has been heavily biased in favour of rigid, hard-coded patterns of production and consumption. Prior to the information age technology was more easily diffused hard-coded in machines and production systems than soft-coded as organizational and management forms. People accept machines and other artifacts more readily than cultural patterns, as evidenced by Britain's early resistance to US management practice while accepting imports of capital and consumer goods. Technological change takes place nonetheless because competition drives the incessant search for advantage. Additionally, technological change has been driven in this century by two world wars, the cold war and major economic crises.

## Human Capital

Human capital is defined as the economically relevant skills and capabilities or the broad-sense 'knowledge' resident in the workforce. This amorphous combination of attributes is a function of economically significant education and competence acquired through work experience; education is mostly an enabling condition for skill acquisition. Economically valuable human capital changes – or depreciates – along with technological change; thus skills developed in the automobile age may lose their value in the information age which generates demand for a very different kind of human capital.

Human capital is the most crucial resource of all: most nations cannot import it or 'buy' it; it must be carefully built up in schools, universities and technical colleges, factories, trading floors, retail outlets, design shops, research establishments and other production, design and marketing arenas (see Lucas's comments on human capital in section 7.2). The primary task of development is to raise human capital to 'higher' levels within the global economic context, so it generates greater incomes for human beings. Liberalized markets and dynamic business organizations are vehicles for achieving the above primary objective and not end objectives in themselves, as pointed out by Stiglitz (1996, 1998a).

The role of human capital as a carrier of technology *complementary* to that embodied in physical capital is now widely accepted. If the essence of economically significant human capital is mastery of technology, then the latter is mainly a learned skill: considerable effort is needed to successfully internalize a capability for a particular technology; a firm needs to have developed skills and knowledge up to one or two steps below that of the target technology for it to be successfully undertaken, even if the capital equipment that provides the vehicle for this learning is imported (Chapter 7).

The crucial point is that in learning to operate particular machines at internationally competitive levels of productivity, workers and firms are compelled to raise themselves to commensurate levels of technological mastery. That is how human capital is built up. Physical capital induces the acquisition of human capital, but not automatically or mechanically or to the same extent everywhere. The above point is a consequence of the key role of learning under competitive pressure, or step-wise upgrading of skills and knowledge in building technological capability. Obviously the more complex the technology the more time, effort and investment needed to indigenize the technology (section 6.3). There also has to be a certain logic of progression determined by carry-over linkages from one technology to a higher one.

## Level of Managerial and Business Efficiency

Business organizations are particular structures for accumulating procedures and techniques which contribute significantly to the productivity and capability of nations. Modern business organizations possess a capacity to preserve, enhance and develop economically useful knowledge that transcend the capacity of individuals or even small groups of skilled people, as defined above. That is the principal reason why this organizational form has developed so strongly over the last hundred years, to establish its present dominance in the economic landscape. No statist or ideological bureaucracy, operating outside the competitive environment of the market, has been able to match the capacity of the business firm in this respect. For want of a better word, such accumulations of organizationally structured knowledge are labelled 'organizational capital,' which along with human capital contributes to the productive capacity of society.

Organizational and business efficiency has developed rapidly over the last one hundred years, its study becoming a formalized discipline in the USA in the early part of the 20th century. Its advance is promoted indirectly by business competition and directly by business school programmes and management consultants. It could be lumped together with human capital to which it is closely related, but that would obscure the value of formalized organizational structures. The level of organization and management is, in a broad sense, a part of the technology of production and identified as a part of the 'software' of economic growth.

## The Quality (Business-friendliness) of Economic Institutions

All societies operate in a matrix of formal and informal institutions which promote or hinder overall efficiency or capability. Formal institutions like banks, stock markets, political systems of governance, schools and universities clearly contribute to national capability. The enormously important role of informal institutions is often not so well understood, because these involve tacit business practices, unwritten rules of interaction patterns, especially relating to business transactions, and so on. Like human capital, institutions cannot be imported or transplanted from one culture to another, but built up with great care and patience, except for small city states.

Outmoded institutions can constitute a serious obstacle to rapid economic development. In fact the task of ridding a nation of its existing dysfunctional institutions is even harder than building up socially productive substitutes. It sometimes takes major social disruptions, such as wars and revolutions, to achieve this necessary objective. It may possibly be the most difficult task of development in any culture. Formal and informal institutions bear a very similar relationship to human and organizational capital as physical infrastructure does to machines and equipment. Together with the quality of organizations and management, institutions can be grouped into a category of 'social infrastructural capital' or even 'social capital'.[13]

---

[13]The above division into 'private' and 'public' components provide formal symmetry with direct physical capital (machinery and equipment) and physical infrastructural capital. However the term 'social capital' is preferred because it is already in currency (Knack and Keefer 1997, Temple and Johnson, 1998). In much of the earlier literature these effects have been ascribed to externalities and scale effects. Clearly the aggregate of human capital and social infrastructural capital of a country is what determines its social capability or NTC.

### The Quality of Institutions that Produce or Mediate Generic Knowledge

The effectiveness of bodies that generate or mediate the acquisition of technological knowledge that is not immediately useful to firms also contribute to national capability. These cover research institutes, technology promoting consortia and technology department of universities. They could have been included with the general category of institutions, but are listed separately on account of their special role. While such institutions have been and are enormously important in advanced industrial countries, such as the USA, their role in developing countries is more limited (Hobday 1995).

### Entrepreneurial Energy or Temperature

Entrepreneurship is the 'business-oriented creativity' that transforms new ideas, inventions and procedures into economic progress. It is the *élan vital* of capitalism. While pre-modern societies could survive for long periods without significant entrepreneurship, no modern country, developed or developing, can prosper for long without promoting and practising private and public entrepreneurship. That is because we live in an interconnected world in which new challenges – problems and opportunities – arise unpredictably with increasing rapidity, and spill across national borders. Much higher levels of innovative energy are needed to survive in this climate.

The evolution of capitalist markets, over the last two hundred years, have secularly – if unevenly – raised the 'entrepreneurial temperature' in most market-oriented societies, not only in business, but in most areas of human activity, ranging from the altruistic and socially desirable to internationally organized crime and piracy. The fire of entrepreneurship exists in all societies to a greater or lesser extent. Successful societies manage to channel this creative energy into socially productive activity. Otherwise the energy expresses itself in violence, crime and socially disruptive activity. Productive entrepreneurship, i.e. the realization of its creative energy, is greatly assisted by well-developed venture capital markets, such as exist in the USA.

## 9.3    IMPLICATIONS FOR ECONOMIC GROWTH

The above analysis suggests that industrial success depends critically on building up technological capability along the six components listed above. But these accumulations involve arduous learning processes which are fast only when demand for output is strong, sustained and intense competitive conditions induce the maximum deployment of human effort at all levels of the firm. Hence a strong feedback loop exists between high growth and high capability accumulation. An alternative equilibrium trajectory would be low growth accompanied by low capability accumulation. The challenge for the government is to create conditions and generate momentum towards the high growth path. Access to export markets, cost and quality competitiveness ensures sustained demand, at least for manufactures. It is intense competition, rather than merely trade liberalization, that ensures superior performance and raises the level of entrepreneurial energy which is the source of longer-term technological upgrading, the movement to higher value-added technologies.

But, as argued above, the separate components are likely to be highly complementary. Hence they must be built-up together in rough balance, which is not guaranteed or even likely as evident from the growth experience of most developing countries over the last half century or so. This is like a coordination problem with regard to complementary investments which are jointly necessary to bring about a desired outcome. Intervention by the public authority is necessary to correct for inadequate development of various components of this system of capabilities. This is a restatement of the point that government intervention is necessary to correct market failure, in the context of balanced capability building.

Two other major roadblocks stand in the way of sustained technological advance which is needed to keep a country on a high growth path. One is the high degree of uncertainty associated with rapid technological change. The other is the public goods nature of crucial aspects of the structure of technological capability, which prevent private firms from recouping most of the gains from their investments. Again, state intervention is needed to address market failures associated with these two problems (see section 9.4), if the tempo of capability-building is to be maintained at a high level. The best examples of such intervention are arguably the USA throughout the 20th century (Mowery and Rosenberg 1998) and South Korea, Taiwan and Singapore in the period after 1960 (Hobday 1995).

The success of East Asia and the relative lethargy of other developing countries show that the pace of accumulation of human and social capital depends on many factors, including the nature of domestic competition and the openness to international competitive pressures and technology flows. Formal education and physical infrastructure are the easiest to build directly. Formal education is only a necessary condition for the advance of skill and efficiency deriving from better organization and management and institutional modernization, i.e. business-friendly changes in the social infrastructure. It is economically significant skill development, rather than the level of formal education, which is the key determinant of effective human capital, even though the two terms are commonly used synonymously.

Skill development and institutional reform, which raise human and social capital, respectively, can be accelerated in two major ways. The first is intensification of competition in product and technology markets, particularly through trade liberalization. That is why the discipline of exporting is seen as crucial to East Asian-style success. The evidence is now very strong that technical efficiency advance and technology development are accelerated by sharpened competition. The second way is the acquisition within the firm of advanced technology embodied in new equipment (usually imported from abroad for many developing countries). Clearly these processes are interrelated, since technology upgrading is accelerated by more competitive environments (World Bank, 1993, Temple, 1999).

## 9.4     THE ROLE OF PUBLIC POLICY IN THE BUILDING OF TECHNOLOGICAL CAPABILITY

The discussion in this section takes off from the analysis of development policy laid out in section 5.3. The crucial question posed is the form of public policy intervention that would build up technological capability fast, so as to generate rates of growth seen in East Asia. The Washington consensus holds that such intervention should be exclusively functional, i.e. targeting generic market failures, such as inadequate investment in education and physical infrastructure. Selective interventions, which involve the selective promotion of particular industrial activities through trade policy or credit subsidies, are deemed to do more harm than good. The argument advanced is that from the experience of the past, the expected cost of any market failures is less than the expected cost of government failure incurred in selective interventions (section 5.3). This argument is examined in terms of the framework developed above.

Following Lall (2000), the dynamics of capability building can be organized under the three broad categories of incentives, factor markets and institutions (in a narrower sense than described in section 7.3). Incentives encompass economic pressures emanating from the macroeconomic environment which induce firms to perform better, as discussed in section 9.3. These are, the competition facing industrial firms, the ease of entry and exit, the nature of the trade regime and industrial policy, domestic competition and state policies towards or against the private sector and the growth of large firms. These have been discussed to some extent in Chapters 4 and 5. The value of relatively stable macroeconomic conditions, fostering competition and the private sector and the promotion of exports, are now accepted almost universally and needs no elaboration.

There is also not much dispute about the value of building up institutions that support the acquisition of technology by firms. These are part of the third component of NTC, the institutions that directly support the building of industrial technology, through education, training, R&D, the determination of standards, technical extension and export support. Adequate information about global product markets and technologies are particularly important to reduce uncertainty and costs associated with rapid technological change (section 7.3). Governments in East Asia and other countries have intervened to build up technological savvy through science-parks, university-based research and governmental research facilities (Lall 1996). Furthermore such intervention has been quite extensive in the USA and other industrial countries as well (Mowery and Rosenberg 1989, Nelson 1993).

Factor market issues relate mainly to the building-up of human capital, technical, scientific and managerial skills and the functioning of capital and information markets. The externalities associated with factor development call for substantial public investment. The conclusion here is that selective intervention, to promote the accumulation of firm and industry capability, was crucial to the success of South Korea and Taiwan. Through industrial targeting, Singapore followed a similar strategy by drawing in a host of MNCs. However, this is not a strategy that is available to large countries, or even to small ones that wish to incubate domestic firms.

The other component, capital markets, are typically weak in developing countries. Market failure arises from imperfect or asymmetric markets where investors and banks, especially those located overseas, have inadequate information about the state of industrial companies. This leads to adverse selection and inadequate financing of long gestation projects involving relatively risky technological investments, those that lead to faster NTC growth. These are typically addressed by state-directed, subsidized, credit to selected firms or industries, often through special development banks.[14] The problems of financial markets in East Asia and how they have been addressed are discussed in some detail by Stiglitz and Uy (1996).

Information failures relate most directly to financial market transactions, as discussed in particular in Chapter 8 and Stiglitz (1998b, 1998c). They also constitute a serious obstacle to the acquisition of technological knowledge by developing country firms, and has been addressed in section 7.1 as well. Business alliances with foreign companies is one way in which these inadequacies have been dealt with by EA-NIE firms. The most direct way of addressing this is through the encouragement of FDI, as in Singapore and

[14]The role of the chaebol conglomerates in South Korea in internalizing financial market transactions is discussed in section 7.1. But this practice needs to change now (section 8.2).

Hong Kong. Where business alliances with foreign firms are not possible or desirable, substitute institutions need to be set up; this is an area in which international agencies could easily help address market failure.

The progress of technology is of course an evolutionary process, which means that it is *rife with uncertainty*, especially at the beginning of an techno-economic paradigm. Even firms that operate on the leading edge of technological change are liable to make disastrous mistakes as evidenced from a casual reading of business journals. There is in fact no evidence that firms are less likely to make mistakes about investing in promising technologies than are governments in formulating industrial policy (Stiglitz 1989, 2000). This is how the system works: while it is unfortunate for the firms that make mistaken forecasts, a market-oriented approach where many alternatives are simultaneously tested out is superior from a systemic, evolutionary point of view. It leads to faster development of technological capacity in the long run. Bureaucrats with a central-planning mind-set may see this as a waste of resources, but experience over the last half century has established the superiority of competitive selection in developing countries.

This seems to be the way that markets operate even in advanced countries with well-formed business institutions. The magic of the market derives from the fact that the success of the few is selected out of the failure of many. It is in fact quite remarkable how frequently the largest firms seem to make bad decisions. The bottom line is that 'resource misallocation' takes place when the private sector makes mistakes as well, except that then it is a matter for the shareholders and the capital markets; it ceases to count as a public policy issue. In advanced countries with well-established exit procedures for failing firms, the overall social costs may not be high. Developing countries with weak institutions and messy bankruptcy rules are likely to find that the social costs are proportionately higher.

An important feature of industrial policy in South Korea, Taiwan and Singapore could well be the reduction of technological uncertainty for private investment, both domestic and foreign. Stiglitz (1996) has also stressed the important 'signalling' effect of state subsidies, even if their quantitative value is not significant. At first glance, it might seem that industrial policy formulation and implementation should be much simpler in developing countries, since the objective is to chart a technological trajectory of catch-up along pathways already explored and mapped out. Lall (2000) points out that information needs in developing nations are less than in advanced countries.

The evolution of technology at the frontier, in advanced countries, should be subject to much more uncertainty, since they are moving into unknown territory. However, as argued in the previous paragraph, the social costs of failure in developing countries are likely to be much higher. Also, unlike in the USA, these countries face the daunting task of building up broad-sense technological capability. It becomes imperative to steer a relatively smooth trajectory of technological evolution to maintain the political legitimacy of the system, while building up overall capability.

It appears that industrial policy worked relatively smoothly in Taiwan and Singapore, and somewhat more untidily in South Korea (Hobday 1995, Stiglitz 1996). Other developing countries have not been able to use industrial policy effectively. The reasons for this have been exhaustively researched and extensively written up by leading authorities on the subject (Lall 1996, Kim and Nelson 2000). Lall shows that industrial policy in these countries targeted the usual market failures. Technology markets in developing countries are particularly prone to market failure. However, aspirant firms in East Asia were also compelled to perform in export markets, i.e. they had to survive against internationally competitive producers. Industrial policy failed in India, and other countries that followed purely ISI strategies, because firms were provided competition-free access to captive domestic markets, with no incentive to accelerate technological learning.

Industrial policy has often been caricatured as the attempt to 'pick winners.' This argument assumes that winners exist ex ante and only need to be discovered. Lall states that the expression 'creating winners' is more appropriate. It follows that simply opening up markets will not work, because underlying market failures will remain. Government intervention is necessary, but it must be carefully crafted to build technological capability by forcing companies to develop their own capability as fast as possible, especially by emulating international best practice. The same point is made by Stiglitz (1996). Research on East Asia is important precisely because it helps us to differentiate between interventions that build market forces and those that lock private companies into cosseted inefficiency.

Industrial learning processes in developing countries, especially the least developed ones in sub-Saharan Africa, face much greater costs, risk, supply side deficiencies and much weaker institutions than those in more industrialized countries. These problems call for public intervention. But the intervention has to be crafted very differently from past ISI strategies where learning was completely neglected. The logical conclusion is that the first step in industrial policy has to be the building-up of government capabilities, information, skills, management systems, autonomy and so on. If this is not possible, then free market responses may be more efficient than government intervention. The downside here is that industrial dynamism will probably not extend beyond exploiting resource-based advantages and low-cost unskilled labour, as is characteristic of the poorest countries today.[15]

---

[15]This paragraph is culled out of remarks made by Sanjaya Lall in a letter e-mailed to the author in October 2000.

In the context of the argument advanced here about the signalling role of public intervention, one important difference between the successful strategies and the less successful ones can be identified. Industrial policy in Taiwan, Korea and Singapore closely tracked and indeed locked onto the market processes in the advanced industrial world. Countries like India and Brazil attempted to develop relatively autonomous industrial systems, asynchronously decoupled from the evolution of technological paths in advanced markets.

In a highly integrated world, the policy of autonomous development, modelled on the early development patterns of the first industrial nations, did not seem to enable a closing of the productivity gap. The East Asian NIEs, on the other hand, made substantial progress in closing the gap by pioneering a new model of growth. China and India now seem to have bought into the East Asian model, orienting towards 'Northern' markets and drawing in the collaboration of advanced country MNCs. Perhaps they should also devote more resources to promoting domestic R&D to encourage private firms to compete more effectively within the new integrated world order, much as German or Japanese firms do.[16] Conditions in the global market are changing and it may be difficult to replicate earlier trajectories of growth. At the same time, India and China have advantages that were not shared by the EA-NIEs.

It is risky to follow even a highly successful model too closely. Thrown into exceptional situations in the early years, each of the four East Asian NIEs worked out development strategies through processes of creative adaptation to a changing global marketplace. In doing this, they were impelled to move beyond the prevailing ISI orthodoxy adopted elsewhere. What is clear from their experience and that of the less successful nations is that history provides no universal formulae that can set development policy on autopilot. This is because the world changes continually and the specific inherited features of countries are different. There exist no simple prescriptions that substitute for creative thinking about problems and solutions.[17]

---

[16]It is well known that Indian software specialists are able to integrate effectively into international markets (*Economist*, May 5, 2001, pp. 59-62). Now the Indian pharmaceutical industry has also demonstrated a capacity for real innovation in the face of competition from the US pharmaceutical giants (*Economist*, September 30, 2000, pp. 66-9).

[17]This point applies to Porter's (1990) activist framework as well, though it is more a set of guidelines than a prescription. It seems to be more relevant to developing countries that have already carried out basic reforms and embarked on a trajectory of industrial development, such as South Korea and Taiwan in the 1970s. His book has little to say about the basic problem of breaking out of low-level equilibrium traps, which afflict many of the most poor developing countries. In fact, Korea is the only developing country considered in the book.

# Bibliography

Abramovitz, Moses (1952), 'Economics of growth', in *A Survey of Contemporary Economics*, edited by Bernard F. Haley, Homewood, IL: Richard D. Irwin, pp. 132–182.

Abramovitz, Moses (1995), 'Elements of social capability', in *Social Capability and Long-term Economic Growth*, edited by Bon Ho Koo and Dwight H. Perkins, New York, NY: St. Martin's Press, pp. 19–47.

Aghion, Philippe and Peter Howitt (1992), 'A model of growth through creative destruction', *Econometrica*, **60**: 323–351.

Aghion, Philippe and Peter Howitt (1998), *Endogenous Growth Theory*, Cambridge, MA: MIT Press.

Aigner, D.J., C.A.K. Lovell and P. Schmidt (1977), 'Formulation and estimation of stochastic frontier production function models', *Journal of Econometrics*, **6**: 21–37.

Amable, Bruno (1994), 'Endogenous growth theory, convergence and divergence', in *The Economics of Growth and Technical Change: Technologies, Nations, Agents*, edited by Gerald Silverberg and Luc Soete, Aldershot, UK: Edward Elgar, pp. 20–44.

Amsden, Alice H. (1986), 'The direction of trade – past and present – and the "learning effects" of exports to different directions', *Journal of Development Economics*, **23** (2): 249–274.

Amsden, Alice H. (1989), *Asia's Next Giant: South Korea and Late Industrialization*, New York, NY: Oxford University Press.

Amsden, Alice H. (1999), 'Taiwan's industrialization policies: two views, two types of subsidy', in *Taiwan's Development Experience: Lessons on Roles of Government and Market*, edited by Erik Thorbecke and Henry Wan Jr., Boston, MA: Kluwer Academic, pp. 95–111.

Argote, L and D. Epple (1990), 'Learning curves in manufacturing', *Science*, **247**: 920–924.

Arrow, Kenneth J. (1962), 'The economic implications of learning by doing', *Review of Economic Studies*, **29**: 155–173.

Arrow, Kenneth (1995), 'Returns to scale, information and economic growth', in *Social Capability and Long-term Economic Growth*, edited

161

by Bon Ho Koo and Dwight H. Perkins, New York, NY: St. Martin's Press, pp. 11–18.

Arthur, W. Brian (1994), *Increasing Returns and Path Dependence in the Economy*, Ann Arbor, MI: University of Michigan Press.

Baetjer, Howard Jr. (1998), *Software as Capital: an Economic Perspective on Software Engineering*, Los Alamitos, CA: IEEE Computer Society.

Balassa, Bela (1971), *The Structure of Protection in Developing Countries*, Baltimore, MD: Johns Hopkins University Press.

Balassa, Bela (1978), 'Exports and economic growth: further evidence', *Journal of Development Economics*, **5** (2): 181–189.

Balassa, Bela (1982), *Development Strategies in Semi-Industrial Economies*, New York: Oxford University Press.

Balassa, Bela (1989), 'Outward orientation', in *Handbook of Development Economics*, edited by H. Chenery and T.N. Srinivasan, Amsterdam: Elsevier Science Publishers B.V., pp. 1646–1689.

Barro, Robert J. and Xavier Sala-i-Martin (1995), *Economic Growth*, New York, NY: McGraw-Hill.

Bartelsman, Eric. J., Ricardo J. Caballero and Richard K. Lyons (1991), 'Short and long run externalities', Cambridge, MA: NBER Working Paper 3810.

Basu, Susanto and John G. Fernald (1997), 'Returns to scale in U.S. production: estimates and implications', *Journal of Political Economy*, **105** (2): 249–283.

Battat, Joseph, Isaiah Frank and Xiaofang Shen (1996), 'Suppliers to multinationals: linkage programs to strengthen local companies in developing countries', World Bank Foreign Investment Advisory Service, Occassional Paper 6, Washington DC.

Baumol, William J., Sue Anne Batey Blackman and Edward N. Wolff (1989), *Productivity and American Leadership*, Cambridge, MA: MIT Press.

Baumol, William J. (1993), *Entrepreneurship, Management and the Structure of Payoffs*, Cambridge, MA: MIT Press.

Bhagwati, Jagdish (1989), *Protectionism*, Cambridge, MA: MIT Press.

Boskin, Michael J and Lawrence J. Lau (1991), 'Capital and productivity: a new view', Department of Economics, Stanford University.

Boskin, Michael J. and Lawrence J. Lau (1992), 'Capital, technology and economic growth', in *Technology and the Wealth of Nations*, edited by Nathan Rosenberg, Ralph Landau and David C. Mowery, Stanford, CA: Stanford University Press, pp. 17–55.

Bosworth, Barry and Susan Collins (1999), 'Capital flows to developing economies: implications for saving and investment', *Brookings Papers on Economic Activity*, **I**: 143–169.

Bradford, Colin I. (1994), 'From trade-driven growth to growth-driven trade: reappraising the East Asian development experience', Paris: OECD Development Centre Document.

Braudel, Fernand (1984), *The Perspective of the World, Volume 3: Civilization & Capitalism 15th–18th Century*, New York, NY: Harper & Row Publishers.

Burki, Shahid Javed and Guillermo E. Perry (1998), *Beyond the Washington Consensus: Institutions Matter*, Washington, DC: World Bank.

Burnside, Craig, Martin Eichenbaum and Sergio Rebelo (1995), 'Capital utilization and returns to scale', in *NBER Macroeconomics Annual 1995, Vol. 10*, edited by Ben S. Bernanke and Julio J. Rotemberg, Cambridge, MA: MIT Press, pp. 67–110.

Caballero, Ricardo J. and Richard K. Lyons (1990), 'Internal versus external economies in European industry', *European Economic Review*, **34**: 805–830.

Campos, Jose Edgardo and Hilton L. Root (1996), *The Key to the Asian Miracle: Making Shared Growth Credible*, Washington, DC: Brookings Institution.

Caprio, Gerard and Patrick Honohan (1999), 'Restoring banking stability: beyond supervised capital requirements', *Journal of Economic Perspectives*, **13** (4): 43–64.

Carlsson, Bo (ed.) (1997), *Technological Systems and Industrial Dynamics*, Boston, MA: Kluwer Academic.

Caves, Richard E. (ed.) (1992), *Industrial Efficiency in Six Nations*, Cambridge, MA: MIT Press.

Caves, Richard E. (1998), 'Industrial organization and new findings on the turnover and mobility of firms', *Journal of Economic Literature*, **36** (4): 1947–1982.

Caves, Richard and David Barton (1990), *Efficiency in US Manufacturing Industries*, Cambridge, MA: MIT Press.

Chakravarty, Sukhamoy (1987), 'Marxist economics and contemporary developing economies', *Cambridge Journal of Economics*, **11** (1): 3–22.

Chen, Edward K.Y., Mee-Kau Nyaw and Teresa Y.C. Wong (eds) (1991), *Industrial and Trade Development in Hong Kong*, Hong Kong: University of Hong Kong.

Chen, Edward K.Y. (1997), 'The total factor productivity debate: determinants of economic growth in East Asia', *Asian-Pacific Economic Literature*, **11** (1): 18–38.

Chenery, Hollis, Sherman Robinson and Moshe Syrquin (eds) (1986),

*Industrialization and Growth: a Comparative Study*, New York, NY: World Bank/Oxford University Press.

Clark, Gregory (1987), 'Why isn't the whole world developed? Lessons from the cotton mills', *Journal of Economic History*, **47** (1): 141–173.

Cline, William R. (1995), 'Managing international debt: how one big battle was won', *Economist*, February 18: 17–19.

Coelli, Tim, D.S. Prasada Rao and George E. Battese (1999), *An Introduction to Efficiency and Productivity Analysis*, Norwell, MA: Kluwer Academic.

Collins, Susan M. and Barry P. Bosworth (1996), ' Economic growth in East Asia: accumulation versus assimilation', *Brookings Papers on Economic Activity*, **2**: 135–203.

Corsetti, Giancarlo, Paolo Pesenti and Nouriel Roubini (1999), 'What caused the Asian currency and financial crisis?' *Japan and the World Economy*, **11** (3): 305–373.

Costello, Donna M. (1993), 'A cross-country, cross-industry comparison of productivity growth', *Journal of Political Economy*, **101** (2): 207–222.

Dahlman, Carl and Richard Nelson (1995), 'Social absorption capability, national innovation systems and economic development', in *Social Capability and Long-term Economic Growth*, edited by Bon Ho Koo and Dwight H. Perkins, New York, NY: St. Martin's Press, pp. 82–122.

David, Paul A. (1988), 'Path-dependence: putting the past into the future of economics', Institute for Mathematical Studies in the Social Sciences, Stanford University, Technical Report 533.

De Long, J. Bradford and Lawrence H. Summers (1991), 'Equipment investment and economic growth', *Quarterly Journal of Economics*, **106** (2): 445–502.

De Long, J. Bradford and Lawrence H. Summers (1992), 'Equipment investment and economic growth: how strong is the nexus?', *Brookings Papers on Economic Activity*, **2**: 157–211.

De Long, J. Bradford (1996), 'Cross-country variations in national economic growth rates: the role of "technology"', in *Technology and Growth*, edited by J.C. Fuhrer and J.N. Little, Boston: Federal Reserve Bank of Boston, pp. 127–150.

De Long, J. Bradford (1997), 'What do we really know about economic growth?'; http://econ161.berkeley.edu.

Dodgson, Mark and Roy Rothwell (eds) (1994), *The Handbook of Industrial Innovation*, Cheltenham, UK: Edward Elgar.

Dollar, David and Kenneth Sokoloff (1990), 'Patterns of productivity growth in South Korean manufacturing industries, 1963–1979', *Journal of Development Economics*, **33**: 309–327.

Dollar, David (1992), 'Outward oriented developing economies really do grow more rapidly: evidence from 95 LDCs, 1976–1985', *Economic Development and Cultural Change*, **40** (3): 523–544.

Dollar, David and Edward N. Wolff (1993), *Competitiveness, Convergence and International Specialization*, Cambridge, MA: MIT Press.

Dornbusch, R. (1990), 'Policies to move from stabilization to growth', paper presented at Proceedings of the World Bank Annual Conference on Development Economics, Washington, DC.

Dosi, Giovanni, Christopher Freeman, Richard Nelson, Gerald Silverberg and Luc Soete (eds) (1988), *Technical Change and Economic Theory*, London, UK: Pinter Publishers.

Easterly, William (1994), 'Explaining miracles: growth regressions meet the gang of four', World Bank Policy Research Working Paper 1250, Washington, DC.

Easterly, William and Ross Levine (2000), 'It's not factor accumulation: stylized facts and growth models', World Bank Policy Research Working Paper, Washington, DC.

Economist (1999), 'Global finance: time for a redesign', January 30: survey pp. 1–18.

Economist (2001), 'Asian business', April 7: survey pp. 1–18.

Edwards, Sebastian (1993), 'Openness, trade liberalization and growth in developing countries', *Journal of Economic Literature*, **31** (3): 1358–1393.

Edwards, Sebastian (1998a), 'Openness, productivity and growth: what do we really know?', *Economic Journal*, **108**: 383–398.

Edwards, Sebastian (1998b), 'Abolish the IMF', *Financial Times*, November 13: A1.

Egan, Mary Lou and Ashoka Mody (1992), 'Buyer-seller links in export development', *World Development*, **20** (3): 321–334.

Eichengreen, Barry (1999), *Towards a New International Financial Architecture*, Washington, DC: Institute for International Economics.

Elster, Jon (1986), 'The theory of uneven and combined development: a critique', in *Analytical Marxism*, edited by John Roemer, Cambridge UK: Cambridge University Press, pp. 54–63.

Enright, Michael J., Edith E. Scott and David Dodwell (1997), *The Hong Kong Advantage*, Hong Kong: Oxford University Press.

Esfahani, Hadi S. (1991), 'Exports, imports and economic growth in semi-industrialized countries', *Journal of Development Economics*, **35** (1): 93–116.

Fagerberg, Jan (1994), 'Technology and international differences in growth rates', *Journal of Economic Literature*, **32** (3):1147–1175.

Faini, Riccardo and Jaime De Melo (1990), 'LDC adjustment packages', *Economic Policy*, October: 491–519.

Färe, Rolf, Shawna Grosskopf and C.A. Knox Lovell (1994), *Production Frontiers*, Cambridge, UK: Cambridge University Press.

Farrell, M.J. (1957), 'The measurement of productive efficiency', *Journal of the Royal Statistical Society, Series A, General*, **120** (3): 253–281.

Feder, Gershon (1983), 'On exports and economic growth', *Journal of Development Economics*, **12** (1): 59–73.

Felipe, Jesus (1999), 'Total factor productivity growth in East Asia: a critical survey', *Journal of Development Studies*, **35** (4): 1–41.

Felipe, Jesus and J.S.L. McCombie (2001), 'Biased technical change, growth accounting and the conundrum of the East Asian miracle', *Journal of Contemporary Economics*: forthcoming.

Fisher, Franklin M. (1993), *Aggregation: Aggregate Production Functions and Related Topics*, Cambridge, MA: MIT Press.

Freeman, Chris (1989), 'Comment 4: "On the economic role of the state" by Joseph E. Stiglitz', in *The Economic Role of the State*, edited by Arnold Heertje, Oxford, UK: Basil Blackwell, pp. 135–143.

Freeman, Chris and Luc Soete (eds) (1997), *The Economics of Industrial Innovation*, Cambridge, MA: MIT Press.

Fried, Harold O., C.A. Knox Lovell and Shelton S. Schmidt (eds) (1993), *The Measurement of Productive Efficiency*, New York: Oxford University Press.

Fujita, Masahisa and Jacques-Francois Thisse (1996), 'Economics of agglomeration', *Journal of the Japanese and International Economies*, **10**: 339–378.

Fukuyama, Francis (1998), 'Asian values and the Asian crisis', *Commentary*, **105** (5): 23–27.

Fuss, Melvyn and Leonard Waverman (1990), 'Productivity growth in the motor vehicle industry, 1970–1984: a comparison of Canada, Japan and the United States', in *Productivity Growth in Japan and the United States*, edited by Charles R. Hulten, Chicago: University of Chicago Press, pp. 85–108.

Galbraith, John K. (1999), 'Challenges of the new millennium', *Finance and Development*, **36** (4): 2–5.

Galenson, Walter (ed.) (1979), *Economic Growth and Structural Change in Taiwan*, Ithaca, NY: Cornell University Press.

Glaeser, Edward L., Hedi D. Kallal, Jose A. Scheinkman and Andrei Shleifer (1992), 'Growth in cities', *Journal of Political Economy*, **100**

(6): 1126–1151.

Goh Keng Swee (1995), The Practice of Economic Growth, Singapore: Federal Publications.

Goldstein, Morris (1998), *The Asian Financial Crisis: Causes, Cures and Systemic Implications*, Washington, DC: Institute for International Economics.

Gore, Charles (2000), 'The rise and fall of the Washington consensus as a paradigm for developing countries', *World Development*, **28** (5): 789–804.

Gort, Michael, Jeremy Greenwood and Peter Rupert (1999) 'How much of economic growth is fueled by investment-specific technical progress?', Economic Research: Economic Commentary Series, Federal Reserve Bank of Cleveland; posted on http://www.clev.frb.org/Research/.

Greenwood, Jeremy (1999) 'The third industrial revolution: technology, productivity and income inequality', *Economic Review: Federal Reserve Bank of Cleveland*, **35** (2): 2–12.

Greenwood, Jeremy, Zvi Hercowitz and Per Krusell (1997) 'Long-run implications of investment-specific technological change', *American Economic Review*, **87** (3): 342–362.

Greenwood, Jeremy and Boyan Jovanovic (1998), 'Accounting for growth', Cambridge, MA: NBER Working Paper Series 6647.

Griliches, Zvi (1988), *Technology, Education and Productivity: Early Papers With Notes to Subsequent Literature*, New York, NY: Basil Blackwell.

Griliches, Zvi (1996), 'The discovery of the residual: a historical note', *Journal of Economic Literature*, **34** (3):1324–1330.

Griliches, Zvi (1999), *R&D, education and productivity: a personal retrospective*, Harvard University, The Simon Kuznets Memorial Lectures.

Grosskopf, Shawna (1993), 'Efficiency and productivity', in *The Measurement of Productive Efficiency*, edited by Harold O. Fried, C.A. Knox Lovell and Shelton S. Schmidt, New York: Oxford University Press, pp. 160–194.

Grossman, Gene M. (1990), 'Promoting new industrial activities: a survey of recent arguments and evidence', *OECD Economic Studies*, **14**: 87–125.

Grossman, Gene M. and Elhanan Helpman (1991a), 'Trade, knowledge spillovers and growth', *European Economic Review*, **35**: 517–526.

Grossman, Gene M. and Elhanan Helpman (1991b), *Innovation and Growth in the Global Economy*, Cambridge, MA: MIT Press.

Grossman, Gene M. and Elhanan Helpman (1994), 'Endogenous innovation in the theory of growth', *Journal of Economic Perspectives*,

**8** (1): 55–72.

Hahm, Joon-Ho and Frederic S. Mishkin (2000), 'Causes of the Korean financial crisis: lessons for policy', Cambridge, MA: NBER Working Paper Series 7483.

Hall, Robert E. (1990), 'Invariance properties of Solow's productivity residual', in *Growth, Productivity, Unemployment*, edited by Peter Diamond, Cambridge, MA: MIT Press, pp. 71–112.

Hall, Robert E. (1995), 'Comment' on "Capital utilization and returns to scale" by Craig Burnside, Martin Eichenbaum and Sergio Rebelo (1995), in *NBER Macroeconomics Annual 1995, Vol. 10*, edited by Ben S. Bernanke and Julio J. Rotemberg, Cambridge, MA: MIT Press, pp. 118–121.

Harberger, Arnold C. (1998), 'A vision of the growth process', *American Economic Review*, **88** (1): 1–32.

Hayami, Yujiro (1998), 'Toward an East Asian model of economic development', in *The Institutional Foundations of East Asian Economic Development*, edited by Yujiro Hayami and Masahiko Aoki, New York, NY: St. Martin's Press, pp. 3–35.

Henderson, Vernon, Ali Kuncoro and Matt Turner (1995), 'Industrial development in cities', *Journal of Political Economy*, **103** (5): 1067–1085.

Hirschman, Albert (1958), *The Strategy of Economic Development*, New Haven, CT: Yale University Press.

Hobday, Mike (1995), *Innovation in East Asia: The Challenge to Japan*, Aldershot, UK: Edward Elgar.

Hobday, Mike (2000), 'East versus Southeast Asian innovation systems: comparing OEM–and TNC–led growth in electronics', in *Technology, Learning and Innovation: Experiences of Newly Industrializing Economies*, edited by Linsu Kim and Richard R. Nelson, Cambridge, UK: Cambridge University Press, pp. 129–169.

Hodgson, Geoffrey M. (1993), *Economics and Evolution: Bringing Life Back Into Economics*, Ann Arbor: University of Michigan Press.

Hsieh, Chang-Tai (1998), 'What explains the industrial revolution in East Asia? Evidence from factor markets', Princeton University Discussion Papers in Economics No. 196.

Hsieh, Chang-Tai (1999), 'Productivity growth and factor prices in East Asia', *American Economic Review*, **89** (2): 133–138.

Hughes, Helen (ed.) (1992), *The Dangers of Export Pessimism*, San Francisco, CA: ICS Press.

Hulten, Charles R. (1975), 'Technical change and the reproducibility of capital', *American Economic Review*, **65** (5): 956–965.

Hulten, Charles R. (1996), 'Capital and wealth in the revised SNA', in *The New System of National Accounts*, edited by John W. Kendrick, Boston, MA: Kluwer Academic, pp. 149–181.

Hulten, Charles R. and Sylaja Srinivasan (1999), 'Indian manufacturing industry: elephant or tiger? New evidence on the Asian miracle', Cambridge, MA: NBER Working Paper 7441.

Hulten, Charles R. (2000), 'Total factor productivity: a short biography', Cambridge, MA: NBER Working Paper 7471.

IEEE (1991), 'Special report on Asiapower', *Institution of Electrical and Electronic Engineers: Spectrum*, **28** (6): 24–66.

IEEE (1994), 'Technology in India', *Institution of Electrical and Electronic Engineers: Spectrum*, **31** (3): 24–53.

IEEE (1998), 'Special report on U.S. education', *Institution of Electrical and Electronic Engineers: Spectrum*, **35** (4): 18–26.

IMF (1997), *World Economic Outlook: Crisis in Asia: regional and global implications*, December 1997, Interim Assessment.

IMF (1997–9), *World Economic Outlook*, various issues.

Ito, Takatoshi (1996), 'Japan and the Asian economies: a "miracle" in transition', *Brookings Papers on Economic Activity*, **2**: 205–272.

Izumi, Y. (1980), *Transformation and development of technology in the Japanese cotton industry*, Tokyo: The United Nations University.

Jones, Charles I. (1998), *Introduction to Economic Growth*, New York, NY: W.W. Norton.

Jorgenson, Dale W. and Zvi Griliches (1967), 'The explanation of productivity change', *Review of Economic Studies*, **34** (3): 249–283.

Jorgenson, Dale W. and Ralph Landau (eds) (1989), *Technology and Capital Formation*, Cambridge, MA: MIT Press.

Kagami, Mitsuhiro (1995), *The Voice of East Asia: Development Implications for Latin America*, Tokyo: Institute of Developing Economies.

Kalpakjian, Serope and Steven R. Schmid (2000), *Manufacturing Engineering and Technology*, Upper Saddle River, NJ: Prentice Hall.

Kendrick, John (1993), 'How much does capital explain?', in *Explaining Economic Growth: Essays in Honour of Angus Maddison*, edited by Adam Szirmai, Bart Van Ark and Dirk Pilat, Amsterdam: North-Holland, pp. 129–145.

Kennedy, Paul (1987), *The Rise and Fall of the Great Powers*, New York: Random House.

Kho, Bong-Chan, Dong Lee and Rene M. Stulz (2000), 'U.S. banks, crises and bailouts: from Mexico to LTCM', *American Economic Review*, **90** (2): 28–31.

Kim, Jong Il and Lawrence J. Lau (1994), 'The sources of economic

170 *Bibliography*

growth of the East Asian newly industrialized countries', *Journal of the Japanese and International Economies*, **8**: 235–271.

Kim, Kee-Young and Boong-Kyu Lee (1996), 'The innovation triangle: stimulating innovation in private and public enterprises', in *Korea at the Turning Point: Innovation-based Strategies for Development*, edited by Lewis M. Branscomb and Young-Hwan Choi, Westport, CT: Praeger Publishers, pp. 45–89.

Kim, Linsu (2000), 'Korea's national innovation system in transition', in *Technology, Learning and Innovation: Experiences of Newly Industrializing Economies*, edited by Linsu Kim and Richard R. Nelson, Cambridge, UK: Cambridge University Press, pp. 335–360.

Kim, Linsu and Richard R. Nelson (eds) (2000), *Technology, Learning and Innovation: Experiences of Newly Industrializing Economies*, Cambridge, UK: Cambridge University Press.

Knack, Stephen and Philip Keefer (1997), 'Does social capital have an economic payoff? A cross-country investigation', *Quarterly Journal of Economics*, **112** (4): 1251–1288.

Krause, Lawrence B., Koh Ai Tee and Lee Tsao Yuan (1987), *The Singapore Economy Reconsidered*, Singapore: Institute of Southeast Asian Studies.

Krause, Lawrence B. (2000), 'The aftermath of the Asian financial crisis for South Korea', *Journal of the Korean Economy*, **1** (1): 1–22.

Krueger, Anne O. (1978), *Foreign Trade Regimes and Economic Development: Liberalization Attempts and Consequences*, Cambridge, MA: Ballinger Publishing Company for NBER.

Krueger, Anne O. (1981), *Trade and Employment in Developing Countries*, Chicago: University of Chicago Press.

Krueger, Anne O. (1995), *Trade Policies and Developing Countries*, Washington, DC: Brookings Institution.

Krueger, Anne O. (1997), 'Trade policy and economic development: how we learn', *American Economic Review*, **87** (1): 1–22.

Krugman, Paul (1990), *Rethinking International Trade*, Cambridge, MA: MIT Press.

Krugman, Paul (1992), 'Towards a counter-counter-revolution in development theory', paper presented at World Bank Annual Conference on Development Economics, Washington, DC.

Krugman, Paul (1994), 'The myth of Asia's miracle', *Foreign Affairs*, **73** (6): 62–78; also posted on http://web.mit.edu/krugman/www/.

Krugman, Paul (1997), 'What ever happened to the Asian miracle?', *Fortune*, August 18; also posted on http://web.mit.edu/krugman/www/.

Krugman, Paul (1998a), 'Paradigms of panic', *Slate*, March 12; also posted on http://web.mit.edu/krugman/www/.

Krugman, Paul (1998b), 'The confidence game', *The New Republic*, October 5; also posted on http://web.mit.edu/krugman/www/.

Lall, Sanjaya (1987), *Learning to Industrialize: the Acquisition of Technological Capability by India*, London, UK: Macmillan Press.

Lall, Sanjaya (1990), *Building Industrial Competitiveness in Developing Countries*, Paris: OECD Development Centre Studies.

Lall, Sanjaya (1991), 'Asia's emerging sources of foreign investment: Hong Kong, Singapore, Taiwan, Korea', *East Asian Executive Reports*, **13** (6): 7, 19–25.

Lall, Sanjaya (1992), 'Technological capabilities and industrialization', *World Development*, **20** (2): 165–186.

Lall, Sanjaya (1994), '*The East Asian Miracle*: does the bell toll for industrial strategy?', *World Development*, **22** (4): 645–654.

Lall, Sanjaya (1996), *Learning from the Asian Tigers: Studies in Technology and Industrial Policy*, New York: St. Martin's Press.

Lall, Sanjaya (1999), 'India's manufactured exports: comparative structure and prospects', *World Development*, **27** (10): 1769–1786.

Lall, Sanjaya (2000), 'Technological change and industrialization in the Asian newly industrializing economies: achievements and challenges', in *Technology, Learning and Innovation: Experiences of Newly Industrializing Economies*, edited by Linsu Kim and Richard R. Nelson, Cambridge, UK: Cambridge University Press, pp.13–68.

Lall, Somik V. and G. Chris Rodrigo (2000), 'Perspectives on the sources of heterogeneity in Indian industry',World Bank Working Paper 2496, Washington, DC.

Landes, David S. (1998), *The Wealth and Poverty of Nations*, New York, NY: W.W. Norton.

Lau, Lawrence J. (1996), 'The sources of long-term economic growth: observations from the experience of developed and developing countries', in *The Mosaic of Economic Growth*, edited by Ralph Landau, Timothy Taylor and Gavin Wright, Stanford, CA: Stanford University Press, pp. 63–91.

Lee Kuan Yew (2000), *From Third World to First: the Singapore Story 1965–2000*, New York, NY: Harper-Collins.

Lee Tsao Yuan (ed.) (1991), *Growth Triangle: the Johor-Singapore-Riau Experience*, Singapore: Institute of Southeast Asian Studies, Institute of Policy Studies.

Leff, N.H. (1968), *The Brazilian Capital Goods Industry 1929–1964*, Cambridge, MA: Harvard University Press.

Leibenstein, Harvey (1966), 'Allocative efficiency vs. X-efficiency', *Ame-*

*rican Economic Review*, **56**: 392–415.

Leibenstein, Harvey (1973), 'Competition and X-efficiency: reply', *Journal of Political Economy*, **81**: 763–777.

Leibenstein, Harvey (1978), 'On the basic propositions of X-efficiency theory', *American Economic Review*, **68**: 328–333.

Levine, Ross and David Renelt (1992), 'A sensitivity analysis of cross-country growth regressions', *American Economic Review*, **82** (4): 942–963.

Levy, Brian and Wen-Jeng Kuo (1991), 'The strategic orientations of firms and the performance of Korea and Taiwan in frontier industries: lessons from comparative case studies of keyboard and personal computer assembly', *World Development*, **19** (4): 363–374.

Levy, Brian (1991), 'Transaction costs, the size of firms and industrial policy: lessons from a comparative case study of the footwear Industry in Korea and Taiwan', *Journal of Development Economics*, **34**: 151–178.

Lewin, Peter (1999), *Capital in Disequilibrium: the Role of Capital in a Changing World*, London, UK: Routledge.

Little, Ian, Tibor Scitovsky and Maurice Scott (1970), *Industry and Trade in Some Developing Countries*, London, UK: Oxford University Press for OECD.

Loungani, Prakash (2000), 'Trade links between China and other East Asian economies', *Finance and Development*, **37** (2): 34–36.

Lucas, Robert E., Jr. (1988), 'On the mechanics of economic development', *Journal of Monetary Economics*, **22**: 3–42.

Lucas, Robert E., Jr. (1993), 'Making a miracle', *Econometrica*, **61** (2): 251–272.

Lundvall, Bengt-Ake (ed.) (1992), *National Systems of Innovation: Towards a Theory of Innovation and Interactive Learning*, London, UK: Pinter Publishers.

Maddison, Angus (1982), *Phases of Capitalist Development*, Oxford, UK: Oxford University Press.

Maddison, Angus (1987), 'Growth and slowdown in advanced capitalist economies: techniques of quantitative assessment', *Journal of Economic Literature*, **25** (2): 649–698.

Maddison, Angus (1991), *Dynamic Forces in Capitalist Development: a Long-run Comparative View*, Oxford, UK: Oxford University Press.

Maddison, Angus (1995), *Monitoring the World Economy 1820–1992*, Paris: OECD, Development Centre Studies.

Mankiw, Gregory N., David Romer and David N. Weil (1992), 'A contribution to the empirics of economic growth', *Quarterly Journal of Economics*, **107** (2): 407–437.

Mankiw, Gregory N. (1995), 'The growth of nations', *Brookings Papers on Economic Activity*, **1**: 275–310.

Mason, E.S., M.J. Kim, D.H. Perkins, K.S. Kim and D.C. Cole (1980), *The Economic and Social Modernization of the Republic of Korea*, Cambridge, MA: Harvard University Press.

Mathews, John A. and Dong-Sung Cho (2000), *Tiger Technology: the Creation of a Semiconductor Industry in East Asia*, Cambridge, UK: Cambridge University Press.

Mayes, David G. (ed.) (1996), *Sources of Productivity Growth*, Cambridge, UK: Cambridge University Press.

McKinsey Global Institute (1993), *Manufacturing Productivity*, Washington, DC: McKinsey Global Institute.

Meier, Gerald M. and Dudley Seers (eds) (1984), *Pioneers in Development*, New York, NY: World Bank/Oxford University Press.

Michaely, Michael (1977), 'Exports and growth: an empirical investigation', *Journal of Development Economics*, **4** (1): 49–53.

Mishkin, Frederic S. (1999), 'Global financial instability: framework, events, issues', *Journal of Economic Perspectives*, **13** (4): 3–20.

Mody, Ashoka (1989), 'Staying in the loop', World Bank Discussion Paper 61, Washington, DC.

Mody, Ashoka (1990), 'Institutions and dynamic comparative advantage: the electronics industry in South Korea and Taiwan', *Cambridge Journal of Economics*, **14**: 291–314.

Mokyr, Joel (ed.) (1999), *The British Industrial Revolution: an Economic Perspective*, Boulder, CO: Westview Press.

Mowery, David C. and Nathan Rosenberg (1989), *Technology and the Pursuit of Economic Growth*, Cambridge, UK: Cambridge University Press.

Mowery, David C. and Nathan Rosenberg (1998), *Paths of Innovation: Technological Change in 20th-Century America*, Cambridge, UK: Cambridge University Press.

Nelson, Richard R. (1964), 'Aggregate production functions and medium-range growth projections', *American Economic Review*, **54** (5): 575–606.

Nelson, Richard R. (1973), 'Recent exercises in growth accounting: new understanding or dead end', *American Economic Review*, **63** (3): 462–468.

Nelson, Richard R. (1981), 'Research on productivity growth and productivity differences: dead ends and new departures', *Journal of Economic Literature*, **19** (3): 1029–1064.

Nelson, Richard R. and Sidney J. Winter (1982), *An Evolutionary Theory of Economic Change*, Cambridge, MA: Harvard University Press.

Nelson, Richard R. (1990a), 'Acquiring technology', in *Technological Challenge in the Asia-Pacific Economy*, edited by Hadi Soesastro and Mari Pangestu, Sydney, Australia: Allen & Unwin, pp. 38–47.

Nelson, Richard R. (1990b), 'Capitalism as an engine of progress', *Research Policy*, **19** (3): 193–214.

Nelson, Richard R. and Gavin Wright (1992), 'The rise and fall of American technological leadership: the postwar era in historical perspective', *Journal of Economic Literature*, **30** (4): 1931–1964.

Nelson, Richard R. (ed.) (1993), *National Innovation Systems: a Comparative Analysis*, New York, NY: Oxford University Press.

Nelson, Richard R. and Paul M. Romer (1996), 'Science, economic growth and public policy', *Challenge*, **39** (2): 9–21.

Nelson, Richard R. (1997), 'How new is new growth theory?', *Challenge*, **40** (5): 29–58.

Nelson, Richard R. (1998), 'The agenda for growth theory: a different point of view', *Cambridge Journal of Economics*, **22** (4): 497–520.

Nelson, Richard R. and Howard Pack (1999), 'The Asian miracle and modern growth theory', *Economic Journal*, **109**: 416–436.

Nishimizu, Mieko and John M. Page Jr. (1982), 'Total factor productivity growth, technological progress and technical efficiency change: dimensions of productivity change in Yugoslavia, 1965–78', *Economic Journal*, **92**: 920–936.

Nordhaug, Odd (1993), *Human Capital in Organizations: Competence, Training and Learning*, Oslo, Norway: Scandinavian University Press.

Norsworthy, J.R. and S.L. Jang (1992), *Empirical Measurement and Analysis of Productivity and Technological Change*, Amsterdam: North-Holland.

North, Douglass C. (1989), 'Institutions and economic growth: an historical introduction', *World Development*, **17** (9): 1319–1332.

North, Douglass C. (1990), *Institutions, Institutional Change and Economic Performance*, Cambridge: Cambridge University Press.

North, Douglass C. (1993), 'The ultimate sources of economic growth', in *Explaining Economic Growth: Essays in Honour of Angus Maddison*, edited by Adam Szirmai, Bart Van Ark and Dirk Pilat, Amsterdam: North-Holland, pp. 65–75.

North, Douglass C. and John J. Wallis (1994), 'Integrating institutional change and technical change in economic history: a transaction cost approach', *Journal of Institutional and Theoretical Economics*, 150 (4): 609–24.

Nurkse, Ragnar (1961), 'Balanced and unbalanced growth', in *Equilibrium and Growth in the World Economy: Economic Essays by Ragnar Nurkse*, edited by G. Haberler and R.M. Stern, Cambridge, MA: Harvard University Press, pp. 241–278.

Pack, Howard (1972), 'Employment and productivity in Kenyan manufacturing', Institute for Development Studies, University of Nairobi, Working Paper IDS 54.

Pack, Howard and Larry Westphal (1986), 'Industrial strategy and technological change', *Journal of Development Economics*, **22**: 87–128.

Pack, Howard (1987), *Productivity, Technology and Industrial Development: a Case Study in Textiles*, New York: Oxford University Press for the World Bank.

Pack, Howard (1988), 'Industrialization and trade', in *Handbook of Development Economics*, edited by Hollis Chenery and T.N. Srinivasan, Amsterdam: North-Holland, pp. 334–380.

Pack, Howard (1992), 'New perspectives on industrial growth in Taiwan', in *Taiwan: from Developing to Mature Economy*, edited by Gustav Ranis, Boulder, CO: Westview Press, pp. 73–120.

Pack, Howard (1994), 'Endogenous growth theory: intellectual appeal and empirical shortcomings', *Journal of Economic Perspectives*, **8** (1): 55–72.

Pack, Howard and John M. Page Jr. (1994a), 'Accumulation, exports and growth in the high performing Asian economies', *Carnegie-Rochester Conference Series on Public Policy*, **40**: 199–236.

Pack, Howard and John M. Page Jr. (1994b), 'Reply to Alwyn Young', *Carnegie-Rochester Conference Series on Public Policy*, **40**: 251–257.

Park, Yung Chul (1996), 'East Asian liberalization, bubbles and the challenge from China', *Brookings Papers on Economic Activity*, **2**: 357–371.

Pavitt, Keith and Martin Bell (1992), 'National capacities for technological accumulation: evidence and implications for developing countries', paper presented at World Bank Annual Conference on Development Economics, Washington, DC.

Phelps, Edmund S. (1995), 'Comment on "The growth of nations" by Mankiw (1995)', *Brookings Papers on Economic Activity*, **1**: 311–313.

Pilat, Dirk (1994), *The Economics of Rapid Growth*, Cheltenham, UK: Edward Elgar.

Porter, Michael E. (1990), *The Competitive Advantage of Nations*, New York, NY: Free Press.

Radelet, Steven and Jeffrey Sachs (1998), 'The East Asian financial crisis:

diagnosis, remedies, prospects', *Brookings Papers on Economic Activity*, **1**: 1–74.

Rao, V. V. Bhanoji and Christopher Lee (1996), 'Sources of growth in the Singapore economy and its manufacturing and service sectors', *Singapore Economic Review*, **40** (1): 83–115.

Roberts, Mark J. and James R. Tybout (1996), *Industrial Evolution in Developing Countries: Micro Patterns of Turnover, Productivity and Market Structure*, New York, NY: Oxford University Press.

Rodrigo, G. Chris and Will Martin (1997), 'Can the world trading system accommodate more East Asian style exporters?', *International Economic Journal*, **11** (4): 51–71.

Rodrigo, G. Chris (2000), 'East Asia's growth: technology or accumulation?', *Contemporary Economic Policy*, **18** (2): 215–227.

Rodriguez, Francisco and Dani Rodrik (1999), 'Trade policy and economic growth: a skeptic's guide to the cross-national evidence', College Park, MD, Department of Economics, University of Maryland.

Rodrik, Dani (1996), 'Understanding economic policy reform', *Journal of Economic Literature*, **34** (1): 9–41.

Rodrik, Dani (1998), 'TFPG controversies, institutions and economic performance in East Asia', in *The Institutional Foundations of East Asian Economic Development*, edited by Yujiro Hayami and Masahiko Aoki, New York, NY: St. Martin's Press, pp. 79–101.

Rodrik, Dani (1999), *The New Global Economy and Developing Countries: Making Openness Work*, Washington, DC: Overseas Development Council.

Romer, Paul M. (1986), 'Increasing returns and long-run growth', *Journal of Political Economy*, **94** (5): 1002–1037.

Romer, Paul M. (1990), 'Endogenous technological change', *Journal of Political Economy*, **98** (5, Part 2): S71–S102.

Romer, Paul M. (1994), 'The origins of endogenous growth', *Journal of Economic Perspectives*, **8** (1): 3–22.

Romer, Paul M. (1995), 'Comment on "The growth of nations" by Mankiw (1995)', *Brookings Papers on Economic Activity*, **1**: 313–320.

Rosenberg, Nathan (1976), *Perspectives on Technology*, Cambridge, UK: Cambridge University Press.

Rosenberg, Nathan (1982), *Inside the Black Box: Technology and Economics*, Cambridge, UK: Cambridge University Press.

Rosenstein-Rodan, P. (1943), 'Problems of industrialization in Eastern and South-eastern Europe', *Economic Journal*, **53**: 202–211.

Rostow, W.W. (1990), *Theorists of Economic Growth from David Hume to the Present*, New York, NY: Oxford University Press.

Sachs, Jeffrey D. and Andrew Warner (1995), ' Economic reform and the process of global integration', *Brookings Papers on Economic Activity*, **1**: 1–95.

Sachs, Jeffrey D. (1995), 'It keeps economy ahead of pack', Singapore: *The Straits Times*: September 21, 1995.

Sah, Raaj Kumar and Joseph E. Stiglitz (1989), 'Sources of technological divergence between developed and less developed countries', in *Debt, Stabilization and Development: Essays in Memory of Carlos Diaz-Alejandro*, edited by Guillermo A. Calvo, Ronald Findlay, Pentti Kouri and Jorge Braga de Macedo, Oxford, UK: Basil Blackwell, pp. 424–446.

Saxonhouse, G.H. (1978), 'The supply of quality workers and the demand for quality in jobs in Japan's early industrialization', *Explorations in Economic History*, **15**: 40–68.

Scholes, Myron S. (2000), 'Crisis and risk management', *American Economic Review*, **90** (2): 17–21.

Schultz, Theodore W. (1961), 'Investment in human capital', *The American Economic Review*, **51** (1): 1–17.

Schumpeter, Joseph (1936), *The Theory of Economic Development*, Cambridge, MA: Harvard University Press.

Schumpeter, Joseph (1942), *Capitalism, Socialism and Democracy*, New York: Harper & Row.

Sen, Amartya (1999), *Development as Freedom*, New York, NY: Anchor Books.

Sheshinski, Eytan (1967), 'Optimal accumulation with learning by doing', in *Essays on the Theory of Optimal Economic Growth*, edited by Karl Shell, Cambridge, MA: MIT Press, pp. 31–52.

Shell, Karl (1966), 'Toward a theory of inventive activity and capital accumulation', *American Economic Review*, 56 (2): 62–68.

Shell, Karl (1967), 'A model of inventive activity and capital accumulation', in *Essays on the Theory of Optimal Economic Growth*, edited by Karl Shell, Cambridge, MA: MIT Press, pp. 67–85.

Shell, Karl (1973), 'Inventive activity, industrial organization and economic growth', in *Models of Economic Growth*, edited by J.A. Mirlees and N.H. Stern, London, UK: Macmillan Press, pp. 77–100.

Shiller, Robert J. (2000), *Irrational Exuberance*, Princeton, NJ: Princeton University Press.

Smith, Stephen C. (1991), 'Industrial policy in developing countries: reconsidering the real sources of export-led growth', Washington, DC: Economic Policy Institute.

Smith, Stephen C. (1993), 'Review of Michael E. Porter's *Competitive*

*Advantage of Nations'*, *Journal of Development Economics*, **40** (2): 399–404.

Solow, Robert M. (1960), 'Investment and technical progress', in *Mathematical Methods in the Social Sciences 1959*, edited by Kenneth Arrow, Samuel Karlin and Patrick Suppes, Stanford CA: Stanford University Press, pp. 89–104.

Solow, Robert M. (1994), 'Perspectives on growth theory', *Journal of Economic Perspectives*, **8** (1): 45–54.

Solow, Robert M. (2001), 'Applying growth theory across countries', *World Bank Economic Review*, (2): forthcoming.

Song, Byung-Nak (1990), *The Rise of the Korean Economy*, Hong Kong: Oxford University Press.

Soros, George (1997), 'Avoiding a breakdown', *Financial Times*, December 31, 1997; also posted on http://www.soros.org/gsbio/.

Soros, George (1998), 'Capitalism's last chance', *Foreign Policy,* Winter 1998–99: 55–66; also posted on http://www.soros.org/gsbio/.

Srinivasan, T.N. (1995), 'Long-run growth theories and empirics: anything new?', in *Growth Theories in Light of the East Asian Experience*, edited by Takatoshi Ito and Anne O. Krueger, Chicago: University of Chicago Press, pp. 37–70.

Stern, Nicholas (1991), 'The determinants of growth', *Economic Journal*, **101**: 122–33.

Stiglitz, Joseph E. (1987), 'Learning to learn, localized learning and technological progress', in *Economic Policy and Technological Performance*, edited by Partha Dasgupta and Paul Stoneman, Cambridge, UK: Cambridge University Press, pp. 125–153.

Stiglitz, Joseph E. (1989), 'On the economic role of the state', in *The Economic Role of the State*, edited by Arnold Heertje, Oxford, UK: Basil Blackwell, pp. 9–85.

Stiglitz, Joseph E. (1992), 'Comment on "Toward a counter-counter revolution in development theory" by Krugman', paper presented at World Bank Annual Conference on Development Economics, Washington, DC.

Stiglitz, Joseph E. (1995), 'Social absorption capability, rent seeking and innovation', in *Social Capability and Long-term Economic Growth*, edited by Bon Ho Koo and Dwight H. Perkins, New York, NY: St Martin's Press, pp. 48–81.

Stiglitz, Joseph E. (1996), 'Some lessons from the East Asian miracle', *World Bank Research Observer*, **11** (2): 151–177.

Stiglitz, Joseph E. and Marilou Uy (1996), 'Financial markets, public policy and the East Asian miracle', *World Bank Research Observer*, **11**

(2): 249–276.

Stiglitz, Joseph E. (1998a), 'Knowledge for development: economic science, economic policy and economic advice', paper presented at Annual Bank Conference on Development Economics, Washington, DC.

Stiglitz, Joseph (1998b), 'Sound finance and sustainable development in Asia', Keynote Address to the Asia Development Forum, Manila; http://www.worldbank.org/knowledge/chiefecon/stiglitz.htm.

Stiglitz, Joseph (1998c), 'The role of international financial institutions in the current global economy', Chicago Council on Foreign Relations; http://www.worldbank.org/knowledge/chiefecon/stiglitz.htm.

Stiglitz, Joseph E. (2000), *Economics of the Public Sector*, New York, NY: W.W. Norton & Company.

Streeten, Paul P. (1984), 'Development dichotomies', in *Pioneers in Development*, edited by Gerald M. Meier and Dudley Seers, New York, NY: World Bank/Oxford University Press, pp. 337–361.

Summers, Robert and Alan Heston (1991), 'The Penn world table (Mark 5): an expanded set of international comparisons, 1950–1988', *Quarterly Journal of Economics*, **56** (2): 327–368.

Summers, Lawrence H. (2000), 'International financial crises: causes, prevention and cures', *American Economic Review*, **90** (2): 1–16.

Taylor, Lance (1988), *Varieties of Stabilization Experience*, Oxford, UK: WIDER & Clarendon Press.

Temple, Jonathan and Paul A. Johnson (1998), 'Social capability and economic growth', *Quarterly Journal of Economics*, **113** (3): 965–990.

Temple, Jonathan (1999), 'The new growth evidence', *Journal of Economic Literature*, **37** (1): 112–156.

Teplitz, Charles J. (1991), *The Learning Curve Deskbook*, New York: Quorum Books.

Thorbecke, Erik (1990), 'Institutions, X-efficiency, transaction costs and socioeconomic development', in *Studies in Economic Rationality: X-efficiency Examined and Extolled*, edited by Klaus Weiermair and Mark Perlman, Ann Arbor: University of Michigan Press, pp. 295–313.

Thorbecke, Erik and Henry Wan Jr. (eds) (1999) *Taiwan's Development Experience: Lessons on Roles of Government and Market*, Boston, MA: Kluwer Academic, pp. 95–111.

Todaro, Michael P. (1989), *Economic Development in the Third World*, New York & London, UK: Longmans, Inc.

Torii, Akio (1992), 'Technical efficiency in Japanese industries', in *Industrial Efficiency in Six Nations*, edited by Richard E. Caves,

Cambridge, MA: MIT Press, pp. 31–119.

Tsao Yuan (1982), *Growth and Productivity in Singapore: a Supply Side Analysis*, Ph.D., Harvard University, Cambridge, MA.

Tunzelmann, G.N. von (1995), *Technology and Industrial Progress: the Foundations of Economic Growth*, Aldershot, UK: Edward Elgar.

Tybout, James (2000), 'Manufacturing firms in developing countries: how well do they do and why?', *Journal of Economic Literature*, **38** (1): 11–44.

Van den Berg, Hendrik (2001), *Economic Growth and Development*, New York, NY: McGraw-Hill.

Vernon, Raymond (1989), 'Technological development: the historical perspective', World Bank EDI Seminar Paper 39, Washington, DC.

Wade, Robert (1990), *Governing the Market: Economic Theory and the Role of Government in East Asian Industrialization*, Princeton, NJ: Princeton University Press.

Wade, Robert (1996), 'Japan, the World Bank and the art of paradigm maintenance: the *East Asian Miracle* in political perspective', *New Left Review*, (217): 3–36.

Wade, Robert (2001), 'Winners and losers', *Economist*, April 28: 72–4.

Wade, Robert and Frank Veneroso (1998a), 'The Asian crisis: the high-debt model versus the Wall Street-Treasury-IMF complex', *New Left Review*, (228): 3–23.

Wade, Robert and Frank Veneroso (1998b), 'The resources lie within', *Economist*, November 7: 19–21.

Wallis, John J. and Douglass C. North (1987), 'Measuring the transaction sector in the American economy, 1870–1970', in *Long-Term Factors in American Economic Growth*, edited by Stanley L. Engerman and Robert E. Gallman, Chicago: University of Chicago Press, pp. 95–161.

World Bank (1987), *World Development Report*, Washington, DC: World Bank.

World Bank (1991), *World Development Report*, Washington, DC: World Bank.

World Bank (1993), *The East Asian Miracle*, New York: Oxford University Press.

World Bank (1998), *World Development Report*, Washington, DC: World Bank.

Young, Alwyn (1991), 'Learning by doing and the dynamic effects of international trade', *Quarterly Journal of Economics*, **56** (2): 369–406.

Young, Alwyn (1992), 'A tale of two cities: factor accumulation and technical change in Hong Kong and Singapore', in *NBER Macro-economics Annual 1992*, edited by Olivier J. Blanchard and Stanley

Fischer, Cambridge, MA: MIT Press, pp. 13–54.

Young, Alwyn (1994a), 'Lessons from the East Asian NICS: a contrarian view', *European Economic Review*, **38**: 964–973.

Young, Alwyn (1994b), 'Accumulation, exports and growth in the high performing Asian economies: a comment', *Carnegie-Rochester Conference Series on Public Policy*, **40**: 237–250.

Young, Alwyn (1995), 'The tyranny of numbers: confronting the statistical realities of the East Asian growth experience', *Quarterly Journal of Economics*, **110** (3): 641–680.

Young, Alwyn (1998a), 'Paasche vs. Laspeyers: the elasticity of substitution and bias in measures of TFP growth', Cambridge, MA: NBER Working Paper Series 6663.

Young, Alwyn (1998b), 'Alternative estimates of productivity growth in the NICs: a comment on the findings of Chang-Tai Hsieh', Cambridge, MA: NBER Working Paper Series 6657.

Yu, Tony Fu-Lai (1998), 'Adaptive entrepreneurship and the economic development of Hong Kong', *World Development*, **26**: 897–911.

# Index